THE
PROMISE OF
PARTNERSHIP

Books by the Whiteheads

THE
PROMISE OF PARTNERSHIP

A MODEL FOR COLLABORATIVE MINISTRY

James D. Whitehead
and
Evelyn Eaton Whitehead

HarperSanFrancisco
A Division of HarperCollinsPublishers

Grateful acknowledgment is made for the use of the following materials by James D. and Evelyn Eaton Whitehead, which appeared previously:

"Conflict—A Discipline of Partnership," *Studies in Formative Spirituality* (May 1989): 221-27. "The Gift of Prophecy," *Spirituality Today* (Winter 1989): 292-304. "Legitimacy and the Religious Leader," *New Theological Review* (May 1990): 5-17. "Obedience and Adult Faith," *Review for Religious* (May/June 1990): 397-406. "Partnership in Ministry," *Emmanuel* (June 1987): 247-69. "Ways to Collaborate: Staff, Team, Community," *Church* (Spring 1990): 29-33. "Women and Men: Partners in Ministry," *Chicago Studies* (August 1988): 159-72.

FIRST HarperCollins PAPERBACK EDITION PUBLISHED IN 1993

Library of Congress Cataloging-in-Publication Data

Whitehead, James D.
    The promise of partnership : a model for collaborative ministry / James D. Whitehead and Evelyn Eaton Whitehead.
        p. cm.
    Includes bibliographical references and index.
    ISBN 0–06–069572–2 (pbk.)
    1. Christian leadership—Catholic Church.   2. Church management.   3. Pastoral theology—Catholic Church.   4. Catholic Church—Clergy.   I. Whitehead, Evelyn Eaton.   II. Title.
    [BX1913.W49   1993]   93–434
    253—dc20

93   94   95   96   97   CWI   10   9   8   7   6   5   4   3   2   1

Contents

For

PEGGY ROACH

Blessed is She Who Hungers and Thirsts After Justice

Foreword

Around the time of my ordination in 1943, I savored the motto of the popes: "servant of the servants of God." Should this not apply to me also?

I promised to try to serve as needed, to be unfailingly obedient to my superiors and to the needs of people. Somehow I would try to share their hopes and dreams, their suffering and their drudgery, and to minister in such a way that the people I was sent to serve would participate in that ministry.

This may sound pompous, as if it came from deep meditation and a rich spiritual life. Yet it did not. The conviction that the ministry I was sent to perform must be shared with partners from whom I would learn, and who in turn might garner some of my insights, came from a very human weakness—and also a strength. I knew that I was not scholarly, sophisticated, learned, or wise. I was grateful for that "gift," because I realized that I needed others if the task was going to be done well.

Much of the rest followed automatically. In my first parish assignment, the sisters in our school taught me how to teach in a grammar school. Then the Young Christian Students and Young Christian Workers trained me in the role of chaplain—not as leader, not as worker, but as listener and enabler. From the experiences I heard, I attempted to help interpret the message of Christ and the rich tradition of the church.

The concept of partnership was beginning to dawn as an integral part of my life as a priest. I was not to be a privileged person except in the multitude of blessings that came to me from my close association with other clergy and with lay people working in the world of graft, corruption, and sin, as well as beauty, generosity, and sacrifice.

Alongside my regular parish duties, young married couples in the parish related to me their struggles of early married life and love and gave me a longing to be of special assistance to them. I enrolled for study under the great Carl Rogers to acquire the counseling skills that I hoped would enhance my ministry and service to others.

Thrown into the midst of ongoing marriage-preparation work on a large scale, I became the diocesan director of the Cana and Pre-Cana Conferences, a growing ministry for the married and engaged. Here my theoretical and practical training with the Young Christian Workers was to be tested.

I had no special training for this work. Providentially, experienced married couples offered me their gracious support; they literally took me in hand and trained me in models of organization, in the beauty of the marriage encounter, in the radical psychological differences between men and women, and in the rich spirituality flowing from the sacrament of Matrimony and the conjugal union.

As in my experience with the Young Christian Workers and the Christian Family Movement, partnership in ministry—with all of its difficulties and challenges—emerged as a beautiful aspect of my life as a priest. I knew that I needed the lay people for my spiritual and intellectual maturity, and they needed and wanted that which I was ordained to bring into their lives—the telling of the Story in the sharing of the Word, the offering of the gifts, the Eucharist of thanksgiving and support.

It did not appear to those of us involved in the marriage-preparation work that we, with so many others in Chicago, were breaking new ground, that we were discovering from our practice and work together that we were the church, the people of God, that our tasks were sacred and collaborative, and that we were united by the love that Christ has for Kingdom, church, and world.

But on a trip to Europe some ten years before Vatican II, I learned that what we had discovered by experience, trust, and faith had long since been a part of the ministry of the church in France, England, and Belgium. While exploring new ideas on the theology of conjugal spirituality there, I found that the mutuality of ministries had both depth and extensive practice. It confirmed to me that the laity with whom I was privileged to work in Chicago were a new kind of Catholic. Our people truly believed that the church was theirs and that their sacraments of Baptism, Confirmation, Marriage, and Eucharist not only gave them full membership but also positioned them for ministry in the church and the world, as collaborators in the redemption of our bloodstained world.

Through those days of trial and error, of success and failure, of excitement and discouragement, I learned what the Whiteheads so brilliantly unfold in this book—the process of partnership in ministry.

Through dialogue and the gift of listening, I learned that values can be shared, that they can be more skillfully internalized, and that the gifts of priest and people complement those that God, training, and experience have given to us.

Prodded by simple and honest prayer, I was made aware that trust and confidence in the other is a precious gift that comes only to those who see themselves as delightfully human, as pilgrims on the way, engaged in a common quest to give hope to the hopeless and love to those who grow weary on the journey.

Through the years, Msgr. Reynold Hillenbrand, Carl Rogers, Father Charles Curran, and a multitude of lay people taught me that listening is a skill, a gift to be cherished, and one of the finest modes of learning. Only with that gift might I be allowed the grace granted to ministers, lay or cleric, of enabling others to grope through the confusion of roles, position, and power to the understanding that together goals can be attained.

Before all this, however, there must be respect—respect for oneself, for the other, for the truth, and for the Spirit who will guide, enlighten, and inspire.

I guess I learned, despite my Irish temperament, that humility is the indispensable virtue. Contrary to the "exalted" role that clericalism imposes and that is part of our Western Christian tradition, humility comes, even now, through suffering, silence, listening, guidance—by standing beneath the cross.

The years have rolled on and the lessons learned early have paid off handsomely in work with community organizations where the lay people are the quintessential leaders, where the priest's role is that of enabler, strong supporter, healing participant. His task is to listen and to try to be a wise counselor during the rough-and-tumble quarrels centering on proposed strategies in a struggle for justice in the community.

In his ministry, Jesus empowered ordinary people—toll collectors, fishermen, women drawing water, tentmakers—to work as partners in the fashioning of the Christian church. He opened their eyes and ears and told them to go forth, generally two by two, to live among their neighbors, to heal, to speak the truth that the time of repentance and redemption was at hand.

It is no different today. The early church was primitive and messy. The church may still be primitive, and it can be awfully messy as it brings Christ into a world suffering from hungers of all kinds, from hopelessness, and from the powerlessness of the poor. Despite our human frailty, the ministry of Christ must go on.

I know that partnership in ministry—collaboration in the work of the church in the building of the Kingdom today—is not intended primarily or even secondarily for anchorites in the desert but for strong and courageous human beings, women and men working together in good humor and humility. I know it because I have done it through forty-seven years. Even today I realize that without my partner in ministry, Peggy Roach, my ministry as a priest in the last twenty-five years would have been done poorly.

Let us say it boldly: the age of patriarchy in the church, which is without a solid foundation in the life of Jesus in whose mission women were integral, must end. It was a cultural aberration. Now, in every aspect of the church's ministry, it must be eliminated as quickly as varying cultures will permit.

Partnership in the church must be taken as a given, neither a privilege nor an exception. It must be taught both theologically and in practice as ministers of whatever sex are being trained and formed, spiritually and intellectually.

Never again in our history as the body of Christ, as the people of God, can we neglect collaboration in our work to bring social justice and peace to the suffering of our peoples across the world.

Ministry within the walls of the church is significant and must be shared, but it is only preparatory to our ministry in the world of work, of organizing, of bringing justice and the fulfillment of human dignity to all; for when we go forth from the Eucharist hand in hand, we are all, in partnership, going through the "servants' entrance" to the world.

I have been inspired for over twenty-five years by the words of Vatican II in its Document on the Church (chap. 32):

For the distinction which the Lord made between sacred ministers and the rest of the People of God entails a unifying purpose, since pastors and faithful are bound to each other by mutual need. Pastors of the Church, following the example of the Lord, should minister to one another and to the faithful. The faithful in their turn should enthusiastically lend their cooperative assistance to their pastors and teachers. Thus, in their diversity all bear witness to the admirable unity of the Body of Christ. This very diversity of graces, ministries and works gathers the children of God into one, because "all these things are the work of one and the same Spirit." (pp. 58–59)

With St. Augustine (quoted in the same chapter of this Vatican II document), I can say in truth, "What I am for you terrifies me; what I am with you consoles me. For you I am a bishop, but with you I am a Christian. The former is a title of duty, the latter, one of grace. The former is danger, the latter, salvation" (p. 59).

In this volume, the Whiteheads draw on their experience, their prayer, and their scholarly learning to give all of us in the ministry those tools that will enable us to build enduring partnerships in the parish, whether on ministry teams or in parish councils. In the total church community, as we collaborate in bringing the life of Christ to the world, the work of ministry will flourish across many nations for years to come.

Msgr. John J. Egan
Assistant to the President for Community Affairs
DePaul University

Acknowledgments

We dedicate this book to our friend Peggy Roach. Peggy serves as mentor in the work of justice and as a gracious model of the gifts of partnership. Involved early in the civil rights struggle in Chicago, Peggy helped inspire the Catholic Interracial Council and the Contract Buyers League and, at the national level, the Catholic Committee on Urban Ministry. Through the 1970s she was at the University of Notre Dame as Director of the Religious Leaders Program and, in collaboration with Msgr. John J. Egan, as Associate Director of the Center for Pastoral and Social Ministry. Peggy returned to Chicago where she joined Jack Egan in the Archdiocesan Office for Human Relations and Ecumenism and, now, in the Office for Community Affairs at DePaul University.

Impressive as they are, her institutional credentials do not fully convey the power of Peggy's personal influence. Generous and talented, practical and visionary, she makes partnership real. In the name of all of us nourished by her example, we salute Peggy Roach—seeker of justice, woman of faith.

This book we dedicate to Peggy has emerged from many discussions. We are especially grateful to the conversation partners in our course "Leadership in Ministry: Power and Authority," offered for the past several years in the Institute of Pastoral Studies of Loyola University of Chicago. The wisdom of these experienced ministers—women and men, religious and lay— continues to shape and energize our work. Other groups have invited us to join their efforts to understand the contemporary demands of partnership: we thank the National Federation of Priests' Councils, Catholic Health Corporation, Maryknoll Missioners, Archdiocese of Edmonton (Canada), Roman Catholic Task Force of Yale Divinity School, All Hallows Centre (Ireland), and Xaverian Brothers' Sponsored Schools for all we learned in these discussions.

Several international colleagues expanded our perspective: we are especially indebted to John Chalmers (Brisbane), Deirdre Collins (London), Therese Kastner (Taiwan), Joan McFedridge

(Wellington), Eric Theriault (Halifax), and Raymond and Noelle Topley (Dublin). And we, like many others, continue to benefit from the insightful analysis of institutional change and organizational loss undertaken by our friend and colleague, J. Gordon Myers.

We address this book to Christian ministers struggling to craft more collaborative styles of leadership and service in a variety of settings: parish ministry, small faith communities, school boards and diocesan commissions, ministry teams in hospitals and other pastoral care agencies, lay boards of trustees of religious institutions, and congregations of vowed religious. While most of our examples are drawn from the Catholic experience, we hope that our analysis may serve the broader Christian community as well. The response to our work that we have received from women and men who minister in mainline Protestant denominations encourages us in this hope.

J. D. W. and E. E. W.

Part One

The Vision of Partnership

1. Christian Leaders: From Parents to Partners

So, James, Cephas and John, these leaders, these pillars,
shook hands with Barnabas and me as a sign of partnership.
(Gal. 2:9, JB)

Christian life is about embraces—the bonds of affection and accountability that unite us in Jesus Christ. When we are children, God's love becomes tangible for us in the warm embraces of our family and friends, in the devoted care of our teachers and pastors. Maturing in faith, we link our lives as disciples and companions of Jesus, and these new embraces build up the church. As adult members of the body of Christ, we hold one another in affection and concern. Gradually, we learn to hold our leaders accountable. We risk the embrace of collaboration as we work together for the coming of God's reign. And in this time of change and crisis, we cannot avoid the painful embrace of conflict.

These embraces challenge a church still growing into adulthood. Clergy and laity, once safely separated, draw close in a new familiarity. Women and men struggle to hold one another in greater mutuality. In this world of adult faith, the model of Christian ministry shifts from parenting to partnership.

The two embraces—parenting and partnership—are as ancient as Christianity itself. Both are essential to a faith community. Each is holy. But they describe very different ways to hold one another. For centuries the Christian community has thrived in the protective embrace of parental leaders. But today the Spirit moves the whole church toward the more adult embrace of partners.

A Hierarchical Family

Most of us grew up in a church that pictured itself as a hierarchy. In a hierarchical cosmos, heaven reigns above the earth, with hell below. In the social hierarchy, the king is superior to the princes, who in turn rule over their subjects. The medieval church used this model of the world to describe its own life: the pope stands above the other clergy, who care for the laity below them.

In this worldview the community of faith is stratified into different levels of responsibility and excellence. This is the world of ecclesiastical rank—"Reverend," "Very Reverend," "Most Reverend," "Unbelievably Reverend." (And that, as the disgruntled lay person might add, leaves all the rest of us "unreverend.") The Document on the Church from the Second Vatican Council (referred to hereafter as Vatican II) quotes St. Augustine's description of this hierarchical world: "From the bishops down to the last lay person."

Good order emerges from the hierarchical vision. The chain of command is clear; we each know where we belong, even if we are not very happy about our place in the arrangement. But for all its administrative clarity, the metaphor of hierarchy lacks emotional warmth. From our earliest days, Christians softened the institutional image by recalling that this community is also a family. We are all the children of God. Jesus encouraged us to address our God as *Abba*, Father, and we speak of Holy Mother Church. The image of family reinforces the bonds of affection and loyalty that unite us in faith. If we are an institution, we are also a religious family. The image of a *hierarchical family* became a guiding metaphor of the developing church's self-understanding.

When we picture the church as a hierarchical family, it is natural to see ministry as an exercise of parenthood. In a family, parents care for those in their charge. This image seemed to capture the blend of concern and authority expected of early Christian leaders. While all Christians remained the children of God, our leaders assumed parental roles in the community. The head of a parish we named "father." The leader of a congregation of women religious was often designated "mother superior." We referred to the pope as our "Holy Father."

The cultures in which Christianity first flourished supported this religious endorsement of the parent metaphor. As theologian Elisabeth Schüssler Fiorenza shows in her influential work *In Memory of Her,* the Roman sense of the *paterfamilias* supported an understanding of the community leader as the group's father. Shepherd and parent soon became the dominant images of religious leadership, expressed in the titles of "pastor" and "father." Both metaphors suggest strong affection, along with a certain distancing of the leader from the group. The shepherd is generically different from the flock; the *paterfamilias* is set apart—by age and maturity and authority—from his children.

A Dangerous Memory

Christians today remember an equally ancient image of our shared life: the mutuality of disciples. Because this recollection challenges established ways, it becomes, in theologian Johannes Metz's phrase, "a dangerous memory." If the church is a hierarchy, it is also a community of disciples. If ministry sometimes looks like parenting, it is more often expressed in the seasoned activity of adult partners. The faith community today recalls a religious world in which we are not parents and children of one another, but sisters and brothers. In this vision, so ancient that it seems novel, the family grows up. We remain kin, but the family members are now adults. In such a family, the rules of obedience and loyalty and dissent all change. The family of faith endures, but the ways we hold one another shift significantly.

This exciting memory, loosed and sanctioned in Vatican II, has deep roots. The Gospels show us Jesus as neither biological parent nor authoritative head of a household. The "Son of God" was prophet, companion, friend, but not father. When he spoke with his disciples about the vocabulary of community leadership, he urged them not to use the title of "father": "You must call no one on earth your father, since you have only one Father, and he is in heaven" (Matt. 23:9, JB). The Creator's parenthood is unique and not to be shared. For this reason Jesus disqualified fatherhood as an apt metaphor for Christian ministry. Our service to one another is the work of siblings— colleagues, friends, partners. Jesus described a community of shared discipleship rather than a hierarchy of parent and child.

This passage, recording Jesus' objection to the most natural metaphor for ministry and leadership, recalls another New Testament story. Jesus was preaching to a crowd when his mother and brothers arrived. Told of their approach, he responded in a strange way: " 'Who are my mother and my brothers?' And looking around at those sitting in a circle about him, he said, 'Here are my mother and my brothers. Anyone who does the will of God, that person is my brother and sister and mother' " (Mark 3:32–35 JB). Jesus demanded that we radically alter the definition and boundaries of our kin. The family metaphor may be apt for Christian life, but only when transformed.

These words of Jesus evoke other "dangerous memories." We recall the early community's conviction about the power of Baptism, expressed in the Pauline letter to the Galatians. Baptism initiates us into a life of radical mutuality. In Baptism we experience a oneness with Christ so profound that the traditional distinctions of social life no longer prevail. Once important boundaries—between Jew and Gentile, between slave and free person, between woman and man—fall away. In the novel partnership of Christian faith these distinctions, so often used to reinforce status and privilege, lose their force.

These scriptural memories bring us today to new insight about the special nature of adult faith. As children we *receive* the faith, a gift from God through the believing community to which we belong. We are, from the first, heirs of our religious tradition. But if the gift is to bear fruit, we must do more than hold on to faith: we need to *do* it. To mature into the full humanity of Jesus Christ, we must live out what we believe. No longer simply heirs, we must author an adult life of faith. And adult faith makes ministers of us all, partners in God's mission for the church. Recognizing our shared call to actions of justice and love, we approach the church's formally designated ministers. But we come no longer as their children. Our hope is not simply "to help out father" but to join in a partnership of ministry.

The last twenty-five years have seen the release of a fierce longing for partnership. Hope for this more adult relationship arises at every level in the hierarchical church. Parishioners ask their pastors to approach them as companions in faith rather than as distant or defensive administrators. Priests look to their bishops for new styles of leadership, more fraternal and less authoritarian. Bishops seek a more collegial relationship with the pope; they seem to be saying, "We already have a father, and he is in heaven. We wish you to be our brother."

Partnership and *Koinonia*

The image of partnership is both ancient and new. In the early days of the church, Paul struggled to form a partnership with the leaders of the community in Jerusalem—a relationship that would be rocky. After his dramatic conversion to the way of Jesus, Paul had begun to preach the Good News on his own. "I did not stop to discuss this with any human being, nor did I go up to Jerusalem to see those who were already apostles before me" (Gal. 1:16–17, JB). But Paul had few credentials: he had not lived with Jesus; at Pentecost he was not present; no one had appointed him an apostle. Lacking official authority, Paul was, in every sense, an outsider. Yet he seemed to assume that his encounter with Christ made him an equal partner in Jesus' mission.

Before long the preaching of this "nobody" attracted attention in Jerusalem. Who was this upstart? Why was he not circumcising those who joined the way of Jesus? Paul and Barnabas, now colleagues in ministry in Antioch, were called to Jerusalem to explain their unorthodox approach. Amid controversy and conflict, this strong-willed assembly hammered out a compromise: Paul would preach to the Gentiles; Peter would preach to the Jews (Gal. 2:7, JB). Paul's words ring with astonishment and pride: "So, James, Peter and John, these leaders, these pillars, shook hands with Barnabas and me as a sign of partnership" (Gal. 2.9, JB).

Koinonia is the Greek word that the Jerusalem Bible renders here as "partnership." Christians have traditionally translated this word as "community" or even "communion." But to describe this relationship of determined adults struggling to resolve their conflict, "partnership" is the more accurate term. *Koinonia* also appears in Luke's account of Jesus calling his first disciples. Walking along the shore, Jesus came upon three fishermen busy about their work—Simon, John, and James. We are told that these three are *partners* in their profession. When Jesus invited them to follow him, they set aside their nets but not their partnership. "From now on it is people you will catch" (adapted from Luke 5:10, JB). Their new partnership would be as disciples.

Partnership, both in the gospel and in contemporary life, is an experience of shared power. In this communal process, we explicitly reject domination of one by the other. Being partners does not mean that we bring the same thing to our relationship or that each of us contributes equally. As societal goals, equal opportunity, and equality under the law safeguard against the prejudices that easily infect social relationships. But using equality as a criterion for partnership is tricky. Equality stresses sameness, while partnership delights in diversity. Partners recognize that their differences often expand and enrich their relationship. Equality, as a quantitative image, hints that we should be keeping score. But measuring our respective contributions more often defeats than strengthens partnership.

More than on strict equality, partnership depends on mutuality. The giving and the receiving go both ways. In a mutual relationship, each party brings something of value; each receives something of worth. Partnership thrives when we recognize and respect this mutual exchange of gifts.

Shadows on the Family

Recapturing the gospel ideal of partnership, we recognize that the family image casts shadows. Uncritical rhetoric about the faith community as a family can generate unhealthy expectations. A parish becomes a place with too many children and too few parents. Ordained leaders feel the press of too much responsibility; parishioners act like needy children or petulant religious consumers. Family images no longer adequately express our devotion to one another and our loyalty to the church. Instead, we trace the links between the passivity of many parishioners and their well-learned status as children. Bad grammar and bad theology combine when the laity are understood as those who just "lay there" waiting to be cared for. This expectation demeans the community of faith, and it burdens our leaders as well. Many priests, yearning to move toward partnership in their ministry, feel trapped by people's expectations that they function in a parental role.

Parental images of ministry cast another shadow: paternalism. A sage priest once remarked, "Too often in the church, we promise care but we deliver control." Authorized as parents, leaders are lured to "care too much" for those in their charge. Subtly, care becomes constraint. Paternalism tempts even those who are not *pater*. Ordained minister or not, biological parent or not, anyone in a position of responsibility may fall victim.

Paternalism is, as sociologist Richard Sennett notes, an "authority of false love," distorting the genuine impulse to provide and protect. The paternalistic leader shields us from the dangers of growing up. But this protection, if effective, stunts our growth and defeats maturing in faith. Paternalism strikes a bad bargain: "I will take care of all your needs. All I ask in return is that you remain dependent on me." Effective leaders, like successful parents, learn the demanding discipline of letting go. Empowering those in their care, genuine leaders nurture others toward maturity and finally welcome them as peers.

The vocabulary of ministry casts its own shadow. For centuries the vocabulary of parenting seemed to fit Christian experience. Calling our religious leaders "father" and "mother" evoked affection and respect. Fewer of us feel these positive nuances today. Now we recognize the pressures on our leaders to be parents without partners. These unspoken demands are grounded less in the requirement of celibacy than in our heroic images of the leader. We have expected our leaders to be independent operators, strong enough to stand alone. Seminary education has often warned against close friendship and belittled the need for personal support. This setting has formed leaders unencumbered by emotional relationships, ready for autonomous action and independent responsibility. But as ministry now moves from parenting to partnership, this heroic expectation becomes a stumbling block.

Partnership in ministry does not require that all our leaders be married; a commitment to shared ministry need not threaten the commitment to celibacy. But ministry today is rooted in the shared resources of the community. Effective leaders—no longer "single parents"—find a place within this ministering community. Coordinating the community's activities and calling forth its gifts, pastoral leaders today work closely with other people. Their ministry requires new, more collaborative strengths. Functioning as a partner challenges a leader trained in the heroic style. But letting go the heroic image, leaders find talented and willing colleagues eager to share the tasks of ministry. Sometimes they also find friends.

The shadows cast by the parental expectations of ministry come to a special focus in the relationship between women and men in the church. For a very long time church leaders skirted the challenge of partnership by seeing women in the sanctioned roles of mother and daughter. These roles kept women at a safe distance, either elevating them in a romanticized ideal of mother or diminishing them with the characterization of docile daughter. Masculine church leaders felt secure in holding mothers and daughters; these were familiar and safe embraces. But women today make a compelling demand. They would be more than mothers and daughters; they wish to be partners in every part of Christian life.

Women as partners: the notion both excites and threatens a masculine church. Part of the dread, and the delight, is the hint of sexual partnership. Here, perhaps, the Catholic tradition bears a special woundedness. Suspicious of sexuality, our church denies sacramental leadership to women and those who marry women. But partnership raises a risk well beyond sexuality. To welcome a partner is to move beyond self-sufficiency. For many men, partnership threatens a loss of control.

Control stands near the heart of masculine spirituality. As men, we strive to be reliable leaders, in charge of the situation. In our personal lives we are eager to master our emotions. Collaborating with women will certainly challenge that control—influencing our decisions, arousing our feelings, modifying our leadership style. We sense that the gain—in pastoral effectiveness and personal support—might be immense, but so is the risk. The conversion for most men lies in the realization that there is something worse than their losing institutional control: denying the faith community the gifts of its women members. Challenging masculine domination will not send the church out of control. Rather, this transformation will open the life of the church to fresh forms of shared responsibility and interdependent action.

Recent events in the Catholic church demonstrate the distress that masculine leaders have with the prospect of women as partners. In 1988 the U.S. Catholic bishops released a first draft of a pastoral letter on women in the church. The text, written by a team composed of bishops and women, was the fruit of public listening sessions held throughout the United States. The document's title announced its orientation: "Partners in the Mystery of Redemption." Included for the first time in an official church text were the testimonies of many women themselves. In both its title and its content, the draft heralded a new, heartening vision of the relationship of women and men in today's church.

A second draft, released April 3, 1990, looked utterly different. The revised title chose the traditional rhetoric of unity ("One in Christ") over the challenging dynamics of partnership. The statements of women were almost entirely deleted. The courage and imagination of the first draft vanished in a safe restatement of the past. The journey to a genuinely adult church took a step backward.

A Clash of Symbols

A promise of partnership continues to enliven the church. A new sense of mutuality shapes our liturgical life; official statements call for greater collaboration among ordained and lay people, women and men. The "National Pastoral Plan for Hispanic Ministry," issued by the U.S. Catholic bishops in 1987, calls for a new *pastoral de conjunto*—ministry together. As Rosendo Urrabazo, the president of the Mexican American Cultural Center, described this plan to the bishops,"efforts are being made to encourage the laity, especially Hispanic laity, *to be partners* with their bishop and clergy in the implementation of diocesan pastoral plans" (italics added). But these hopes stir within a church that still operates as a hierarchical bureaucracy. If this institutional situation is schizophrenic, so—for many of us—is our own experience. "Parenting" and "partnership" live side by side in our own expectations. We know times when our own ministry is close to parenting: educating the very young, giving solace to someone deeply wounded or distressed. But more and more we face both the demands and the benefits of partnership.

In our confusion we may demand, Is the church a hierarchical organization or a partnership in Christ? The answer, of course, is yes! We are *both*. As a bureaucracy of international scope, the church has a complex structure and a formal chain of command. But the hope of partnership gains force at all levels of ecclesial life.

The Document on the Church developed by Vatican II dramatically witnesses to this ambivalence. Its second chapter describes the church as "the people of God" in the rich imagery of mutuality and adult partnership. The third chapter then outlines in exquisite detail the different levels of excellence in a hierarchical institution. The original draft submitted for the bishops' consideration placed the hierarchy chapter first. By a resounding vote the council members reversed the order. While both hierarchy and mutuality may describe the church, the participants of the council voted for a priority of adult partnership.

This clash of metaphors continues to sound among us. In every parish there are some who ask the pastor to be their brother in faith, but others insist that he continue to be father. Many ministry staffs use the language of partnership even when the structures for hiring and firing remain firmly hierarchical and the final decision lies outside the group. The tension generated in this contradiction reveals the struggle of our church in the midst of change. Some leaders long for "the good old days" when the faithful obeyed promptly and without question. Many lay people regret the loss of that time of innocence when the church knew all the answers, freeing them from the need to form and trust their consciences.

The promise of partnership demands that we give up both childish behavior and paternalistic roles. If faith takes shape in the many ways we hold one another, the challenge today is to learn to hold one another as partners. In the chapters ahead we trace the contemporary demands of these robust embraces of faith.

Reflective Exercise

In a time of change and purification, identifying our own experience is important. A reflective exercise appears at the end of each chapter to assist that process. The goal of each reflection is discernment—to come to a clearer and more confident awareness of your own convictions on a particular question or theme. The exercises are designed so that they may be used by a single reader, but their value is often greatly enhanced when they are shared with a colleague or in a small group discussion.

Recall your life in the community of faith these days: in your parish, in a prayer group or ministry team, as part of the wider Christian body. Do not undertake an analysis: just be present to your ongoing participation in the church. Take time with this initial reflection.

Now identify a recent experience where "the church as hierarchy" was real for you. Spend some time with the experience itself: What was the setting? Who was involved? What was the outcome?

As you look back to this experience of hierarchy, what do you see as its strengths? What, for you, are its limitations?

Then identify a recent experience where "church as partnership in faith" was real for you. Again spend time with the experience: the setting, the people involved, the outcome.

From your perspective, what were the strengths of this experience of partnership? What were its limitations?

Additional Resources

In *Transforming Parish Ministry: The Changing Roles of the Catholic Clergy, Laity, and Women Religious* (New York: Crossroad/Continuum, 1989), historian Jay Dolan and his colleagues chart recent changes in ministry and their influence on the religious experience of U.S. Catholics. We discuss pastoral issues raised by the movement from parenting to partnership in *The Emerging Laity: Returning Leadership to the Community of Faith* (New York: Image Books/Doubleday, 1988). William Bausch describes practical ways in which the values of partnership can shape the local community of faith in *The Hands-On Parish* (Mystic, CT: Twenty-Third Publications, 1989).

Virginia Hoffman envisions the future of an adult church in *Birthing a Living Church* (New York: Crossroad/Continuum, 1989). William V. D'Antonio and his associates survey the shifting experiences and expectations of American Catholics in *American Catholic Laity in a Changing Church* (Kansas City, MO: Sheed & Ward, 1989).

In *Dangerous Memories: House Churches and our American Story* (Kansas City, MO: Sheed & Ward, 1986), Bernard Lee and Michael Cowan use Johannes Metz's provocative image in relation to small faith communities. For discussion of the leader's role, see Michael Cowan, ed., *Leadership Ministry in Community*, vol. 6 of the Alternative Futures for Worship series (Liturgical Press, 1987), and James Bacik, *The Challenge of Pastoral Leadership: Putting Theology into Practice* (Cincinnati: St. Anthony Messenger Audiocassettes, 1990).

Elisabeth Schüssler Fiorenza, in *In Memory of Her: A Feminist Theological Reconstruction of Christian Origins* (New York: Crossroad/Continuum, 1983), argues that the first generations of Christians envisioned a discipleship of equals. Sociologist Richard Sennett analyzes the destructive dynamics of paternalism in *Authority* (New York: Vintage Books, 1981).

The quotation of St. Augustine on the hierarchical structure of the church was quoted in the Vatican II document on the church (*Lumen Gentium*), paragraph 12; see p. 29 of Walter M. Abbott, ed., *The Documents of Vatican II* (New York: America Press, 1966). The initial draft of the U.S. Catholic bishops' pastoral letter "Partners in the Mystery of Redemption" appeared in *Origins*, the documentary service of the National Conference of Catholic Bishops, on April 21, 1988, pp. 757–88. The second draft, entitled "One in Christ: A Pastoral Response to the Concerns of Women for Church and Society," appeared in *Origins*, April 5, 1990, pp. 717–40.

The National Pastoral Plan for Hispanic Ministry is available from the Printing Office of the United States Catholic Conference. Rosendo Urrabazo's address appeared in *Origins*, August 17, 1989, pp. 202–6.

We discuss the practical shape of *koinonia* in contemporary Christian life in our *Community of Faith: Crafting Christian Communities Today* (Mystic, CT: Twenty-Third Publications, 1992).

2. Worlds of Scarcity, Promise of Abundance

I came that they may have life and have it abundantly.   (John 10:10, RSV)

We live these days in a religious world of scarcity. Vocations to priesthood and religious life, once in abundant supply, have decreased dramatically. Lacking priests, parishes consolidate or risk being closed. Diocesan budgets shrink, forcing a reduction in needed services. Catholic hospitals and schools shut their doors, victims of escalating operating costs. Throughout the church a mood of diminishment spreads as parts of our cherished past pass away.

In this season of loss, the gospel alerts us to paradox, urging us to expect the unexpected. Looking again at our shortages, we see a startling abundance. Everywhere people come forward, yearning to give their lives to God's saving mission. Parishes abound with gifted adults eager to minister to the needs of the world and the church. Generous women—vowed religious and lay, well trained in the Scriptures and theology—stand ready for roles of pastoral leadership. Do we dwell in scarcity or abundance?

To Have Life More Abundantly

Jesus proclaims a special economy of scarcity and abundance. In the Gospel of John, he announces, "I came that they may have life and have it *abundantly*" (10:10, RSV). Jesus' presence among us generates abundance.

15

One gospel story especially illumines the paradox of scarcity and abundance. A group gathers around Jesus, eager to hear him speak. As the day progresses, he is aware that the people are hungry, but no provision has been made for feeding so large a group. Jesus asks his friends to gather up what they can find. They report only some fish and a few loaves here and there. When these scarce resources are collected, Jesus has them distributed to the crowd. Amazingly, there is enough food!

In this event, traditionally called "the multiplication of loaves and fishes," Jesus turns fragmented resources and privately held sustenance into bountiful nourishment. By sharing their meager amount of food, the people seemed to multiply it; breaking their bread, they made more of it. Apparent scarcity was transformed into abundance.

The Invention of Scarcity

Surprised by this gospel plenty, we look more deeply into our want today. Scarcity is often genuine: the poverty that afflicts so much of the world; the enduring lack of strength that accompanies a long illness; our inability to heal problems in our own family. Scarcity can be quite real.

Often, however, scarcity is more apparent than real. Another town lacks food, but our granaries are full. Or we become depressed and are convinced that we have no friends, though people remain eager to be admitted to our life. Sometimes scarcity is not merely apparent but fabricated; it can be a human invention and a cultural institution. A Rolex watch is valuable because there are so few; the status a fur coat or an expensive car confer depends on their scarcity. Only if we can keep these objects in short supply, can we guarantee their value. Consumerism trains us in this illusion of scarcity and need.

The church is also tempted to invent scarcity. Attempting to control the profligate outpouring of the Spirit, we manufacture scarcity. When the church decides that lay people should not preach, it makes the Good News more scarce. When we restrict ordained leadership to unmarried men, we guarantee that the sacraments will be in short supply. This invention of scarcity reached its height with the theological judgment that "there is no salvation outside the church." (Imagine God's surprise upon hearing this!) In this classic statement, now disavowed, the church sought to reduce God's extravagant grace to official channels. We made grace scarce, captive to institutional guidelines.

Leadership and an Abundance of Power

Scarcity and abundance come to special focus around issues of leadership. Conflicting visions vie for our allegiance. One view, crafted in the medieval church, sees leaders as having power. Power, conferred in ordination, belongs solely to the leader, not to the community. As a *possession*, power may be delegated or shared—but only leaders can make that decision, because power actually resides in their hands.

The vision of power as an individual possession dominates our cultural imagination as well. People either have power or they do not. The athlete and politician and police officer possess power; most women, the poor, and the elderly do not. Whether we identify power with wealth or education or ordination, we tend to see it as a commodity that is held by individuals. As a possession, power is like private property: it is always in short supply. Your increase in power comes at my expense. Competition and defensiveness abound in a world where there is never enough power to go around.

Power as a Community Dynamic

In the New Testament we enter a different world of power. The chief word for power in the gospel message is *dynamis*—a "dynamic." Power is not a commodity possessed by a few leaders but the dynamic interaction—for better or for worse—that moves through a group of people. This dynamic may be the power of hope that guides a group through a crisis, or it may be a shared rage that binds a community in its hatred of an enemy. Throughout the New Testament we see God's power moving through Jesus to arouse hope, heal illness, and confront destructive patterns of domination.

As Jesus and his friends were making their way through a crowded street, a woman who was ill struggled to get near him,

convinced that even touching his clothes might bring her healing (Luke 8). When she succeeded in reaching him, Jesus
stopped and asked, "Who touched me?" His friends reminded
him that many people had bumped against him as they passed
through a busy avenue. But Jesus recognized a special touch: "I
felt that power had gone out of me" (v. 46, JB). The woman's
touch released the power of God in Jesus, and that power flowed
out to heal her illness. Jesus did not stop and decide to dispense
some of his personal power. The woman's touch tapped God's
power alive in Jesus, and he suddenly felt it moving through
him.

This story portrays power not as an individual possession but
as a movement of saving energy. Jesus is the special channel of
this dynamic force, but it is the woman's faith that makes it flow.
God's power is not the private possession of any individual but
the very dynamic (*dynamis*) that links and nourishes the members of a faith community. As a group of Christians share their
faith—and doubt and grief—they feel this power energizing
and renewing them. When a congregation is able to face conflict
honestly, it experiences God's power reuniting the members in
reconciliation.

Perhaps the central story of God's power surging through a
group of believers, empowering them to act in new and creative
ways, is the story of Pentecost. Jesus' death was a bitter blow to
his friends; they felt impotent and defeated. In the days before
this disaster, Jesus had urged them, "Stay in the city then, until
you are clothed with the power from on high" (Luke 24:49, JB).
His death, he seemed to be warning them, would leave them
powerless. But God, stronger than death, would soon "clothe
them with power."

On the day that we call Pentecost, some of the disciples gathered in a mood of bewilderment and grief. Suddenly they felt
the stirring of a wind among them. A new mood of hope moved
through the group. Confidently they left this room and their
desolation behind, eager to tell others about Jesus and to bring
healing where they could. A gift of power had transformed this
fragile community.

At Pentecost we celebrate a new advent of power into the
first community of believers. There were no individual heroes in
this upper room; neither Peter nor any other apostle did any-

thing for the group. The unexpected abundance that stirred on this day was not dispensed to an individual leader; it was poured out over the entire group.

Charism and Conscience

Pentecost keeps happening. God's abundant power continues to stir our faith today. Christians experience the power of the Spirit in the everyday dynamics of charism and conscience. These powers come from the Spirit to strengthen us and to link us as a community of faith.

In the New Testament *charism* refers to a personal strength or ability. In his letter to the Christians in Corinth, Paul mentions the gifts of preaching, healing, prophecy, and discernment (1 Cor. 12). In parishes today we meet innumerable strengths: abilities to counsel, to manage finances, to preach, to deal with conflict. All these are charisms needed by a faith community.

Charisms, as specific abilities, come to us as gifts that surprise and even dismay us. I am surprised to find that, in a business meeting, I am effective in raising questions of the ethical dimensions of our work. Before you began volunteering at the AIDS hospice, you did not suspect that you had the ability to comfort people in their grief. In fact, some charisms come to us more like curses than gifts. I sense that I am called to raise questions of justice in our parish's use of money. I would prefer to contribute in some other way; I even ask God to give me another means of serving the community. But—I realize with trepidation—this is what I must do.

Charisms are concrete ways in which we feel the power of the Spirit stir within us. Because of this, even when we are reluctant recipients, we call them gifts. And we come to see that they are gifts *to be given away.* Our abilities are not meant for our private enjoyment or to give us an advantage over others. They are how we help build up the community of faith. Because this is the work of God, we can expect some surprising turns. A woman comes through a very painful divorce. After several years of anger and guilt and loss, she realizes that she has not merely survived this crisis; she is stronger than she had been before. What are this new confidence and this new strength for? Stirred by a new ability, she gathers a support group of divorced and separated women. Out of her woundedness a charism grows. If this is paradoxical, it also rings true to the gospel.

Our charisms are for the community in another sense. Through our strengths and gifts we link ourselves to a group of believers. These charisms bond us to a specific community and its needs. Our charisms rescue us from isolation and insert us in a community. They show us how to belong. If we have no strength or gift to give this group, we can belong only as a child or consumer. For a very long time the church did not expect lay people to have charisms for preaching, pastoral care, and other leadership tasks. Yet today we are startled at the gifts that overflow in our parishes. Where have these people been? They have been here all this time, of course, but we are only now learning to recognize their gifts.

Another dynamic of God's power stirs in our conscience, that inner, hard-won authority that guides our adult decisions and commitments. In its richest sense, conscience refers to *who I am*. It is a deepening sense, rooted in our youth and developed through our twenties and thirties, of what we are to do with our life. Only through many efforts, some false starts, and numerous failures do we come to trust our own decisions. Slowly we learn our special rhythms of social involvement and solitude. We come to a sense of our own special strengths and limits and how these will be part of our following of Jesus. This awareness and confidence gives authority to our choices and makes us conscientious.

Like the power of charism, the authority of conscience links us to the community of believers. It does not lead us to do whatever we want, distinct from the demands of authorities. Rather, conscience is a profoundly *social* strength: in this interior authority our parents and early teachers continue to thrive. Their values and best hopes still shape our inner judgments. The communities of our past survive by shaping our conscience.

Our past, of course, leaves other traces in our heart: voices not of conscience but of wounds inflicted by our family or religious heritage continue to play within us. An inner voice warns us that anger is always bad, to be avoided at any cost. Another voice warns us against undertaking projects because we are only "lay people." Our conscience is our own maturing voice, able to distinguish healthy and unhealthy sounds from our past. This authoritative voice, like our charisms, anchors our contributions to a community of faith. Without a reliable conscience we may docilely comply, but we cannot become adult partners in faith.

But conscience, like charism, has not always been prized in the church. In a religious world dominated by parental leaders, the children of God seemed not to need a conscience. When Catholics began to reclaim these religious powers of charism and conscience, in the first years after Vatican II, they were tempted to see them as personal powers. These two strengths equipped us to withstand the paternalistic persuasions of our religious institution. But soon we saw the deeper truth: charism and conscience do not set us free from community; they link us to both God and other believers. These strengths bind us to God in gratitude and to our community in generosity. They empower us to belong.

From Abundance to Scarcity

But many Christians are still unfamiliar with their charisms and uncomfortable with their conscience. They are heirs to another vision of God's power—a vision of scarcity. How did this spiritual poverty come about?

As Christianity expanded in the third and fourth centuries, ministry began to shrink. The rich variety of charisms, scattered throughout the earliest Christian communities, was gradually absorbed into the ministry of the priest. The powerful gifts for teaching, healing, prophesying, and community administration were seen as belonging uniquely to the priest and bishop. Other Christians, now called "laity," were told that they lacked these powerful charisms. The abundance of power that Christians had known in Jesus Christ began to dwindle into scarcity.

In the twelfth century, church officials described sacramental leadership in a new fashion: the priest was defined as *having the power* to perform the sacraments, apart from his union with a community of faith. This vision of leadership as the individual possession of power had been developing for some centuries: the appearance of the private Mass suggested that this community celebration belonged, essentially, to the individual leader.

The church had come to picture the priest not as orchestrating the shared power that is a faith community but as uniquely supplying to this receptive group God's power in the sacraments.

In this hierarchical world, Christians came to perceive pastoral power as belonging exclusively to the clerical leader. Lay Christians, as ungifted consumers, were unqualified to select their leaders or raise questions of accountability. This vision of power still binds many parishes. The pastor, by both canon law and common consent, has all the power. No one celebrates the liturgy or undertakes ministry in this community except at his discretion. He is able to dismiss other ministers in the parish without accountability. When he arrives at a new parish, he can abolish programs that have been in effect for years.

This view allows us to forget that God's power has been active in the community prior to this leader's arrival and will be active long after his departure. It lets us neglect the charisms and consciences of the other adults in the community. We forget that the power of the *Spirit* shapes Christian ministry, not the power of the *pastor*. In such an environment the church mimics the culture's view of power as a scarce possession instead of announcing the gospel vision of power in abundance flowing through a community.

Shrinking the abundance of God's power into scarcity results in the malaise of clericalism. Clerical leaders weave a controlling web around charisms and ministries, carefully guarding their own priority and privilege. As a recent study of clericalism, published in *Religious Life at the Crossroads*, observes, clericalism "is neither identical with nor a necessary consequence of priesthood, but a diminishment and distortion of it." Priesthood, in its best expression, announces an abundance of power: a priest's ministry is meant to multiply power. A minister's preaching and anointing remind the community of its priestliness. Ordained leaders do not forgive and make Christ present because others cannot; they preside in these symbolic actions to celebrate the reconciling and nourishing that the community is already performing, daily, in Christ's name. These sacraments remind us of our calling and renew our enthusiasm for forgiving and nourishing one another.

Clericalism, like paternalism, is not restricted to priests. Any leaders who use their positions to protect their privileges make power scarce and foster clericalism. If others preach and forgive and nourish, then the clerical leader sees his special power as diminished. The laity are not to usurp his status and priority. Instead, a few officially designated leaders replace the abundance of charism in the group; the clerical priest rules a community that has been stripped of its priestliness. When deacons and lay leaders succumb to a possessive sense of power, they join the ranks of clericalism.

In this milieu of invented scarcity, clerical leaders see ministry as their domain and possession. "This is *my* parish," the pastor insists, "and I will do it my way." The word goes out: power is in short supply. Others can be strong only at the leader's expense. There is not much grace available here. Clericalism is, finally, a failure to recognize that God's power does not belong to any person or office but flows freely and abundantly through the community.

The Sacraments: Abundant Power

If God's grace is a dynamic that stirs in a group, then the sacraments are the ordinary channels through which this saving energy moves. But these rituals are the actions of a community, not just its leaders. The fundamental sacrament is the church itself: every genuine faith community, in its witness and healing, makes Christ visible and tangible. It acts sacramentally in the daily faith and courage of its members. At times we celebrate our sacramental life in special rituals of the seven sacraments. An ordained leader presides at and orchestrates these communal events. Only in a clerical world does a leader absorb all the initiative and render others in the community dependent and passive.

The central sacrament of the Eucharist has changed most profoundly under this vision of the community as sacrament. Not long ago we pictured the Eucharist as what the priest did; all others simply attended or "heard" Mass. The priest said all the prayers and distributed Communion, and he alone could preach. He said Mass whether others were in attendance or not. Today we are recovering the Eucharist as the action of a community. Some in the group guide the singing; others read the Scriptures and give the homily; others distribute Communion. We are less likely to see the Eucharist as the priest's private domain or possession. This sacrament is not his to do, at his discretion; it is the community's celebration of God's nourishing presence among us.

For this vision to become real, we must have an experience of this communal nurturance. Many Catholics testify that they attend Mass but find little nourishment. Fulfilling their Sunday obligation, they take Communion; but they are not fed. They go to Mass but experience no Eucharist. But when we take the time, often in a much smaller group, to break bread together with prayer and forgiveness, we taste the presence of God among us. We feel again the energizing force that consoles and challenges us. Bringing our different gifts and needs to a focus in this sacrament, we experience God's abundant power. And in this nourishing celebration we are empowered: we grow and make more of our shared life. In this saving ritual we also recognize that the power is not the leader's or even the community's. The pulse that renews and enlivens us is the power of the Spirit.

Recent transformations in the sacrament of Baptism further illustrate the community's reclaiming of abundance out of scarcity. Baptism is not merely the brief ritual performed by the parish priest; it is also the long process of bringing a child or adult into the community of faith. Parents instruct their child in the ways of faith; relatives and neighbors model the shape of Christian charity and justice. Many members of the community, through the abundant power of their faith, make Baptism real and effective. We bring this sacramental process to a focus in the ritual of Baptism. In the Rite of Christian Initiation of Adults, communities express their shared responsibility in introducing new members into their shared life. As a parish welcomes new members baptized at the Easter Vigil, God's power expands and strengthens the community. The priest performing the sacrament in seclusion cannot substitute for the transforming process of a baptizing community. This is not how Christian power works.

The sacrament of Ordination was, in early Christianity, a more communal exercise as a community helped select and prepare its new leader. Centuries later, this sacrament was collapsed into the ritual action of the ordaining bishop; he alone seemed to have the responsibility for training and appointing parish leaders. Today, in dioceses with priestless parishes, communities are once again invited to participate in the selection of their pastoral leaders. In this tentative movement many hear hints of the rescue of Ordination from a world of scarcity.

The sacrament of Reconciliation is a striking example of the paradox of absence and plenty. Very few Catholics go regularly to confession these days. As a private exchange between penitent and priest, the sacrament continues to wither. Yet when we look more closely at the faith community, we see an abundance of reconciliation. In Marriage Encounter and Cursillo, couples are extending and receiving forgiveness. In faith-sharing groups and counseling, many Christians are healing ancient wounds rooted in their families of origin. Parishes and other religious groups develop prayerful services of communal forgiveness. Reconciliation is plentiful—though not where we have been trained to expect it.

The sacrament of Reconciliation rediscovers abundance as it comes out of the dark confessional into the light of the community. Ritual and leadership remain important to this sacrament, but these must serve the communal process of forgiveness.

In each of the sacraments we meet the paradox of scarcity and abundance. We carry new wine in old wineskins. The challenge may be to find the abundance—where nourishment and forgiveness and leadership are happening—and move our sacraments there.

In Jesus Christ, God has given us great abundance. We, the church, have invented scarcity. And yet clues and hints abound, in this world of scarcity, of God's surprising and abundant power.

Reflective Exercise

Consider your own experience of scarcity and abundance. Where is the pain of scarcity most real for you these days? Perhaps an experience of material poverty or a lack of sustaining relationships; maybe an unrewarding job or a lingering personal limitation. How does this scarcity affect your life? Be concrete; give some examples.

Where do you most often feel graced with abundance? In your family? In the world of your work and civic involvement? In your prayer? In your awareness of goodness and beauty? Again offer examples of this abundance in your life these days.

Finally, have you experienced the paradox of scarcity and abundance—an apparent lack that led to new life; a deprivation that proved to be fruitful? Recall the experience in detail, savoring the shape of this paradox in your own life.

What learnings from your personal experience might help illumine the experience of scarcity and abundance in the church?

Additional Resources

Leaders in many sectors of American life are learning to manage for scarcity; see, for example, A. M. Pettigrew's early examination of this challenge in "On Studying Organizational Cultures," *Administrative Science Quarterly* 24 (1979): 570–81. For a sobering account of the increasing scarcity in priestly leadership, see the overview of Richard Schoenherr's study, sponsored by the U.S. Catholic bishops, "Study of U.S. Diocesan Priesthood Statistics: 1966–2005," in *Origins*, September 6, 1990, pp. 206–8. Dean R. Hoge discusses the current situation and future trends in priesthood in *The Future of Catholic Leadership: Responses to the Priest Shortage* (Kansas City, MO: Sheed & Ward, 1989).

In the 1980s the Conference of Major Religious Superiors of Men commissioned a task force to undertake a critical analysis of clericalism in ministry; see Francine Cardman and others, "In Solidarity and Service: Reflections on the Problem of Clericalism in the Church," in David Fleming, ed., *Religious Life at the Crossroads* (New York: Paulist Press, 1985), pp. 65–87; quote taken from p. 67. This discussion continues in Rémi Parent, *A Church of the Baptized: Overcoming Tension Between the Clergy and the Laity*, trans. Stephen W. Arndt (New York: Paulist Press, 1990).

John Dominic Crossan explores the abundance of meaning in the parable of the sower and seed in his *Cliffs of Fall* (New York: Crossroad/Continuum, 1980). The last two decades have seen an explosion in theological studies of power. See, for instance, Bengt Holmberg's *Paul and Power: The Structure of Authority in the Primitive Church as Reflected in the Pauline Epistles* (Philadelphia: Fortress Press, 1978) and the more pastoral work of Walter Wink in *Naming the Powers: The Language of Power in the New Testament*, (Philadelphia: Fortress Press, 1984).

3. Healing the Wounds of Authority

> For this Law that I enjoin on you today is not beyond your strength or beyond your reach. . . . It is not beyond the seas, so that you need to wonder, "who will cross the seas for us and bring it back to us, so that we may hear it and keep it?" No, the Word is very near to you, it is in your mouth and in your heart for your observance. (Deut. 30:11, 13–14, JB)

Partnership includes the embrace of authority. The root meaning of *authority* is "augment"—to make more of. Parents are our first authority figures. Good parents encourage their children's first steps and support their later leaps. They learn to correct without stunting the child's movement toward maturity. Success as a parent comes through nurturing another's growth, inviting the child into adulthood. This standard holds for other authorities as well. All genuine authority expands life, making power more abundant. Religious authority succeeds by nurturing spiritual growth. This genuine religious authority calls us to greater responsibility, finally welcoming us as partners.

But the mature embrace of authority sometimes eludes us. Many of us move into adult life wounded. From early experiences in our own families and from messages reinforced in our society, we develop an image of authority as external. Authority, we have come to believe, is "beyond the seas," so that we must wonder, "Who will cross the seas for us and bring it back to us?" We picture authority as existing in important institutions and special people but not in ourselves. Those in authority—parents, pastors, police—seem to *have* power, holding on to it as a permanent and privileged possession. But if power is a possession, authority escapes accountability. Those in authority can use their power as they see fit. Their actions may help us or harm us, but the decision is theirs to make.

This vision of external power provokes a variety of responses. Sometimes we see ourselves as children, needing "their" power because we do not have any, or at least not as much as we need. Sometimes we see ourselves as victims, subject to the arbitrary use of power but unable to influence those who wield it.

Seeing ourselves as children or victims, we cannot become adult partners in faith. Both images carry a judgment about ourselves and an expectation about external authority. The judgment is that we are vulnerable; when we deal with those in authority we are likely to be hurt. The expectation is that authority is dangerous; people in authority will shame us, punish us, turn against us in our need. These attitudes sabotage our efforts to grow into the full adulthood of Jesus Christ.

Burdens on Religious Leadership

Our wounded attitudes toward authority lead us to make irrational demands of leaders, especially religious leaders. We want them to be—we *need* them to be—larger than life. We expect them to be all-knowing, capable of telling us what we should do. We demand that they be all-providing as well, accessible to us at all times and ready to care for our needs. We require that they be perfect—accountable to standards of morality, generosity, and excellence that far exceed those to which we hold ourselves.

These unreal expectations confirm a sense of authority as *other*. People in authority are not like me; they are somehow *different* from the rest of us. We treat people in authoritative roles as if they possessed special qualities—wisdom or talent, insight or holiness—that somehow explain their difference and justify our demeaning response.

The psychological process of distancing our leaders has negative consequences, but it pursues a primitive personal gain. Picturing our leaders as endowed with magical qualities of wisdom and generosity and courage, we try to hold off a deeper terror of maturity—the recognition that we are accountable for our own lives. As long as our leaders are superior to us, we do not have to be responsible. We can count on them to make things turn out right. They are properly in charge because they are better—more talented, more mature, wiser, closer to God. We resist finding out that our leaders are like the rest of us—insightful and confused, gifted and wounded. This realization drives us from our hiding places; no person or group stands as a buffer, protecting us from the demands of life.

Our leaders are like us: this is a hard saying. Though it is the beginning of adulthood and the basis of religious maturity, we strenuously resist its truth. To accept the truth leaves us both more vulnerable and more responsible than we want to be. Believing that leaders have all the answers comforts us, especially when we have so few answers ourselves. Once we recognize a leader's access to truth as being like our own—often partial and conflicted, sometimes wounded by bias and error—then we are no longer relieved of responsibility. Leaders cannot protect us; we are all in this together. Our own participation, no longer a luxury, is now required.

Partnership in an adult church depends on our participation. Authority in the community of faith is not simply what *they* do to the rest of us—whether we judge them to be good-hearted or malicious, enlightened or hopelessly out of touch. The rest of us are more than just beneficiaries or victims, more than simply observers of how religious authority functions. We are all active participants in authority.

The Transformation of Authority

How do we move beyond our wounded images of authority? The transformation often begins in a moment of crisis, as I realize that I am locked in a pattern that just doesn't work. Whatever my actual behavior—whether I always try to avoid authority or I always fight authority or I am intent to win authority's approval—it simply causes too much pain.

WITHDRAWAL

Recognizing that my awareness of authority has been focused almost exclusively outward—on a leader or boss or set of laws—I withdraw that focus. This modest step, often made in a mood of quiet desperation, may remain hidden. Nothing needs to change on the outside. I may still behave the same way, but a process has begun. I start to experience myself as set apart from the influence of authority, at least in some interior way. People in authority just do not "get to me" so much.

In my head and my heart, I can turn off authority: transformation begins here. The process may stop here as well. Moving away from a wounded stance toward authority is dangerous business. Letting go these accustomed attitudes may demand that I behave in new ways. Aware of the risks involved if I start to act differently toward authority, I may settle instead for this private inner freedom. I have a place of interior refuge to which I can retreat. Here I can feel safe—but nothing more is asked of me.

DISBELIEF

But for most of us the process does not stop with withdrawal. We move into disbelief, a second moment of purification. Disbelief comes as a moral conversion. Until now my sense of self and my feelings of self-worth have depended on how those in authority have viewed me. But I am *not* just what authority says of me: I am more than that, even different from that. This simple affirmation brings a surge of personal power. I can stand on my own, apart from "the powers that be."

Refusing to accept the way that those in power define me is a radical act in the strictest sense: it goes to the root of my relationship with authority. I start to question leadership's right to define my experience. At first, disbelief has a defensive edge: "Who says . . . ?" Who says that blacks are less intelligent than whites? Who says that men are more dependable than women? Who says that poor people do not know their own best interests? Who says that gay and lesbian love is disordered? Who says that the proper role of the laity is to pay, pray, and obey? "Who says . . . ?"—especially if my own experience or my own aspiration says otherwise.

Disbelief accelerates my withdrawal from authority understood as outside me, located exclusively in a particular leader or a certain set of laws. As the influence of "outside" authority diminishes, I see things anew. I find my own experience trustworthy. My unthinking loyalty to the way things are begins to erode. I recognize that the way things are is not always the way things *should* be, not the only way things *can* be. Much of what I used to accept as necessary now seems arbitrary, or at least changeable. Initially a conviction that the people in charge were always right guided me. Now I am not so sure. I see that "the way things are" often comes down to the way that people with power have decided—and sometimes for their benefit more than mine. The moral superiority of those in authority, which until now seemed self-evident, is suddenly in doubt.

The risk here is that disbelief may sour into skepticism—a contemptuous suspicion of every exercise of power, a repudiation of any structure of authority. Such skepticism often turns personal, emerging as a preoccupation with the faults and frailties of the people in charge. We are eager for evidence that diminishes them in our eyes. The success of the *National Enquirer* and its clones in the tabloid press attests to this morbid fascination with the weaknesses of the powerful. Institutional gossip gives skepticism another forum. By sharing rumors about their misconduct, we knock the powerful off the pedestals we had built. We do not yet see ourselves as their equals, but at least we can bring them down to our level.

SELF-SCRUTINY

For me to move beyond skepticism's impasse, I must refocus my gaze. A challenging self-examination awaits me. I have to face what I am like in my relationship with external authority. Not until I confront my own behavior can I determine the proper place of authority in my life.

Transformation stalls if this scrutiny bogs down in self-absorption. Then my attention remains focused on me—my wounded history with authority figures, my fears of approaching the people in charge. Under the weight of this internal agenda, I excuse myself from any real change in the way I act. In my case, I explain, it is just too tough.

But examining how I act toward authority challenges this sense of powerlessness. The facts force me to recognize how active I have been all along. My authority relationships have been shaped as much by *my* attitudes—whether fear or defiance or shame—as by the demands of the people in charge. This insight invites me to acknowledge my collusion. It has been easier to blame "them" than to take responsibility for my own actions; I do not like being told what to do, but I would rather acquiesce than risk failure on my own. A painful recognition dawns: I am not *simply* a victim in the unhappy relationship I have with authority. In good measure, I have been doing it to myself.

Confronting my part in this unhealthy pattern helps me to see authority anew. Authority is not a distant, magical force; it is not a power that leaders possess and others do not. Instead, authority is a dynamic between people; it is what goes on among us. Authority is a way of interacting—not a possession but a process. Together, Americans give authority to our Constitution; Catholics actively give their assent to the authoritative reforms of Vatican II. In these processes we are all participants. Our own attitudes and behaviors are part of the interplay, sometimes confirming the way things are, sometimes moving toward change.

Each of us is already a participant in authority: this realization is a milestone on the journey of personal transformation. If I have participated in my own oppression, I can contribute to my empowerment as well. I start by identifying the attitudes and behaviors that keep me subservient, and—instead of giving myself over to self-pity or blame—hold myself accountable to act differently.

By freeing me to look at how authority actually functions in my life, self-scrutiny readies me for the next movement of purification. Now I can ask the question, When is the influence of external authority—a leader, a value system, a set of laws—legitimate in my life? Earlier this was not an open question, because my response was predetermined. Before I began the journey of transformation, my automatic response would have been "always." Authority as I understood it then—existing outside me as a morally superior force—was always legitimate; its demands were to be obeyed without question. At the stage of disbelief, my predetermined response would have to be "never." Authority, now unmasked as a sham, is never legitimate in its attempts to influence my life.

But life with others is impossible if I simply refuse to be influenced by structures and needs beyond my own. Marriage, friendship, ministry, civic life—these thrive only if I am willing to accommodate myself to demands that come from outside me. But when do external requirements take precedence over my own preferences? Richard Sennett reminds us that only when this question comes at the end of a journey of personal transformation can it be asked freely, "with neither the compulsion to give a negative answer nor the desire to satisfy a hidden agenda." Not until I reach a certain level of intellectual and emotional flexibility can I weigh the evidence that leads to a mature response. Only then can I develop trustworthy criteria to help guide my practical discernment of when and how to obey.

AUTHORITY-MAKING

Transformation attains its goal when I can raise the issue of legitimate authority. Now I can reenter the process of authority-making—that is, of granting others some influence over me. I have always been doing this—conferring authority by giving certain persons and procedures the right to influence my own beliefs and behavior. But before, I was largely unconscious of my own role. Seeing authority as an external force, I understood my role as simply giving in or going along. Now I recognize my own participation in the processes of social power: both my negative contribution—through fear or apathy or magical thinking—and my positive contribution—through personal assertion and a willingness to face controversy and conflict.

At this stage of transformation, now aware of my own strengths and wounds in regard to authority, I can unite with others in pursuit of a common purpose. I can recognize both the benefits and the limits of the patterns of authority that we have established among ourselves. I am able both to take initiative and to obey, to assert my needs and to accommodate myself for the common good. Now partnership in faith becomes possible for me.

Finally, a crucial clarification is in order. The importance of the personal agenda—healing wounded attitudes toward authority—does not excuse me from the public task. I cannot wait until I am healed before I become involved in social change. I cannot wait until all my own motives are pure before I actively participate in institutional reform. As we saw at the outset, I am already a participant. My actions always influence the patterns of power around me, either reinforcing the status quo or moving toward some other way of doing things. To excuse myself from conscious participation is simply to reinforce that the way things are is the way things have to be. For me to drop out in this way is of obvious advantage to people who are eager for things to stay as they are.

There is an obvious political intent in strategies that urge the out-group—whether this be women, people of color, or groups that are economically deprived or politically marginal—to "clean up their own act" before they have the audacity to question the actions or intentions of the people in charge. But we cannot wait that long! We cannot wait until we are pure, until our personal motives are unambiguous, until all our wounds are fully healed. Processes of personal transformation and social reform must proceed together.

The process of personal transformation must go on. Refusing the painful purification of my own demons around authority only undermines my participation in institutional reform. Even without much insight into my own wounds regarding authority, I may be able to help "throw the rascals out." But my positive contribution will be crippled. I am unlikely to offer much to the structural purification demanded of a church that is truly adult.

Authority in the Body of Christ

"The Word is very near to you, it is in your mouth and in your heart for your observance." The ancient author uses the intimate images of mouth and heart to express the nearness of God's truth. Religious authority is within us—in our social body, in our seasoned communal experience. Psychologist Eugene Kennedy takes this corporeal image a step further. Genuine authority, he says, is always sexual.

Authority and sexuality are both powers that shape our shared life. Sexuality refers to much more than genital activity; its energy attracts us to one another and arouses us to commitment. Sexuality promotes life and leads us to be fruitful. Genuine authority likewise fosters life and seeks fruitfulness.

Our parents, those first and enduring authorities, not only gave us life but encouraged us to grow up and to act responsibly. Similarly, religious authorities engender faith, foster our growth, and stir us to virtuous action.

Both parents and religious authorities fail when they use their power to inhibit and defeat our maturing. When authorities threaten and coerce others, their influence no longer promotes life; it become asexual. Authoritarian leaders, suspicious of change and growth, cling to control. Stifling the responsible actions of others, their style of leadership becomes barren.

Partners in faith yearn for fruitful embraces. Ministering together, we slowly learn the rhythms of mutual influence and shared control. In these new collaborative settings, we struggle to shape more life-giving patterns of religious authority. This effort helps heal the wounds around authority that we still carry as the body of Christ.

Reflective Exercise

Trace your own maturing in authority, using the model in this chapter as a guide. Begin by identifying, over the past five or ten years, a significant shift in your attitude toward external authority. Spend time with this experience. What triggered this shift? What thoughts and feelings accompanied the change?

Then consider the process of personal transformation discussed in this chapter (withdrawal, disbelief, self-scrutiny, and authority-making). What shape did these stages take in your own experience? Offer some concrete examples.

Finally, what awareness do you now have of your positive contribution to authority? For you, what wounds around authority remain to be healed?

Additional Resources

This chapter follows sociologist Richard Sennett's analysis of the personal transformation of authority; see his *Authority* (New York: Vintage Books, 1981); quote taken from p. 133. Social analyst Elizabeth Janeway develops the significance of disbelief in personal and social change in *Powers of the Weak* (New York: Knopf, 1982); see also her *Improper Behavior: When and How Misconduct Can Be Healthy for Society* (New York: Morrow, 1987).

Eugene Kennedy explores the conflict between genuine authority and authoritarianism in *Tomorrow's Catholics, Yesterday's Church* (San Francisco: Harper & Row, 1988), part 2. In *Household of Freedom: Authority in Feminist Theology* (Philadelphia: Westminster Press, 1987), Letty Russell examines authority from the perspective of feminist theology. We discuss religious authority as a social interpretation of God's power in *The Emerging Laity: Returning Leadership to the Community of Faith* (New York: Image Books/Doubleday, 1988); see especially chapter 4.

Rosemary Radford Ruether and Eugene Bianchi bring together a series of significant essays on the transformation of institutional authority in *A Democratic Catholic Church* (New York: Crossroad, 1992).

4. Shadows on the Journey: Absence, Conflict, Failure

> At every stage of their journey, whenever the cloud rose from the tent the children of Israel would resume their march. If the cloud did not rise, they waited and would not march until it did.   (Adapted from Exod. 40:36, JB)

A cloud passes over. Does its shadow cool us or darken our day? In the midst of a long walk in August, we welcome this overshadowing. If we are planning an autumn picnic, this cloud may appear on our horizon as a threat.

Clouds have played a creative role in the Judeo-Christian tradition. The book of Genesis pictures the Spirit of God *overshadowing* the primeval waters (1:2). The mystery of creation is ignited when this Spirit hovers over the "formless void." During their long journey through the desert, our religious ancestors recognized some clouds as signs of God's presence. In the heat of the desert, clouds gave God's people both relief and direction.

The image of God's creative presence as a cloud reappears in the gospel story of Jesus' conception. Mary is told that "the Holy Spirit will come upon you . . . and the power of the Most High will *overshadow* you" (Luke 1:35). This second creation intentionally echoes the account of Genesis.

The provocative image of a potent overshadowing of God appears only twice more in the New Testament. In the story of the transfiguration, Jesus' three friends are given a sudden, overwhelming insight into who he is (Matt. 17). They remember this revelation as a cloud overshadowing them and a voice telling them that Jesus is God's specially chosen one. Such a shadow does not cloud their life but illumines it. This image appears again in an account of the apostles' extraordinary ministry after Pentecost. So impressed are people by Peter's ability to heal that they set their ill relatives on the street "in the hope that at least *the shadow* of Peter might fall across some of them as he went past" (Acts 5:15, JB, italics added). The story suggests that certain shadows fall with potent healing effect.

The memory of Hiroshima may have erased for us today the nuances of healing in the overshadowing cloud. Our vulnerable imaginations now picture clouds as signs of destruction rather than of God's presence. Clouds are carriers of acid rain or worse. But the ambiguity deep within the human imagination endures: the approach of both friend and enemy casts a shadow over us; clouds rain on our parades, but drought-stricken farmers shower gratitude on any rain cloud. In our efforts to minister together in the church, three special shadows cross our paths. These are the ominous clouds of absence, conflict, and failure. Might these frightening shapes signal more than approaching darkness? Could these clouds conceal, as they once did, God's special presence?

The Shadow of Absence

A spirit of absence hovers over the church these days. Like the mood of scarcity we discussed in chapter 2, absence often threatens our fragile faith. A rural rectory, formerly occupied by a resident priest, now stands empty. Elsewhere a parish school, once a thriving center of religious education, is shuttered. The human heart recoils from absence, because it suggests failure and death; it evokes a sense of peril. But might the shadow of absence carry another meaning? Could this cloud, too, come bearing gifts? We must look into the absence itself to find the answer.

We honor absence by neither fleeing from it nor trying to cover it up. If we look into the face of absence, we begin to see that it is a curious gift. A campus ministry team is disrupted when the ordained leader is transferred. The two remaining staff members panic; deprived of his customary leadership, how are they to manage? Yet they are surprised to discover how well they do over the next weeks and months. They are more capable

than they had guessed! With a strong leader, they had not needed to test their abilities or try anything new. Now, in his absence, they are compelled to create programs on their own. But
their new-found abilities needed this experience of absence. The
threatening cloud of absence becomes benevolent.

A new pastor faces a challenge in an area where his own
skills are minimal. Should he just stumble ahead, trying to ignore the problem? When he has the courage to look to the community, he will find others capable of dealing with the problem.
An absence in his repertoire of skills becomes an opportunity for
others to minister. Their strength is challenged to grow in this
environment of absence. If the leader sees his lack of skills as
humiliating and others' strengths as threatening, he will not
honor absence and the gifts of the community will not increase.
His resistance restrains the group's power.

Sensing the special potential of absence, we return to the intriguing stories of emptiness in the Scriptures. Reading again
about the long romance of our ancestors with God in the desert,
we suddenly see how empty a place the desert is. One can walk
for days without any sign of progress. Apparent oases turn out
to be mirages. Often the Israelites felt their hope slipping away.
They complained to their leaders: Did you bring us out here to
die? But in this seemingly sterile absence, they felt the stirring
of God's presence. Setting up a tent at the edge of their campsite,
they listened for the movement of the wind and looked for the
appearance of a cloud—any sign of the mysterious presence of
God. "The pillar of cloud would come down and station itself at
the entrance to the Tent, and Yahweh would speak with Moses"
(Exod. 33:9, JB). Our ancestors' earliest experiences of God were
an epiphany: the sudden and momentary appearance of this saving power. God's presence, whether in a campside tent or burn-
ing bush, flashed out in a milieu of emptiness. Absence was the
deserted stage where this saving presence walked.

Many Christians today are heartened by this dynamic. Our
fleeting glimpses of God in the midst of absence echo our ancestors' experience. A long crisis generates not only pain but, surprisingly, a heightened sense of God's presence in our life. A
community, feeling the deprivation of having no resident priest,
gradually recognizes its own gifts and responsibilities; only the
absence of a leader led them to this realization of abundance.

Faith blooms in unexpected places. God's presence still walks through absence and surprises us with its epiphanies.

Awakened to this creative dynamic of absence, we look again at the New Testament. Jesus' prayer at the Last Supper turned to a threatening absence. Steadying himself to face his death, he told his friends that he had to leave them: "In a short time you will no longer see me" (John 16:16, JB). But his departure was not an abandonment. After his death and resurrection, Jesus appeared to his friends in the kind of epiphany found in the Hebrew Scriptures. At the seashore and on the road to Emmaus they sensed his presence, and then suddenly he was gone.

At Pentecost the disciples gathered in an upper room, frightened and confused by Jesus' absence. In this domestic desert, they suddenly felt the stirring of God's power; fear turned into courage, and confusion into confidence. Finding themselves strangely gifted—to speak out and heal and celebrate—they felt Christ's enduring presence in these abilities. They began to understand the potency of Jesus' absence. As long as he was physically with them, they could totally depend on him. Asking his advice, face-to-face, they would remain forever disciples. Only when he absented himself were they forced to take responsibility for their lives and their shared faith. Jesus' absence did not diminish their faith but expanded it.

The Shadow of Conflict

If absence is an ominous shadow, conflict comes as a storm cloud. Disagreements overshadow our best efforts to work together and cool off our friendships. Is this cloud only destructive or might it also bear some hidden good?

Uncomfortable with absence, many of us positively hate conflict. Why do we have such a strong reaction to this cloud in our life? Conflict threatens our relationships. Our pulse quickens when we remember a quarrel that gravely injured a friendship. Such memories can paralyze us when we face a new conflict: if I confront my boss, I may be fired; if our ministry team allows this simmering disagreement to come out in the open, it might destroy us. Conflict has earned its reputation for destruction.

Conflict bewilders us because our distress is so often misdirected. After being humiliated at work, I come home and start an argument with my teenage son. Or a co-worker comments on my late arrival for a meeting and I react in rage—hearing a parent's scolding voice in my colleague's remark. Or I become extremely angered at a minor decision of a religious official. In these painful encounters, my conflict is not with my child or colleague or religious authority, but with an "absent other." Our unfinished business, especially with deceased parents and former authorities—the absent others who still populate our life—often generates conflict in us. If we project these struggles onto a friend or colleague, we are starting a fight that we cannot finish. And though we may not know why, we often sense that these conflicts are about the wrong thing.

At other times our fear of conflict arises from an uneasiness with strong emotions. Many of us have not learned to distinguish anger from its destructive relatives. We assume that all anger runs inevitably to rage. Our only strategy becomes avoidance. When our anger finally boils over, the conflict it induces is much more difficult to resolve.

Finally, many of us have learned to identify disagreement with disloyalty. We may have been taught that, for good Christians, obedience means agreement, belonging demands conformity. To challenge others—especially those in authority—is to be disobedient and disloyal. Thus conflict is outlawed. These biases about anger and disagreement cripple our efforts to face the necessary conflicts in our life.

Yet even in our fear of conflict we often have a hunch that it is more than an outlaw. Could this threatening cloud ever suggest the presence of God? To answer this question we turn to the Hebrew and Christian Scriptures.

PARABLES

Religious narratives such as our Scriptures are made up of two kinds of stories: myths and parables. A myth is not a falsehood but a story with a plot. (The Greek word *mythos* means "plot.")

The stories of the Jewish and Christian Scriptures develop a plot about God's love for humans. These stories help us make sense of our life. But parables, a very different kind of story, introduce conflict into the flow of our life with God; they complicate the plot.

The book of Ruth in the Hebrew Scriptures is such a story. Ruth was a foreigner, a non-Jew, and Israelites had been told by God not to marry outsiders. In a troubled time an Israelite journeyed to Ruth's land and married her. From their family line King David was born. At the heart of this lovely tale of friendship and fidelity lies a parable: if Ruth's husband had followed the rules, the Jewish people would have been deprived of one of their great leaders. Parables surprise us, catch us off guard; they remind us that God's ways are not ours.

In the life of Jesus we meet this same blend of plot and parable. Jesus' daily activities of preaching, healing, and eating with friends all weave a plot—the appealing story line of his life. About the time we think we are following the story, Jesus introduces a parable to throw us off stride. We know who our neighbor is until he tells the story of the good Samaritan. We understand how to treat a selfish son who runs off and squanders his inheritance until we hear the parable of the prodigal son. But these confusing stories are but sparks given off from the central parable: Jesus' own life. God's specially chosen one, he constantly acts in ways that confuse us. He consorts with public sinners, with women of poor reputation, and with men of questionable occupations (such as tax collectors). He disregards religious law by gathering corn to be eaten on the Sabbath. Is this any way to act? When his friends jockey for preference, he assures them that, with God, the last will be first. This makes no sense.

Theologian John Dominic Crossan observes that the parable brings not peace, but the sword. If the plot of a story connects the many threads of a life into unity, a parable unravels them. If the plot of our life roots us in certain convictions, parables uproot us, leaving us uncertain. And it is the conflict between the sensible plot and the confusing parables that gives our life its energy and vitality.

Parables, as Crossan observes, are the dark night of our story. Crises are the guise that modern parables wear: in our family troubles and crises of faith, our control of the plot is broken. But in these dark nights we learn amazing lessons: we are stronger than we thought; and there is something better than total control.

Parables are about "graceful" conflict. They break the flow of the narrative—in Jesus' life as in ours. We would like the story to be tidy and under control, neat around the edges even if a bit romantic. But Jesus insists that parables are part of the plot. Conflict is not just an unfortunate footnote; it is essential if we are to tell the full story.

HARMONY AND AGONY

Western Christians carry two very different heritages of conflict. Aristotle and Thomas Aquinas speak for a tradition emphasizing harmony as the highest ideal of human life. In their view conflict and tragedy signal a special peril—the loss of the ideal. The world has been created good; its parts are meant to fit harmoniously together. In such a vision there is no room for a conflict of goods. Conflict, the cousin of failure and sin, always foreshadows evil. In *After Virtue* Alisdair MacIntyre summarizes this position: "If we encounter genuine moral conflict, it is always because of some previous wrong action of our own." Thus the specter of conflict evokes both threat and guilt. It is a sign of disorder and also an indication of personal failure. Thus linked with wrongdoing, conflict can bear no good fruit. Like its sibling, anger, conflict is to be evicted from the Christian community. Only it will not leave. When conflict is repressed, it goes underground, accumulating more strength for its next visit.

This vision of harmony is in sharp contrast to a more tragic vision of life. Homer, Aeschylus, and other Greek poets believed that struggle is an integral part of human life. Conflicts arise not only due to personal flaws but because the human situation is unavoidably tragic at times. The Greek word *agon* ("contest" or "agony") conveys this conviction: humans must struggle their way toward good decisions and a just life. The Greeks developed this idea of *agon* first in the physical contests of the Olympic Games, then in the political debates and philosophical disputes of Athens. As MacIntyre observes, these Greeks came to see that "it was in the context of the *agon* that that truth had to be discovered."

Conflict and the discovery of truth are linked! We uncover truth, but the effort is agonizing. If harmony is a goal of life, conflict is often the route to this ideal. Turmoil and conflict are normal dynamics in human life. The friction of conflict often generates insight: we reclaim a value that, in the midst of a well-protected "harmony," we had taken for granted. As MacIntyre reminds us, "It is through conflict and sometimes only through conflict that we learn what our ends and purposes are."

So it was with Jesus. In his own agony, the night before he died, Jesus struggled with his fate. He prayed to God—as we do—to avoid this impending conflict. He, too, preferred harmony. But in the pressure of this agonizing evening he came to see what he was to do. Because of the gracefulness of this conflict, Christians honor his agony in the garden. The parable of his suffering and death was a necessary part of God's plot. And today we search for the courage to honor the agony in our church—the disruptions and crises that portend not only death but new life.

The Shadow of Failure

As we minister together as partners in faith, we meet another shadow: the experience of failure. We try things that do not work; we form relationships that, despite our best efforts, come to an end. Whatever our education or goodwill, each of us fails at many tasks.

For Christians, failing can bear an extra weight, because we expect the best from ourselves and find our failures humiliating. Our perfectionism makes it difficult for us to forgive ourselves. "Good enough"—that humble blend of success and failure—is *not* enough. An unholy insistence on perfection turns the shadow of failure into a toxic cloud. This idealism casts a special weight on our leaders. We place them high above us and expect them to be wiser and holier than the rest of us. They must exhibit exceptional patience and charity and courage; they should never fail. In the last century Catholics have come to see their leader as in-fallible, one who cannot fall. This claim burdens not only the pope but the whole community.

A THEOLOGY OF FAILING

We begin to heal our vision of failure by remembering that falling is part of the parable of our life. It is not an unfortunate exception that has nothing to do with the plot of our vocation. Falling is part of the story, an integral part of our journey.

We are helped to recognize this paradox by returning to our Scriptures. In the Easter liturgy Christians celebrate the *happy fault* of our first parents. In the account of creation in the book of Genesis, we read of Adam and Eve's sin. They fell from grace and were forced to leave the garden of paradise. This story recalls an enormous failure that influences all of human history. Here lies the mysterious root of our brokenness, our injustice, and our failures at loving.

Yet in this Easter prayer the church celebrates a *felix culpa*—a felicitous failure. It was, after all, this disastrous failure that brought Christ into our midst. The fall of Adam and Eve bore a strangely paradoxical fruit: the coming of Jesus Christ. In a most peculiar way this fall seems to be part of the story, part of the plot of our salvation. It is a cloud that is not all bad.

A second place that Christians honor falling is in their devotion to the stations of the cross. In this pious exercise Catholics journey with Jesus through the "stations" that led to his death on the cross. At several points in this devotion we honor Jesus' falling. "Jesus falls the second time." As in our celebration of Adam and Eve's fall, we recognize here the mysterious role of falling and failing in every human journey.

Jesus reached the goal of his journey by falling. That is how he got there. The road that led to his death and resurrection came through the valley of failure. This should not sound too strange to an adult Christian. When we look back at our own peculiar journey, we may remember a mistaken career move in our twenties or a failure at love in our thirties. Earlier we may have tried to forget these embarrassing failures. Now, however, we begin to see that they are part of the journey; they are turns in the road that leads to our present life. This is the way we have come.

Reconciliation is a central part of Christian life. It does not always mean "the forgiveness of sins." Often it challenges us to acknowledge our failures—the stumblings and wrong turns that are part of our vocation. Reconciliation invites us to honor falling, not to flee it or deny it. We are all experienced in falling; maturity comes in our response to it. A wise commentator once observed: if we can touch the nerve of failure, we will be delivered from a failure of nerve. To touch the nerve of failure: this is to admit and forgive our falling. We taste our own failure and recognize that we have survived it. With this new knowledge we are equipped to try new jobs and make new friends. We can afford to risk failing, for we have been delivered from a failure of nerve.

When we become more tolerant of failure in our own life, we begin to give our leaders room to fail. We have been tempted to place our leaders on pedestals; from these heights they should not fall, ought not let us down. But these heroic expectations twist the meaning of infallibility, which is a gift of God to the church, not an attribute of a leader. Matthew's Gospel ends with Jesus' assurance: "Know that I am with you always; yes, to the end of time" (28:20). This gift of Christ's guiding presence is a promise to hold us through all the turmoil of human history. Whatever our blunders and blindness, God will not let us fall fatally. We will err grievously—history bears emphatic witness to this truth—but God will see us through, holding us firm in faith. This is God's gift, given to the community of Christians. Because of this guarantee, we can risk creativity and change. Christians can allow their leaders to risk falling in their service of the community.

Both falling and infallibility belong within the community. If our life is solitary, if we labor as a soloist, we perform alone and so, fall alone. It is much better to play out our life in a community—a place of friends with strong arms to hold us, a safe place to fall. In a supportive community we can take risks and large leaps. If we fall, our friends and colleagues will catch us. A network of friends forms a net that cushions our fall and protects us from major injury. A community also comforts and holds us after a scary fall until we are bold enough to try again.

The shadows of absence, conflict, and failure fall on every human journey. Yet our Christian heritage gives us optimistic clues about these threatening clouds. They are about more than loss or humiliation. At times these clouds announce the surprising presence of God. If we can befriend absence and conflict and failure, we can become more graceful partners in faith and ministry.

Reflective Exercise

An adult church, like an adult life, must learn to befriend these shadows—absence, conflict, failure. Consider where these shadows fall as you experience the community of faith.

Absence. What shape does absence take in the faith community most important to you? How does the community respond? What feelings accompany this absence? What actions? What gift does this absence bring?

Conflict. Identify the conflicts that are part of this community's life these days. Can you trace an underlying pattern here? What attitudes and feelings about conflict are dominant among us? How are these feelings and attitudes usually expressed? When has conflict been "graceful" among us?

Failure. How is failure real for this community? Do we have a characteristic response?: denial? blame? forgiveness? Give some examples. What is the best lesson that failure has taught this group?

Additional Resources

Theologian Martin Marty offers a prayerful reflection on the experience of absence in *A Cry of Absence* (San Francisco: Harper & Row, 1983). Frederick Busch examines the continuing influence of absent others in his collection of short stories, *Absent Friends* (New York: Knopf, 1989). Mary R. Thompson examines Mark's Gospel as an account of failure and struggle in *The Role of Disbelief in Mark* (New York: Paulist Press, 1989). In *Seasons of Strength: New Visions of Adult Christian Maturing* (New York: Image Books/ Doubleday, 1986), we explore the religious significance of failure (chap. 1) and absence (chap. 14).

John Dominic Crossan's continuing examination of the biblical form of parables highlights conflict's power to instruct and transform; see his *Dark Interval: Towards a Theology of Story* (Chicago: Argus Press, 1975). Alisdair MacIntyre looks at the positive role of conflict in *After Virtue* (Notre Dame, IN: Notre Dame Press, 1981); quotes taken from pp. 167, 129, and 153. For an excellent discussion of parables, see John Donahue's *The Gospel in Parable: Metaphor, Narrative and Theology in the Synoptic Gospels* (Philadelphia: Fortress, 1988). Organizational consultants Kenwyn K. Smith and David N. Berg analyze the role of group conflict in *Paradoxes of Group Life: Understanding Conflict, Paralysis, and Movement in Group Dynamics* (San Francisco: Jossey-Bass, 1987). In *Dealing with Diversity: A Guide for Parish Leaders* (Mystic, CT: Twenty-Third Publications, 1987), Greg Dues offers parish leaders practical strategies for managing the stress of conflict.

For a discussion of the emergence of the doctrine of infallibility, see William Bausch's *Pilgrim Church* (Mystic, CT: Twenty-Third Publications, 1989). Philip Kaufman offers a more comprehensive look at the gradual development of this papal prerogative in *Why You Can Disagree and Remain a Faithful Catholic* (New York: Crossroad/Continuum, 1989); see also Peter Chirico's *Infallibility: The Crossroads of Doctrine* (Wilmington, DE: Glazier, 1983).

For help in facing conflicts generated by pluralism, see Joseph Fitzpatrick, *One Church, Many Cultures: The Challenge of Diversity* (Kansas City, MO: Sheed & Ward, 1990) and Stephen Kliewer, *How to Live with Diversity in the Local Church* (Washington, DC: Alban Institute, 1990).

Part Two

Ministry in a World of Partners

5. Ways to Collaborate: Staff, Team, Community

"It is not right," the father-in-law of Moses said to him, "to take this on yourself. You will tire yourself out, you and the people with you. The work is too heavy for you. You cannot do it alone." (Exod. 18:17-18, JB)

You cannot do it alone! Throughout the church—in parishes and schools, justice networks and prayer groups, social agencies and health-care institutions—ministers affirm this conviction. The church today needs all the gifts that the Spirit of God gives to the community. But how do we rally our diverse strengths? Finding better ways to collaborate is a practical response. The image of committed and competent persons working together in the complex tasks of ministry captivates us. We sense the power that this shared ministry releases in ourselves and in the church. We can do more together than any of us on our own!

Enthusiasm for collaboration surged in the 1970s. Women and men, ordained and lay, rejoiced in new opportunities to share faith. Convinced that joint action would accomplish more than individual effort, people sought out colleagues. Small faith communities offered members support in their work and family life. Neighboring parishes committed themselves to coordinated planning. People involved in difficult and frustrating work—prison ministry, for example, or justice education—formed alliances. Co-operation became more than a management strategy; ministry co-workers saw their ongoing effort to work together in honesty and respect as part of the Good News that the gospel proclaims.

But over the past decade, this initial enthusiasm for shared ministry has mellowed. Still aware of the advantages of collaboration, we now know its costs as well. The benefits of effectiveness and support are paid for in the coin of compromise and change. As Archbishop Thomas Murphy of Seattle notes, "Collaboration has become the major challenge for all people who minister in the church today." But today's commitment to shared ministry is less naive and, for that reason, more willing to face the messy demands that collaboration makes.

What can we do to improve our collaboration in ministry? Ministry groups everywhere grapple with this question. To collaborate is to "labor together," to work together for a common goal. This "laboring together" takes many different forms; no one style emerges as the "right" way for every ministry setting, so collaborative ministry groups do not all look alike. In fact, several organizational styles can support greater collaboration. This diversity shows up in the terms that people use to describe their ministry efforts—ministry staff, pastoral team, ministering community.

Staff, team, community—some people use these words interchangeably, referring to the same ministry group. But the terms suggest different ways of working together. In consulting with ministry groups these days, we incorporate these three terms in a model of clarification. The model uses *staff, team,* and *community* as distinct images offering three ways to conceptualize how collaborative groups function. Each image carries a set of expectations about how a group sees itself and how it organizes its work. The images are merely tools for understanding; real groups are always more complex than the model suggests. For example, working together does not demand that a group choose one of these organizational patterns and eradicate signs of any other. In practice the styles overlap; many successful ministry groups incorporate elements of all three.

We will look at each organizational style, examining both its strengths and challenges for shared ministry. The model is not a prescription for how collaboration *should* look. It serves best as a guide for discussion, helping co-workers evaluate their current style to see what needs to be reinforced and what needs to be renegotiated.

Ministry Staff

A staff is a work group organized into different levels of responsibility. The person in charge holds a higher position than others on the staff. The chain of command moves vertically: directives come down from levels above; staff members are accountable to "higher-ups." Staff members have distinct areas of responsibility. Co-workers may share information and coordinate schedules, but they usually work alone. The leader's role is highly visible, pictured at the top of a pyramid or at the hub of a wheel. This official leader—understood as manager, supervisor, boss—directs the activities of other staff members.

A staff is often part of a larger system: a care unit in a hospital, a department in a school, an office in a social-service agency, a parish in a diocese. While staff members locally report to the leader, the leader reports to organizational superiors outside this group. Accountability goes one way only—up the chain of command.

Many ministry groups, especially in large parishes and diocesan agencies, function as a staff. Working as a staff brings clear advantages to an organization with broad outreach and a wide range of programs. The manager/staff design is orderly and efficient. In a well-run staff organization, job descriptions state what each worker's duties are and how much authority each has; established policies and procedures announce ahead of time what behavior is expected. Staff members can thus appreciate the group's larger goals but are not responsible for everything. Recognizing the chain of command, individuals know their own place in the power structure. These established procedures help staff members act with confidence.

But operating as a staff carries some risks for collaboration. The first is isolation. Staff procedures typically do more to separate co-workers than to bring them together. Official lines of communication move to and from the person in charge. This group leader, as manager, tends to deal with staff members individually. Organizations often emphasize these links with the leader, downplaying connections among staff members. Any ongoing cooperation among co-workers must be initiated or at least tacitly approved by the person in charge. Sometimes this separation serves the work, by keeping people out of one another's way and focused on their own responsibilities. But collaboration depends on connections. A staff that wants to work collaboratively has to overcome its built-in separatedness.

Let us reiterate: a work group organized as a staff *can* function collaboratively. The leader can expand staff participation in decisions even while retaining final review. Co-workers can co-operate in an overall plan that leaves them considerable autonomy in carrying out their part. Staff members can look to one another for peer support and criticism, even as they respect areas of distinct responsibility. But effective collaboration comes neither easily not automatically on a staff; people have to work hard to make it happen.

Because a staff setting highlights the leader's role, the person in charge usually has to take the first steps to broaden collaboration: setting up opportunities for members to work together, supporting joint planning efforts, encouraging direct communication among the staff. Even then, if the person in charge fails to *model* the behavior being asked of others, these leadership initiatives seldom succeed.

A second risk to collaboration comes from the pull of formal procedures. Functioning as a staff means working within established roles and rules. By formulating policy and issuing guidelines, organizations make clear what is expected of staff members. These structures help the group act with consistency: people do not have to work out a plan of action for themselves. But sometimes structures harden. Collaboration demands that staff members can contribute to keeping the structure flexible.

Some organizations resist giving staff members much leeway. Decisions made by people higher in the organization leave little discretion to those who actually carry out the job. But a staff unable to influence operating procedures risks being smothered by its own structure. Following common policies works well when these procedures fit the circumstances. But established procedures do not always suit the circumstances. In fact, procedures already in place sometimes blind us to new, more appropriate ways of doing things. In highly structured work settings, this causes problems. Policies intended to strengthen the staff's effectiveness instead burden its life. Procedures are justified less by their actual benefits than by custom: "That's the way we do it around here." When structure becomes master rather than servant, collaboration suffers.

In many staff settings, collaboration hangs on the question of mutual accountability. A bureaucracy holds the leader accountable only to those on a higher organizational level. Local leaders may be urged to communicate with staff members and to keep relations cordial, but only their formal superiors are competent to judge their work. Collaboration implies that designated leaders "render an account" to their co-workers as well. How this is done differs widely, but some forum for open discussion of the leader's role is essential for collaboration.

FIGURE 1: STAFF/TEAM/COMMUNITY

	Style	Strengths	Challenges
Staff	Distinct responsibility; vertical accountability	Order and efficiency	Encourage connections; keep structure flexible
Team	Interdependent action and accountability	Complementary strengths; flexibility and spontaneity	Befriend structure; establish workable patterns for ongoing activities
Community	Strong value components; explicit concern for task, vision, and support	Group witness to values; commitment to mutual support	Move values beyond rhetoric; develop structures that hold belonging in tension with effectiveness

Pastoral Team

A team is a work group organized for interdependence. People come together *intentionally*, convinced that coordinated planning and joint action accomplish more than working alone. To operate as a team means that people call on one another for help, for advice, for support, for critique. Co-workers are available to one another by design, not just by chance. If staff members are organized to stay out of one another's way, team members get in one another's way—on purpose.

Pastoral teams benefit from the strengths of this interdependent style. Working together expands a group's scope, because it is not limited to what individuals can do on their own. Team members make their experience and skills available to one another; that is part of the promise of team ministry. Functioning as a team, each member has a *right* to the others' resources.

Flexibility is a second strength. While a pyramid captures the stable hierarchical pattern that many staffs follow, an effective team operates more as an amoeba does: responsive to its environment, the organism is able to change its shape to meet new opportunities or demands. On a ministry team, job definitions and rules of procedure typically stay tentative; work patterns shift in response to changing pastoral needs. Responsibilities can be shared among team members or transferred from one person to another without too much strain. The team's leader operates as "first among colleagues" more than as administrative superior, as facilitator of the group's activities more than as the person ultimately in charge.

Spontaneity is a third strength. Teams accommodate change more readily than most formal organizations. Because established procedures carry less weight, teams more easily improvise. Unanticipated needs provoke alternate methods; unexpected problems stimulate novel solutions. Spontaneity does not always guarantee success, of course, but members are free to experiment creatively.

These strengths of team ministry come with risks. Pastoral teams sometimes generate suspicion. By intent, work groups that function as teams do not play by the rules that guide most organizational behavior. Others on the scene often wonder, "What are they up to?" A pastor committed to functioning as a member of the ministry team may be accused of abdicating leadership. An irate parishioner may resist having to deal with the team member—a lay woman—now serving as financial administrator. A disgruntled chancery official may demand, "Who's *really* in charge over there?" When suspicion grows, people working in team settings are dismissed as idealists or treated as rebels. In either case, the larger institution is wary of their influence.

To be honest, pastoral teams are often wary as well. Many people join a team after other ministry experiences have left them frustrated. Suspicious of hierarchical structures, skeptical of formal procedures, they long for more life-giving ways to work together. Team ministry attracts them with its promise of freedom and flexibility. They carry their caution with them when they come to this new ministry scene, however. Disillusioned by the organizational patterns in their past, they resist efforts to organize *this* team. But operating without structure seldom serves collaboration. Without organization, the team loses focus. What starts out as flexibility becomes lack of common purpose; what first looked like spontaneity now shows up as an inability to complete group projects.

Teams need to *befriend* structure. Policies and procedures exist to help groups function at their best. Granted, structure often fails at this high objective. But the challenge then is to change the faulty pattern, not to abandon organizational patterns altogether. For collaboration to thrive in a team setting, co-workers often have to overcome their reluctance to get organized. By putting some regular procedures in place, a team rescues energy for its more important work. Who does what around here? How do we keep everyone informed? What is the best way to make decisions? How will we deal with conflict? Getting these things down in writing does not have to mean setting them in stone. In this necessary organizational process, team members who remain skeptical often help the group by insisting on safeguards to prevent the procedures from becoming sacrosanct.

Ministering Community

People in pastoral work today often describe themselves as a ministering community. The word *community* is hard to pin down, especially in religious discussions. For some people, the word signifies the strong emotional ties of family or close friendship. For others, the word simply means a group that they like, a place where they feel at home. But *community* can be used more precisely, to describe a way of collaborating in ministry. A community is a ministry group in which *shared values* lead to *common action* undertaken in a spirit of *mutual concern*. Values, action, and concern are not absent from other collaborative groups. But in a community each of these elements demands *explicit* attention.

The image of a searchlight may help. A ministry group that understands itself as a staff focuses its light primarily (though not exclusively) on the common task. Co-workers are likely to hold many values in common, but these are seldom discussed explicitly. Staff members interact as they carry out their ministry, but this interaction seldom comes under scrutiny unless it gets in the way of the work.

As a team, a ministry group's focus widens to include a more explicit concern for their interaction. Like a staff, a team gathers for a task. But unlike most staffs, teams intentionally involve one another in their work. On a team, interdependence is both practical and emotional. Because they work together more intensely, team members often develop stronger ties than do colleagues on a staff. These ties do not mean that team members necessarily become close friends or function as a support group. But teamwork engages people in one another's lives in ways that go beyond staff functioning. Because teams draw their strength from this broader interdependence, members have to be conscious of how they deal with one another. For a team to be effective, the quality of the group's life cannot remain just a background issue; explicit attention must be paid to it.

In a ministering community, the searchlight widens its focus again. Now common values become a priority, and mutual support is an explicit goal. Values, task, support—in a community each of these elements is crucial. A ministering community wants to *be* something as well as get something done. Members work together, guided by the theological insight that Christian ministry is essentially communal. Their commitment to a collaborative working style testifies to a deeper conviction: a gift of the Spirit to the whole church, ministry is not meant to be done alone.

In a ministering community, each member feels committed to *practice* what its common values *preach*. In doing so, the group becomes a visible "we." People outside can see that something special is going on. A Christian community sets out to enact the gospel. Aware that actions speak louder than words, we shape our ministry accordingly. In our work style and in the way we treat one another, we explicitly hold ourselves accountable to patterns reflected in Jesus' life. We hope to make the gospel visible in our pastoral practice as surely as we announce it in our words. Many pastoral groups consider this public witness central in their ministry.

The ministry of witness is a risky undertaking, leaving our behavior open to these questions: Who is watching, and what do they see? Some ministry groups get lost in rhetoric. Theological statements are issued; religious convictions are proclaimed. But people looking on have a hard time tracing connections between these value declarations and how the group operates. When this happens, a group in ministry risks becoming a countersign. We are in trouble as a witnessing community if the only way people recognize the values we serve is by reading our mission statement.

In a community, witness is central to the leader's role as well. People in the group and on the outside expect the community's leader to embody the values that the group professes. Some ministering communities go further, burdening the leadership position with heroic expectations. Then the leader is cast as exclusive guardian of the community's dream, charged with challenging members to live up to its ideals. Or the leader becomes the group's chief spiritual guide, a kind of guru nurturing each member on a personal journey of faith. These heroic expectations distance the leader from the rest of the community, even as strong bonds of dependency are forged. Communities—both leaders and the rest of us—have to work hard against the force of these larger-than-life expectations. To fail is to fall into the trap of paternalism, a communal style that ultimately defeats collaboration.

A ministering community is challenged simultaneously on several fronts: to nurture a common vision, to show their concern for one another in genuinely appropriate ways, and to act together effectively.

COMMON VISION

In a community, what we believe in common nourishes our common action. But for this vision to fuel our action, we must acknowledge what we hold in common. A sense of community requires some agreement (but only *some* agreement) about values. Acknowledging the values that we share takes time—time to look together at what we believe, time to develop the trust that makes this honest discussion possible, time to accept the value differences that are sure to exist, time to deal responsibly with disagreement and dissent.

MUTUAL CONCERN

For many in pastoral work, a ministering community's greatest benefit comes in mutual concern. Community attracts us with its sense of belonging, promising opportunities to share with others at a significant level and to express genuine care and concern. We like knowing that we are in this together, part of a close-knit group with a strong sense of solidarity. But a supportive community does not come easy. People collaborating in ministry these days come from diverse life-styles: clergy, religious, and laity; married, single, and celibate. Diversity enriches the collaborative experience—but also adds complications. Often members carry different expectations of support and mutual concern. For some, the most significant personal relationships are with ministry colleagues. Others have dense networks of family and friends beyond this ministry group. Some of us look to the ministering community for close friendship; for others, it promises an ongoing commitment to faith sharing and common prayer. And whatever the shape of the expectations, mutual support demands time and emotional energy—resources that are in short supply.

EFFECTIVE ACTION

Ministering communities are about more than solidarity and support. Important work needs to be done, and doing the work of ministry makes organizational demands. Ministers must reach agreement about tasks and roles and responsibilities. Lines of authority and accountability need to be sketched; patterns of decision making have to be determined. Without these structures our efforts will lack focus and force, displaying nothing but ineffective good intentions.

Community groups take seriously both their tasks and the quality of their life together. This dual orientation often creates strain. Sometimes tasks dominate, crowding out the time needed for mutual support. Or commitment to proceed by consensus delays an important decision. Activities that help in one area of communal ministry may cause problems in another: a program of performance evaluation may improve the quality of work but foster a destructive sense of competition; a regular schedule of communal prayer may strengthen the group's cohesion but draws the complaint that it diverts the group from ministerial work. Ministry groups that become successful as communities learn how to live with these tensions, balancing commitment to one another with shared responsibility for the pastoral task.

Staff, team, community: using this sequence in our model of clarification does not suggest an order of preference. Ministry groups function well in each of these organizational styles. Collaboration demands that people who work together discuss the pluses and minuses of their current organizational arrangement, whatever style prevails. The reflective questions that follow may be a good place to start this discussion.

Reflective Exercise

Identify a ministry group important to you. This may be a small faith community or an ongoing parish committee, a formal ministry staff or an established pastoral team. Spend time with your memories of this group: recall the people and events from your history together, as well as the group's purpose and task. Take some notes about the group, including both the facts and the feelings that are part of your experience.

Most ministry groups include elements of more than one organizational style. Is this true in your case? Read again through the description of a ministerial staff, listing ways that your group fits that style. Then read through the section on the pastoral team, noting ways that your group fits that style. Finally, read through the section on the ministering community to find ways that your group fits that style.

When you have completed this, look at your ministry group and consider the questions that follow. Give examples to support your answers. Discussing your responses with other members of the ministry group can itself be a step toward greater collaboration.

1. Which organizational style is dominant, as you see it?
2. How does this way of operating help collaboration?
3. Does this style get in the way of collaboration?
4. What one change do you suggest to improve collaboration?

Additional Resources

Thomas Sweetser and Carol Holden explore the dynamics of collaboration in *Leadership in the Successful Parish* (San Francisco: Harper & Row, 1986). In *Improving Your Multiple Staff Ministry: How to Work Together More Effectively* (Minneapolis: Augsburg, 1989), Anne Marie Nuechterlein discusses collaborative ministry from the perspective of family systems theory. Bernard Swain describes the range of the leader's behavior in shared ministry in *Liberating Leadership: Practical Styles for Pastoral Ministry* (San Francisco: Harper & Row, 1986); see also Robert D. Dale, *Pastoral Leadership* (Nashville, Abingdon Press, 1986), and Arthur Baranowski, *Creating Small Faith Communities* (Cincinnati: St. Anthony Messenger Press, 1989).

Archbishop Thomas Murphy's discussion of collaboration appears in "The Host of Challenges Priests Face," *Origins*, Aug. 4, 1988, pp. 1–4; quote taken from p. 2. For helpful discussions of interdependent ministry, see Loughlan Sofield and Carrol Juliano, *Collaborative Ministry* (Notre Dame, IN: Ave Maria Press, 1987), and Keith Clark, *The Skilled Participant: A Way to Effective Collaboration* (Notre Dame, IN: Ave Maria Press, 1988).

In "Work Teams: Applications and Effectiveness," *American Psychologist*, Feb. 1990, pp. 120–33, Eric Sundstrom, Kenneth DeMeuse, and David Futrell look at work groups across a range of organizational settings to discover factors that increase their effectiveness. For fuller discussions, see J. R. Hackman, *Groups That Work (and Those That Don't)* (San Francisco: Jossey-Bass, 1989), W. G. Dyer, *Team Building: Issues and Alternatives*, 2nd edition (Reading, MA: Addison-Wesley, 1987), and Glenn H. Varney, *Building Productive Teams: An Action Guide and Resource Book* (San Francisco: Jossey-Bass, 1989).

6. How Leaders Gain Legitimacy

The apostles continued to testify to the resurrection of the Lord Jesus with great power, and they were all given great respect. (Acts 4:33, JB)

After Jesus died and was raised, the community faced a crisis of leadership. Jesus had spoken with authority. But what about Peter, John, and the other disciples? Could they be trusted to speak in Jesus' name? Were they worthy leaders, deserving of the community's recognition and respect? And who was this Paul? What right did he have to preach so authoritatively? The book of Acts and the letters of Paul and his associates give us glimpses of the ways in which the early Christian communities came to embrace this new generation of leaders.

The church today faces another crisis of leadership. The decades since Vatican II have transformed the shape of ministry. Now women and men, lay and ordained, salaried professionals and committed parishioners all minister among us. These new faces raise complicated questions of religious leadership.

Today, as in the past, communities confer legitimacy on leaders who earn their trust. Canonically, church leaders are legitimate when proper procedures are followed to bring them into the job. Being duly appointed by the bishop, for example, gives the pastor legal jurisdiction. But, as most pastors realize, jurisdiction is not enough. To carry out their responsibilities in the community of faith, pastoral leaders need the active support of the community. Legitimacy comes when a group recognizes the leader's *right* to be in the position, the *right* to make the demands that are part of the leader's job. In a very practical sense, then, a group grants legitimacy when it accepts the leader's right to be heard and heeded.

Consider these two examples. The people of St. Malachy's parish have a special affection for Father Keller. Pastor among them for many years, he has baptized their children and buried their parents. His sermons, admittedly somewhat rambling, alert them to the signs of God's enduring love in their lives every day. Father Keller is not good at raising money and his singing voice is terrible. But the people love him! Parishioners pitch in willingly to get the work of the community done. Father Keller is *their priest*, his authority acknowledged in their respect and esteem.

St. George's parish is another matter. When their pastor retired two years ago, the diocesan personnel board announced that no priest was available to replace him. Parishioners were outraged: "Eighty years a parish, and we don't deserve even a priest!" Several weeks later two Catholic sisters arrived. The bishop's letter designating them as "pastoral administrators" pleased no one. As the months went by, those active in the parish came to admit, at first somewhat begrudgingly, how much the sisters were contributing to the community's life. Sister Connie is a fine teacher and an even better organizer. After conferring with a number of parishioners, she started a Bible study program and recruited volunteers for a community ministries committee. A worship commission now meets regularly to design community prayer for "priestless Sundays" twice a month. There is talk about a leadership training program to prepare candidates for a parish council. Sister Ruth devotes much of her time to the needs of the children and young people. A parents' support group now meets regularly. Teenagers are welcome at the parish hall and, more surprising still, have started spending time there. The sisters have accepted an invitation to join the monthly clergy conference, an ecumenical gathering of local pastors. Gradually the parish community is embracing these two nontraditional ministers, granting the legitimacy of their leadership.

Conferring Legitimacy

An organization can appoint the people in charge, but organizations cannot create leaders. Practically, leadership depends on the consent of the group. To be effective, people in leadership positions must be accepted by the rest of us. We need not see them as likable, as someone we would have chosen, or as the best candidate for the job. But we must at least grant that their authority is in some way justified.

Properly speaking, then, organizations may assign *headship*, but groups make *leaders*. They do this by accepting the *right* of the designated person to influence their lives. "She's not my first choice for chairperson, but she came by the job fair and square. Now that she's in the position, I think she deserves our support." This is a statement of legitimacy.

Legitimacy gives the leader breathing space, room to move, the benefit of the doubt. Without that kind of acceptance, the leadership role grows increasingly burdensome. Dissatisfaction mounts; people squander their energy in mutual suspicion. Group members resist the leader's influence—raising obstacles, finding fault, delaying action. And the leader often responds defensively—demanding compliance, threatening punishment, tightening control.

A group empowers its leaders when it is open to their initiative, accepts their influence, and responds to the challenge their ministry brings. A readiness to cooperate out of choice rather than coercion, a willingness to accommodate ourselves to the inconveniences and even sacrifices that are required—these are the signs that we accept a leader as legitimate.

To serve the Christian community today, people in ministry have to win this practical acceptance. What leads us to embrace our religious leaders? How do they earn credibility? What evidence do we use to confirm a pastoral minister's right to be heard and heeded? The process of gaining legitimacy is complex and still not well understood. We look here at several factors that seem significant in the community of faith today. These are *institutional factors* that are part of our shared life as Catholics, *personal qualities* that leaders display, and *extra-rational dynamics* that arise in the relationship between the religious leader and others in the community.

The Institutional Bases of Legitimacy

In this chapter we consider only the institutional factors listed in Figure 2. In the following chapter we will explore the personal factors and the extra-rational dynamics of religious legitimacy.

FIGURE 2: THE LEGITIMACY OF THE RELIGIOUS LEADER
Institutional Factors
Theological justificaton
Office or formal role
Personal Factors
Demonstrated competence
Personal vision
Extra-Rational Factors
Symbolic role of the leader
Religious authenticity

THEOLOGICAL JUSTIFICATION

Theology provides an important foundation for the legitimacy of the religious leader. Theology is the Christian community's reflection on its life of faith. From the earliest disagreements between Peter and Paul, Christians have debated the source of the leader's authority. How is Christian leadership rooted in charism? In the selection of leaders, how active should the community be? What is the role of Baptism? of ordination? of formal office? of an active life of faith? But across these debates, theological answers to the question, "Who are our religious leaders?" have carried considerable weight.

Until quite recently Catholics shared a broad consensus about *who* our religious leaders were and *why* their authority was justified. Our leaders were priests. The deep respect and ready obedience they inspired was rooted in a generally accepted theology of priesthood. Clergy and laity alike understood the priest to be an essential mediator of God's grace, through the sacraments (to which the priest alone had direct access) and through the otherness of his life as a sacred person. The priest was the primary, even exclusive, minister to the spiritual needs of the Catholic community. His soul marked with the indelible character of the sacrament of Holy Orders, the priest was essentially different from others in the community. Whatever the limits of his personal ability or even his moral rectitude, the priest was "another Christ." For these reasons, his authority was legitimate.

But Catholics' deep respect for the priesthood carried some negative consequences. The faith community made few demands. Poor preaching passed without question; parishioners were expected to reconcile themselves to a domineering pastor's autocratic behavior. Priests themselves suffered from this too-easy acceptance. Their need for continuing education was downplayed or denied. Ordination seemed to dispense with a need for further study. Evidence of a priest's personal problems was often overlooked. Bishops were reluctant to remove an alcoholic chaplain or incompetent pastor, because the then-dominant theology of priesthood argued that the priest's legitimacy resided in his ordination and official appointment. These made him, legally speaking, "competent." To remove him from ministry risked undermining this interpretation of religious authority.

The experiences of the Catholic community over the past twenty-five years have called this theological understanding into question. Many priests today find the conventional definitions of priesthood at odds with their own experience. But efforts to express a post–Vatican II understanding of ordained ministry are still in the early stages. As yet, no clear or widely convincing reformulation replaces the consensus that has been lost.

If the theology of priesthood remains in flux, the theological understanding of other ministries is even less well developed. Vowed religious, along with growing numbers of lay women and men and married deacons, now staff parishes, diocesan offices, and religious agencies that were once the exclusive world of the priest. In this atmosphere of shared ministry, legitimacy—who ministers here and by what right—emerges as a lively concern.

Theology lags behind these developments in ministry. The documents of Vatican II reiterated the links between Baptism and the call to ministry, but the church struggles to appreciate the practical implications of this connection. While nonordained persons exercise considerable pastoral leadership, no compelling theological statement supports their legitimacy. What is the theological relevance of the religious education director or youth minister? What theological weight secures the position of a woman pastoral associate or lay teacher in a Catholic school? People may bring to these roles a rich personal awareness of the religious significance of what they do, but no well-developed or publicly accepted theology of ministry supports their private conviction.

Today lay people gain credibility in roles once open only to priests, but this acceptance is hard-won. Often these nonordained leaders are welcome for reasons that lie outside theology: they have proved themselves dedicated and competent, for example, or they accept a job for which no priest is available. A well-trained lay chaplain, for example, is often rebuffed in her first encounters with Catholic patients. "Where is Father?" or, "Is there no priest in the place?" Initially, her ministry seems like a weak substitute for "the real thing." But soon she will be asked to anoint a person approaching death—asked by a family that knows she is not a priest. Gently she reminds them that she is not able to perform the sacraments. Nonetheless they want *this* minister, who has cared so well for them and their loved one during the hospital stay, to provide the church's final blessing. Their confidence confers legitimacy on this person and validates her ministry.

Administrators serving parishes without a resident priest have similar experiences. At first, a person in this position bears the brunt of the parish's pain and grief. Unable to celebrate the Eucharist or to provide the sacrament of Reconciliation, this minister seems useless. But after months of generous service, the situation changes. The administrator, lacking customary credentials, secures another source of credibility: showing the community the believable face of Christian care, he wins their acceptance and trust. As Peter Gilmour observes in *The Emerging Pastor*, in practice the community ordains these ministers. But we await the development of a theology of ministry reflecting these movements of the Spirit in our own time.

As controversy continues over the theological foundations upon which religious leadership *is* and *should be* based, people in ministry feel the strain. Many serve in leadership positions that as yet have little theological weight. Roles once religiously potent—priest, pastor, bishop—have suffered a loss of credibility as theological consensus shifts. As a result, theology's contribution to the practical legitimacy of religious leaders is not as strong today as in our recent history. This situation will improve as a richer theology of ministry comes into wide acceptance, but that development lies somewhere in the future.

THE LEGITIMACY OF OFFICE OR ROLE

Beyond theological formulations, legitimacy comes from *formal role*. To be properly designated as a leader—whether by appointment or election—strengthens credibility. Occupying a recognized leadership position reinforces the right to be heard and heeded.

A leadership "role" depends on mutually agreed-upon expectations of how a person in that position *should* act. These expectations, shared by leaders and other group members alike, encourage certain kinds of behavior and limit others. When the role is clear, leaders find it easier to perform acts that otherwise they might shy away from or avoid altogether. Many of us approach a leadership position with some trepidation, not at all sure we are up to the job. For example, embarrassed to give other people directions, we may hesitate to confront anyone older or more experienced. But expectations of us as leaders pull us into situations that demand different, initially uncomfortable, behavior. Amazed, we find ourselves acting with new confidence. We sense ourselves "growing into the role."

The leadership role seldom supports total freedom of action: structures of accountability and systems of evaluation remind leader and other members alike of the boundaries of the leader's power. But members *expect* the leader to take initiative in particular circumstances, to make certain demands on members, to act in ways that have an impact on other people. And more important for legitimacy, members *accept* this as appropriate leadership behavior. The very acceptance makes it easier for the leader to act. In this sense leaders inherit legitimacy. The role comes with some recognized authority already attached. New leaders rely on this inherited credibility to give them room to move as they begin the job.

In the church of the 1940s and 1950s, religious leaders—and the rest of us—knew what was expected of them. Their roles were clear. By and large, priests and parishioners shared the same expectations of how priests should act and how lay Catholics should respond. The religious leader's role was itself deserving of reverence, even if one had misgivings about a particular person in the job. The pastor was to be respected even if he was an unsavory character; the religious superior was to be obeyed even if she was not a very pleasant person.

Catholic theologians have struggled to separate the legitimacy of the leadership role from the limitations of the person filling it. Examining the sacramental role of the priest, they developed an understanding of *ex opere operato*. In this Latin phrase the church argued that the sacraments are effective apart from considerations of the minister's worthiness. God's grace, available in the sacraments, cannot be subject to the whims and flaws of the minister. However poorly the priest officiates at the Eucharist, the graces of the communal sacrament become available to the believing community. However uncaringly the priest anoints the dying, God's consoling grace touches them.

Like most historical formulations, the concept of *ex opere operato* lies open to misunderstanding. We sense its true meaning when, in the midst of a most ordinary homily, a phrase strikes us to the heart. Moved, we are brought to conversion. The minister's lackluster preaching was the occasion of our change, but hardly its cause. Or we experience the truth of God's presence as the community gathers for the Eucharist—a presence that does not depend on the presider's liturgical flair or communication skills. Sometimes *through* our official ministers, and sometimes *despite* them, God's grace reaches out to us.

But insistence on *ex opere operato* rings false when it neglects the intimate ties between nature and grace. At this extreme, the concept suggests that a miserable worship service celebrated by an inept priest conveys guaranteed grace—a view that taxes God's inventiveness and insults our partnership in salvation. One unhappy result of this misinterpretation is a piety of priesthood in which the role becomes unimpeachable: the priest's ministry produces grace-filled results, apart from his responsible performance. The role's legitimacy now becomes magical and unaccountable.

What is the role of the priest? Theologians, bishops, and priests themselves differ widely in their response. Is the priest a nurturing parent of the children of God, devoted to direct care for the spiritual needs of the laity? Or a responsible steward in an adult community of faith, called to facilitate and coordinate the multiple ministries of the people of God? Should the pastor stand as prophetic herald of the reign of God, challenging the congregation to assume greater responsibility for peace and justice? Or does he stand as wounded healer in our midst, witnessing to God's tender mercy toward those broken by personal pain and loss?

If the role of the priest is unclear, the status of other ministries is even less sure. Few mutually agreed-upon expectations exist for the role of the director of ministry effectiveness in a Catholic hospital or the diocesan coordinator of justice ministries or the lay person witnessing to faith in the context of her business career. The ministry of the permanent diaconate suffers particularly from such a lack of shared expectations. An initial enthusiasm for the reinstatement of this ancient ministry has given way to more practical questions: What does this person do? How is the deacon's ministry, which explicitly excludes presiding at the Eucharist or administering the sacrament of Reconciliation, different from the service of other Christian adults? Should an ordained deacon be brought into a parish to proclaim the Word when many lay people in that community already stand gifted and ready to preach?

That these questions exist does not mean that people involved in new ministries do not know what they are doing. Out of necessity, those in the newly emerging ministries have to develop clear personal goals. With so few established guidelines in their work, they wisely insist on written job descriptions and clear lines of accountability. But this personal clarity does not ensure that other people will see their ministerial responsibilities the same way.

Some difference between the minister's understanding and the group's expectations is to be expected, is even healthy. Without this tension, religious leaders risk becoming embedded in the group. Like the priest portrayed by actor Jack Lemmon in the film *Mass Appeal*, the leader who simply conforms to the group's expectations easily falls victim to subtle pressure to please everyone. When this happens, challenge falls out of bounds; conflict is taken as a sign of the leader's failure. But leaders have to be willing—and able—to lead, to move the group beyond the status quo. Without a prophetic edge, leadership sinks into a cautious defense of the way things are.

But when the gap between the leader's goals and the group's expectations looms too large, leadership suffers as well. A social role rests on mutual expectations. We recognize as legitimate those whose activities as leaders match our understanding of what their responsibilities are. When this connection is not clear, the leader loses credibility. Ministers trapped in a web of conflicting expectations become increasingly ineffective. Caught up in the struggle to justify what they are doing, these leaders feel their influence wane.

In the church today we are reexamining the roots of legitimacy. But consensus eludes us at this time. Theological opinion is divided; official role expectations remain in dispute. In the face of this institutional dissonance, religious leaders find their legitimacy elsewhere. In the next chapter we look at several of these alternate sources of effective religious authority.

Reflective Exercise

Call to mind a religious leader who has been influential in your life—someone you trust and admire. Spend time with these memories. Recall your favorite examples of this person's influence; note the behaviors and attitudes that you see as most characteristic of the person's leadership style.

Make a list of the factors contributing to this person's effectiveness as a religious leader, as you see it. Consider factors in the leader, in the group, in the larger setting. Give yourself enough time to draw up a full list.

From this list identify the two or three factors that contribute most to this person's stature in your eyes. Consider why these particular factors are important to your sense of legitimate religious leadership.

Finally, keep these factors in mind as you read through the discussion of legitimacy in the next chapter.

Additional Resources

Kenan Osborne provides an excellent overview of the changing sense of priesthood and its legitimacy in *Priesthood: A History of the Ordained Ministry in the Roman Catholic Church* (New York: Paulist Press, 1989). In *The Priest as Person* (Mystic, CT: Twenty-Third Publications, 1988), Robert Lauder examines the meaning and experience of priesthood. Henri Nouwen reflects on the role and responsibilities of Christian leaders in *In the Name of Jesus: Reflections on Christian Leadership* (New York: Crossroads, 1989).

For a discussion of authority and legitimacy in the history of Christian ministry, see John Howard Schütz's *Paul and the Anatomy of Apostolic Authority* (Cambridge: Cambridge Univ. Press, 1975). On the medieval theology of the special "character" of priesthood, see H. M. Legrand, "The 'Indelible' Character and the Theology of Ministry," in Hans Küng and Walter Kasper, eds., *The Plurality of Ministries; Concilium*, vol. 74 (New York: Herder & Herder, 1972), pp. 54–62.

In *Gifts That Differ: Lay Ministries Established and Unestablished* (New York: Pueblo, 1980), David Power considers the connection between theological legitimacy and the ritual commissioning of lay ministers. For a practical study of the ministry and legitimacy of lay parish administrators, see Peter Gilmour's *The Emerging Pastor* (Kansas City, MO: Sheed & Ward, 1986). See also *Laborers for the Lord* (Washington, DC: United States Catholic Conference, 1990), Leonard Doohan, *Grass Roots Pastors: A Handbook for Career Lay Ministers* (San Francisco: Harper & Row, 1989), and Patrick Brennan, *Re-Imagining the Parish* (New York: Crossroad/Continuum, 1990). For a comprehensive look at the issues that shape contemporary Catholic priesthood, see Donald Goergen (ed.), *Being a Priest Today* (Collegeville, MN: Liturgical Press, 1992).

7. The Authentic Religious Leader

> Jesus had now finished what he wanted to say, and his teaching made a deep impression on the people because he taught them with authority.   (Matt. 7:28–29, JB)

As he spoke to the people, Jesus emanated authority. Conviction in his voice and posture won him credibility. But when Jesus preached nearer to home, a different scenario unfolded. Here, too, his listeners were astonished and wondered at his wisdom. But they remembered: "This is the carpenter, surely, the son of Mary, the brother of James and Joseph and Jude and Simon" (Mark 6:3, JB). Being a local boy seemed to invalidate his credentials—"and they would not accept him."

The legitimacy of the religious leader is a complex story. More than official appointment is demanded; more than charismatic gifts is required. In this chapter we will examine both the personal qualities through which a leader earns legitimacy and the more mysterious forces in the dynamics of religious authority.

Personal Qualities of the Leader

Duly appointed leaders arrive on the scene invested with authority. They begin their jobs cloaked in robes of legitimacy. Experienced leaders count on an early grace period, when their motives and actions receive the benefit of the doubt. But unquestioned acceptance does not last long.

DEMONSTRATED COMPETENCE

Soon we start to evaluate our leaders by how well they do the job. As this happens, the leader's competence becomes an important source of legitimacy. Competence supports legitimacy: we respect those who are good at what they do. The checkered history of official ministry shows that those who function incompetently do not *automatically* lose their influence in religious groups. Over time, however, an incompetent leader loses credibility, and eventually the legitimacy of the role itself falls under question. On the other hand, a capable and generous leader wins appreciation: "Agnes Jancowski is the most effective president the parish council has ever had. She really does her homework!" Or, "I respect the way Bishop Colletti deals with controversy in the diocese. He doesn't shy away from the tough issues, and he's always ready to listen to an opposing view." We allow leaders such as these to make demands on the rest of us, because our esteem and gratitude make them credible in our eyes.

But defining competence is complicated. We call people competent when we judge them to be successful in a particular role. Thus if we lack agreement on what the role requires, we have a hard time deciding who does it successfully. Discussions of the proper role of religious leaders generate more argument than agreement these days. When we disagree about what the leader's job actually is, then no matter how well leaders perform the job as *they* see it, they are likely to be judged incompetent by some in the group.

An example helps make this clear. An experienced religious educator understands her primary responsibility to be recruiting and training adults in the parish as educators of their own children. In line with this understanding, she spends most of her time with the adult community, supporting active volunteers and contacting new families. An ongoing program of adult formation in faith stands as the centerpiece of her creative effort. The formation program has won wide acclaim: participating parishioners testify that their spiritual lives have been enriched; religious educators in neighboring parishes eagerly adopt her materials for their own use. And yet her competence comes under question. Some parents object to her focus on adults, expecting her to teach classes for the children herself. Another group grumbles that in offering the program of adult spiritual enrichment she is taking on responsibilities that really belong to a priest. Disagreement over her proper role clouds their judgment about her competence.

PERSONAL VISION

Another quality that adds to the legitimacy of religious leaders today is personal vision. As proclaimers of the gospel's vision of charity and justice, Christian ministers might be expected to have a strong personal vision. But vision has not always been expected or encouraged among pastoral personnel. Most institutions reward orthodox belief and dutiful behavior—qualities that are stressed in the selection and training of those preparing for official ministry. Recent directives from Vatican sources urge seminary staffs to ensure that candidates for the priesthood accept church doctrine and follow official procedures. Men who find these disciplines of belief and behavior too confining are not to proceed to ordination. In such a system of training, loyalty to the organization and obedience to institutional authority are highly valued.

Most Catholics respect loyalty and obedience as qualities to be admired in our leaders. But today we are increasingly aware of their shadow side. Excessive allegiance to an organization can turn leaders into functionaries, persons who see themselves simply as representatives of the official line. The community of faith soon grows impatient with leaders who are no more than functionaries. We do not demand that our pastors become rebels, but we want them to be more than just "company men." We expect them to have a personal vision of ministry, to be able to share with the faith community some statement of their leadership goals. A personal statement does not guarantee that the community will accept the leader's view without question. But we want to be assured that anyone in a role of pastoral leadership among us *has* a dream, a practical vision of what we are about as a Christian group.

Sharing one's vision means more than promoting a ready-made mission plan. The leader's role is not to supply the community with a vision but to help us discover our communal dream. Each faith community must trace the connections between its daily tasks of love and work and the gospel vision of the reign of God. An effective leader does not free the community from the arduous process of dialogue and compromise in which this communal vision emerges. Rather, a visionary leader reminds us of the spiritual significance of the task. We respect ministers who challenge us in this way; their legitimacy is thereby enhanced.

Extra-Rational Dynamics in Religious Authority

The sources of legitimacy we have considered thus far—theological interpretation, shared expectations, demonstrated competence, personal vision—are somewhat public and open to direct analysis. Other factors contribute to legitimacy in ways that may be less obvious but no less influential. We consider here two of these sometimes-overlooked dynamics of religious authority: the symbolic role of the leader and the leader's religious authenticity.

To describe these dynamics as *extra-rational* is not to diminish their significance but to recall that legitimacy involves more than cognitive factors. Authority has emotional roots as well. Exploring the leader's symbolic role and religious authenticity, we are dealing with the evocative, emotional dimensions of authority.

THE SYMBOLIC ROLE OF THE LEADER

Leaders, especially religious leaders, often serve a symbolic function. They stand for "something else" or "something more." A priest gives an example: "Frequently in my ministry people respond to me in ways that have little to do with me. Sometimes I get more praise than I deserve; often enough I get more grief than I merit! This used to confuse me a lot. I'm less bothered by it these days. I've come to accept that very often people are responding to much more than 'just me.' They're responding to something I represent—God's mercy or God's judgment, some pastor who gave them a hard time in grade school, or a church that has changed without asking their permission."

"Sometimes I get more praise than I deserve; often enough I get more grief than I merit." Anyone who has been in ministry for a while has had this experience. Taking up a religious role puts us in a powerful, if perilous, position. The force of this symbolic function invites closer examination, even if its dynamics are not fully understood. In chapter 11 we consider in greater detail the theological and pastoral implications of the leader's symbolic role. Here we examine one way in which the symbolic function contributes to the legitimacy of the leader.

Religious leaders function as lightning rods, drawing the emotional energy that surrounds people's experiences of God. This dynamic especially affects the traditional roles of priest, bishop, and vowed religious, but others in ministry also feel the effects. Those in ministry become the target of other people's religious hopes and fears. Some people respond to religious professionals as if these ministers themselves possessed qualities that are part of a magical image of God. The minister, endowed with godly attributes, is seen as an all-providing parent or all-knowing judge, able both to reassure and to punish.

Attributing "godly" qualities to the professional minister is risky business, especially when the dominant image of "God" arises more from unreflected religious longing than from the gospel witness. But however risky, this psychological process affects ministry relationships. Having endowed the minister with these attributes, the believer then responds to the minister as if these were personal qualities. Sometimes this projection evokes fear and anger, sometimes respect and awe. In either case, the minister's influence is magnified.

Such an unadorned psychological explanation may suggest that symbolic interaction is always detrimental, that religious leaders should purge these projections from their relationships. This is not the case. The psychological dynamics here are complex, and they can be confusing. But their effect can be beneficial. Consider a similar dynamic between therapist and client. People in crisis go to a psychological counselor looking for help. They feel powerless and overwhelmed, unable to see a way out of their present difficulties. In distress, a client approaches the counselor with a desperate hope: "I may be weak and confused, but this person has the power to make me better."

Experienced therapists realize that this is not the case. Sources of healing lie within the wounded person—not in the counselor's superior knowledge or sophisticated technique but in the client's courage and commitment to growth. The wise counselor, then, knows where the power actually resides—in the person's capacity for self-determination and choice. But an effective counselor does not force this realization on the client prematurely.

As a therapeutic relationship begins, distressed people are seldom able to claim their own power. Inner resources seem unavailable or unreliable, so they look outside for help. In doing so, clients project their resourcefulness onto the therapist, recognizing power only in the counselor's insights and actions. This is a natural dynamic in the therapeutic process. This projection—the illusion that healing will come from the outside rather than from within a client's own resources—is dangerous only if the counselor succumbs to its illusion. In the hands of a skillful counselor, the illusion serves the healing process. The therapist holds the client's power in trust and gradually, over the course of therapy, returns it. Slowly the client regains the strength and confidence to assume responsibility once more for the direction of his or her life.

Those of us in pastoral ministry also participate in this delicate exchange of power. People often approach the minister keenly aware of God's absence in their own lives. Earlier images of who God is, previous understandings of what God asks, once-satisfying ways of relating to the church—these no longer sustain them. Overwhelmed by grief or guilt, they feel cut off from God. Feeling themselves bereft of God, they turn to the minister for help.

Convinced that God is absent from their own experience, they want the minister to "give" God to them. They have, in a sense, projected onto the pastoral minister something that really resides within themselves—the loving presence of God in their daily lives. When a person comes in this distress, wise ministers do not begin by providing a theologically correct instruction to make clear that the minister is not God! More likely such pastoral counselors try to honor the person's distress. They receive with care the misdirected emotions (whether of love or hate) actually meant for God; hold in trust the misplaced expectation that they can supply God; then gradually return to the believer the responsibility—and confidence—to continue on the journey of faith.

This symbolic dynamic, by which believers vest their religious leaders with special power, comes into play in many pastoral settings. An effective minister learns to appreciate the value of this necessary, if dangerous, resource. The call to hear and heed a leader who stands in the place of God is compelling for most people of faith; being seen in this symbolic role strengthens the minister's legitimacy.

Such symbolic power, unpurified and unrestrained, can have disastrous effects; the diabolical power exercised by Adolf Hitler and, with more limited but equally devastating results, by Jim Jones among his religious followers in Guyana attests to this danger. The way out of the danger is neither to deny that this symbolic dynamic is real nor to declare it unacceptable in ministerial relationships. To begin with, such protestations simply will not work. Elements of projection and fantasy cloud most of our significant relationships. But beyond the practical futility of trying to rule the symbolic function out of bounds, there are other reasons to appreciate its presence. The ambiguous power of the symbolic interaction can be constructive in ministry. Sometimes, to be sure, the community of faith must confront its illusions around religious leadership, so that leaders and community members can deal with one another as real persons rather than as projections of unfulfilled needs. But it is equally important for religious leaders to befriend their symbolic role, learning to draw on its power in ways that serve and strengthen the community of faith.

RELIGIOUS AUTHENTICITY

The community of faith today asks of its leaders more than institutional orthodoxy and administrative efficiency. People of faith look for religious authenticity. We long for ministers whose professional behavior clearly flows from a personal life of faith. We are hungry for the witness of leadership styles that are congruent with the gospel. Leaders who act with such spiritual integrity are welcomed among us, their legitimacy confirmed.

What is the shape of the authenticity we ask of our religious leaders? The Alban Institute, an interdenominational study center focusing on parish life, has explored this question in depth. In its reflections, three themes emerge as central. Pastoral leaders are recognized as religiously authentic when (1) they are seen as personally genuine, (2) they adopt a leadership style that is nondefensive, and (3) they are willing to exercise spiritual leadership.

The religious leader recognized as genuine is available to the group. Time is less at issue here than presence. Workaholic ministers in compulsive pursuit of being "all things to all people" seldom seem genuine. Too often their ministerial responsibilities or professional competencies serve as a screen, helping them avoid actually dealing with people. Leaders judged to be authentic are more open in their professional relationships, able to respond to people at a human level. They are present in ways that go deeper than the official role.

To be appreciated as genuine, ministers must be recognized as spiritual people. In our religious leaders—pastoral ministers, bishops, priests—we hope to meet not just guru or guide, more than judge or manager. We hope to find a companion in faith. We embrace the leader who is also a fellow disciple, one whose life of faith is like ours, one who is familiar with hope and doubt alike, strengthened by both crisis and consolation.

Increasingly in this time of institutional purification and structural change, the spiritual depth of pastoral leaders contributes significantly to their legitimacy. Ministers who allow us to glimpse the hope and struggle of their personal journey gain credibility. The religious leader who gives no evidence of a personal life of faith becomes, quite literally, incredible.

A second theme in authenticity is a nondefensive leadership style. Most of us know from bitter experience the tension that develops around a leader with a fragile sense of self. Emotions run high as the group polarizes. Some members enlist in an ongoing effort to protect the leader (and, often enough, themselves) from information that contradicts the image of an ideal leader. Others rush to expose the leader's pretense. A defensive leader thus undermines group effectiveness. Personal loyalty overshadows questions of truth; dissent becomes the enemy. Communal life disintegrates as productive energies drain away.

The nondefensive leader functions in a way that "fits." First, the style fits the leader. Groups quickly sense leaders who are comfortable with themselves, who expend little energy defending an unreal image of "who I should be as a leader." Leaders seen as genuine are at ease with who they are; they have befriended their limitations. No longer embarrassed by personal weaknesses, they devote little effort to hiding these from view. Leaders like this, not burdened by an idealized sense of self, display more flexibility. Comfortable with an image of self that fits, they are freer to work out with other people a style of leadership than fits the situation at hand.

Nondefensive leaders negotiate practical questions of how their actions can best serve the group's shared hopes and common goals. "Out of this process of negotiation," as John Harris of the Alban Institute reminds us in *Stress, Power, and Ministry*, "evolves an authentic professional image of the pastor, integrated into the church in a way that reflects his actual talents and limits and builds upon the authority of his internal vision for the church." Leaders who are open to examining their leadership style and flexible in responding to feedback can help liberate religious groups from the "tyranny of the ideal"—the fears and fantasies around authority that frustrate religious maturity.

The third theme in authenticity is spiritual leadership. Authentic leaders do not shy away from the most demanding task of ministry: helping people find meaning in their own lives. Among the distractions and satisfactions of our ordinary days, daunting questions disquiet us all: Is love possible? Why do the innocent suffer? Does my own life have purpose? Can justice prevail? On our own, these questions are hard to face and harder still to resolve. We yearn for some way to bring the everyday experiences of our lives, as well as the extraordinary ones, within a context of larger significance. Those who stand with and strengthen us in this search we recognize as spiritual leaders.

Pastoral ministers support the quest for spiritual meaning by helping people become sensitive to their own experience of

God. Many of us see spirituality as the realm of the religious specialist, somehow out of bounds for people like us, whose lives are so taken up with the ordinary. "Religious experience" may be available to the spiritually elite, but our own access to God seems sorely limited. Spiritual leaders expand our religious awareness. Challenging us to take our own experience seriously, they bring us to see what so often remains invisible—the abundance of God's power and presence in all of life.

Pastoral ministers often serve as spiritual mentors, inviting us into the daily discipleship of Christian living: praying with the Scriptures, acting for justice, forgiving those who wrong us, showing compassion toward those in need. As these disciplines develop, we come gradually to find our own religious experience trustworthy. Those who open to us this new level of spiritual maturity we recognize as legitimate spiritual leaders.

Ministers act as spiritual leaders by bringing the religious tradition to life. Some adults carry their religious heritage as a burden. Their image of God is as righteous judge; they see the church as moral censor; they experience religion primarily as a source of guilt. Others seem to treat the tradition as a guarantee: "If I just play by the rules, I've got it made. Nothing more will be asked of me." An authentic spiritual leader invites people to a different relationship with their religious heritage. Beyond guilt and guarantees, the tradition carries forward an unfolding story of God's faithful love. Opening this story to people, helping them trace its connections with the story of their own lives—this is the exercise of spiritual leadership. In ministry like this the religious tradition comes alive as a resource in the search for spiritual meaning.

Finally, authentic religious leaders stand with us when life's absurdity—the death of a child, the disintegration of a marriage, the tragedy of senseless violence, the unremitting plight of the poor—tests the resilience of our faith. In these dark moments, they offer us not easy answers but their companionship in courage. They hold out the hope embodied in the paradoxes of Jesus' life—that loss sometimes brings grace, that failure can be fruitful, that letting go may be a path to life. Their mettle having been tested in the crucible of crisis, we account their authority legitimate among us.

Finding Legitimacy in a Time of Change

In this and the previous chapter we have examined several factors supporting the legitimacy of religious leaders. Our intent has not been to suggest that some of these are better than others. Theological meaning and assigned role, personal talent and vision, dynamics of symbolism and authenticity—all these come into play in pastoral leadership. But not all carry equal weight in every religious setting. Some religious groups give highest priority to official role; when duly appointed by proper religious authority, the leader has the right to their support. To be sure, the group welcomes a leader's prayerful spirit or gracious personal manner. But these personal attributes are not the foundation of their respect. An official leader who lacks any such appealing qualities remains deserving of loyalty, because for them the role counts more than any personal qualities.

But personal and ecclesial changes over the past three decades have shifted the religious priorities of many Christians. When these people evaluate pastoral leaders, the institutional criteria of clerical role and official appointment carry less weight than other factors. In some parishes competence is key; here the pastor who refuses theological updating and consistently performs poorly sees his credibility slip away, even though he has been properly appointed. Another group ranks religious authenticity high, valuing a "nontraditional" leader who is spiritually mature even when the theological interpretation of her role remains unclear.

A three-pronged goal for the whole church in this time of transition should be (1) to reformulate the institutional bases of legitimacy—theological statements and role expectations—so that they actually relate to the current experience of the community of faith; (2) to contextualize the personal factors—competence and vision—so that they resist the cult of personality and remain in service of the larger goals of the group; and (3) to clarify the extra-rational factors—dynamics of symbolism and authenticity—so that their power can be purified and used. This purification of ministry is crucial for ordained ministers, whose legitimacy comes under question as the persuasive power of the earlier formulations of religious authority continues to erode. It is also important for the many new ministers in the community whose generosity remains unmatched by an official legitimacy.

Faced with the multiple challenges of the leadership role today, all pastoral ministers recognize the importance of strengthening their credibility. As leaders, they need room to move, to take some risks, to try new things. The more evidence the group has to reinforce the minister's *right* to lead, the easier the task becomes. Personal vision *and* theological justification, symbolic power *and* demonstrated competence in the work, official appointment *and* an active spiritual life—these elements of leadership are not mutually incompatible. Rather, they are the strengths that shape the service of leadership today.

Reflective Exercise

Return to the influential leader you considered at the end of chapter 6. Look at the four sources of legitimacy discussed in this chapter—competence, personal vision, symbolic power, and religious authenticity. As you see it, which of these factors contributed to your leader's credibility? Give examples to show these factors at work.

Now turn to your own exercise of religious leadership. Recall your various involvements in the faith community—through communal worship, in ministry, or as a member of a small group, parish commission, or network of support and action. With these involvements in mind, recall a time when you were particularly effective as a religious leader. Use your own criteria for what *effectiveness* means; select an example that has special significance for you and let your memory bring back the experience in rich detail.

Look over the factors of legitimacy we have discussed in these two chapters. Which of these sources support your own exercise of religious leadership? Give examples to show these factors at play in your own experience.

Additional Resources

John Snow explores the crisis of legitimacy in ministry in *The Impossible Vocation: Ministry in the Mean Time* (Cambridge, MA: Cowley, 1988). In *Staffing Tomorrow's Parishes: Experiences and Issues in Evolving Forms of Pastoral Leadership* (Kansas City, MO: Sheed & Ward, 1990), Maurice L. Monette compiles a compelling assessment of issues affecting the legitimacy of new forms of pastoral leadership.

The organizational disciplines today show concern for the spiritual discipline of leadership: see Max DePree, *Leadership Is an Art* (New York: Doubleday, 1989), and Richard E. Walton, *Management as a Performing Art: New Ideas for a World of Chaotic Change* (San Francisco: Jossey-Bass, 1989). James Autry reflects on the spirituality of the organizational leader in *Love and Profit: The Art of Caring Leadership* (New York: William Morrow, 1991).

Over the past twenty years the staff and associates of the Alban Institute, an interdenominational study center based in Washington, DC, have been examining the links between leadership and religious authenticity. Their insightful work has contributed significantly to an appreciation of the extra-rational dynamics of legitimacy. See especially the following materials, available through the institute's publication office (4125 Nebraska Ave. N.W., Washington, DC 20016): John C. Fletcher, *Religious Authenticity in the Clergy;* John C. Harris, *Stress, Power, and Ministry,* quote taken from p. 22; Cecilia A. Hahn and James R. Adams, *The Mystery of Clergy Authority;* and Bruce Reed, *The Task of the Church and the Role of Its Members.* For a thoughtful reflection on the vital role ritual plays in a group's life, see Tom F. Driver, *The Magic of Ritual* (San Francisco: HarperSanFrancisco, 1991).

8. Embracing Conflict

> And Jacob was left alone; and something wrestled with him
> until the breaking of the day. When it saw that it did not prevail
> against Jacob, it touched the hollow of his thigh; and Jacob's
> thigh was put out of joint as he wrestled with it.   (Adapted
> from Gen. 32:24, RSV)

Ministry bring us in touch with one another. In the faith community today we cross boundaries that once separated clergy from
laity, women from men. Becoming better colleagues and companions on the journey of faith, we aspire to become partners in ministry as well. Partnership draws us by its benefits: more effective
action, shared burdens, mutual support. But in the practice of partnership we become conscious of its costs: the demanding requirements of conflict, negotiation, and compromise.

The Embrace of Conflict

Partners hold each other in respect and sometimes in affection.
In efficient cooperation and genuine friendship alike, we know
partnership's graceful touch. But we must acknowledge another
ordinary embrace: partners sometimes quarrel and disagree.
These episodes can be frightening, imperiling our good feelings
toward one another. The question looms: Will this relationship
survive? Our distress introduces a necessary strength: the ability
to hold one another in conflict.

The risks of this threatening embrace make conflict difficult
to face. A provocative tale in the book of Genesis illumines the

dynamics of this painful embrace. The story can teach us about
the rigors of partnership today.

> And Jacob was left alone; and something wrestled with him until
> the breaking of the day. When it saw that it did not prevail against
> Jacob, it touched the hollow of his thigh; and Jacob's thigh was put
> out of joint as he wrestled with it. Then it said, "Let me go, for the
> day is breaking." But Jacob said, "I will not let you go, unless you
> bless me." And it said to him, "What is your name?" And he said,
> "Jacob." Then it said, "Your name shall no more be called Jacob, but
> Israel, for you have striven with God and with humans, and have
> prevailed." Then Jacob asked it, "Tell me, I pray, your name." But it
> said, "Why is it that you ask my name?" And there it blessed him.
> So Jacob called the name of the place Peniel, saying, "For I have
> seen God face to face, and yet my life is preserved." The sun rose
> upon him as he passed Peniel, limping because of his thigh. (Adapt-
> ed from Gen. 32:24–31, RSV)

The story's theme is intimacy—a deepening relationship between Jacob and Yahweh. But the tale is told in the metaphor of
wrestling. One night these partners fell into the troubling embrace of conflict. The ancient story captures the anxiety of the
encounter: Jacob is alone in the dark; something unrecognizable
grabs hold of him. Jacob struggles with this "partner," demanding to know what it wants of him. He cannot escape this embrace, nor can he control his "nocturnal assailant." Through the
night they struggle, with injury and complaint, toward a different relationship.

In their sweaty encounter each is changed. Jacob receives a
new name—Israel. And he limps away seriously wounded. But
his partner, recognized later as Yahweh, is forced to surrender
something as well: upon demand, God gives Jacob a blessing.
These combatants end the night exhausted and changed, together in a new way.

Partners in ministry recognize Jacob's story as their own. The
tale recalls our own terror as we face conflict. Locked in disagreement, we struggle with one another or with the institutional church. We debate the role of women in ministry. We
wrestle over power and authority in the parish. On the broader
scene we grapple over the demands of social justice, the significance of sexuality, the shape of institutional reform. Often the

struggle is with former parents ("fathers" in Mother Church), themselves still learning to be partners. Previously terrified by conflict, we strive now to hold one another in its difficult embrace.

Responses to Conflict

Jacob's story leads us to examine our own responses to conflict. When facing a simmering conflict seems too frightening, a temptation for some of us is flight. If my colleague and I addressed our differences, the relationship might explode or we might injure each other; so I flee. Various strategies help me in my flight: retreating behind humor, absenting myself from a meeting, changing jobs. Sometimes, of course, the wisest course *is* to flee conflict. Avoiding an unfair fight makes sense. But if I generally avoid conflict, my flight may be fueled by more than good judgment. Jacob's behavior invites me to reconsider my own.

Some of us move in another direction. When an impending conflict frightens me, I try to control the situation. I tightly monitor the agenda of the meeting; I refuse to discuss certain issues if boundaries are not clear from the start; I rule out feelings and emotions as acceptable topics between us.

Seeing partnership as a dance helps us recognize the difference between flight and control. The "fleer" in us says, "I don't dance. Dancing is for sissies." And so we skirt the embarrassment that awaits the dancer: being out of step, perspiring in public, stepping on the other person's toes. But we do not get to dance. To avoid conflict, we sacrifice partnership.

The "controller" in us says, "Let's dance. I'll lead." We dance only if we remain in charge, controlling the tempo and determining the direction. We engage conflict only with an edge, an advantage of authority or role that leaves us in control.

An inclination to give in too easily tempts others. We have learned that conflict is un-Christian, that wrestling holds no virtue. The embrace of conflict—with a spouse, a colleague, a church official—triggers immediate surrender. We give in, we comply, we "roll over and play dead." As religious persons, we sometimes cloak this behavior with virtuous names—docility or meekness or obedience. But returning to the image of dance, we see the special liability of this response. Dancing with a corpse is difficult. The contest fizzles when one of us refuses to engage the struggle. And the conflict, uncontested, goes unresolved.

In his conflict Jacob does something different. His response—murkier than those just mentioned—is to hold on. Unable to flee or to control the encounter, he seizes hold and does not let go. In sophisticated vocabulary, he sustains the ambiguity of this nocturnal embrace. In ordinary terms, he tries to outlast the night. Bewildered but determined, he holds on to his partner until it dawns on him who this contestant is and what it wants of him. In this dark tale, the metaphor of "dawning" originates. Jacob's faith tells him that from the night of struggle—if he holds on—will come illumination and grace.

Our History of Conflict

Even strengthened by this encouraging story, we continue to find conflict difficult. Its destructive effects sear our memories: we have seen friendships destroyed and partnerships broken. But our experience holds another conviction: conflict sometimes brings grace. Most of us can recall a painful time in a friendship or among a ministry team when struggle severely threatened the relationship. Perhaps we had stagnated into a familiar but unsatisfying way of interacting. Or we were locked in old and increasingly sterile expectations of each other. These patterns had to be broken for the relationship to mature. Developing more fitting patterns of partnership demanded a difficult, even wounding, period of conflict. Only by facing the conflict could we heal and deepen the relationship. Here conflict turned out to be graceful, but only because we had courage to hold one another in its confusing embrace.

These precious experiences, recalled and celebrated, empower us to recognize the role of conflict in Christian history. Our religious heritage does not unfold simply, a cordial account of sure consensus and mutual concern. We find, upon reexamination, a communal history not unlike our personal journeys. Recall the New Testament account with which we opened this book. In the decades after Jesus' death, serious disagreement arose around inducting new members into the company of believers. Jesus' followers in the Jewish community in Jerusalem naturally considered circumcision the ritual sign of entry. Working in Antioch, Barnabas and Paul grew uneasy with this requirement. The ritual did not seem to fit: Did one have to become a Jew in order to become a Christian? When Paul and Barnabas decided not to circumcise their Gentile converts, Jerusalem protested this unorthodox behavior. The conflict heated up. Barnabas and Paul were called to Jerusalem, and a prolonged debate ensued. The very identity of the movement seemed to be at stake. Those in Jerusalem insisted that circumcision was essential: this ritual had always distinguished the chosen people from those others who did not share the covenant with God. But Barnabas and Paul held on: they argued that following Jesus broke traditional ethnic boundaries. Former venerable practices—circumcision, kosher food—no longer fit this religious way of life.

In the conflict, and because of it, a new awareness gained strength among the earliest Christians. Their assembly was to be more than a reform movement within Judaism; following Jesus initiated a way of life that dissolved the traditional boundaries between Jew and Gentile, between free person and slave, even between woman and man (Gal. 3:28). This conflict among the first generation of Christians was both painful and generative. The disagreement brought deeper understanding. In this struggle, who we are as a church began to dawn on us.

A Conflict of Goods

Memories of grace-filled disagreement encourage us to look more closely at the dynamic of conflict. Sometimes conflict arises between good and evil, challenging us to abandon selfishness or cowardice and choose the righteous path. But conflict also erupts around competing goods. Making a career decision, for example, I struggle to choose one option from many good possibilities. Or I feel called to change my job not because my current work is suddenly wrong but because some new value emerges as crucial for me. In the midst of life, God invites me to something different. To follow this call, I have to let go something already cherished; I must choose among competing goods.

Catholics experienced such a conflict in the liturgical reforms of the 1960s. The traditional value of having a universal language for worship came into conflict with an urgently increasing desire: to participate more fully in the sacramental life of the church. Anger and acrimony swept through parishes as the vernacular, with its too-familiar phrases and often-secular nuances, replaced a more sacred—if less intelligible—Latin. When tempers cooled, we recognized that the choice was not between good and evil; neither of the options was wrong. We were choosing between two conflicting goods—the positive value of a single, shared language and the value of everyone's understanding the liturgy. To use English as our liturgical language does not discredit our past. A new value appeared among us, and in our fidelity to the Spirit that leads us, we chose this new good.

Faith communities regularly face conflicts of value. A large downtown parish considers replacing its ancient organ. As the parish council moves toward a decision, conflict arises. Would the money not be better spent on projects of social care—a shelter for survivors of family violence or a food kitchen? Camps form: one group objects to liberal social programs that only encourage the passivity of the poor. Other people argue that the purchase of an organ is selfish and un-Christian. Still others urge the importance of the community's liturgical celebrations as both worthy in themselves and generative of funds for social action. Although this debate threatens us, it can also deepen our shared life. Staying in the conversation, neither abusing one another nor docilely giving in, we come to a better understanding of our values. Forced to clarify what we are about, we mature as a Christian community.

The Scandal of Dissent

God reveals us gradually to ourselves. Often this revelation is ignited by conflict. For twenty centuries dissent and conflict have been a central dynamic in the church's maturing. When we confess that the church is *semper reformanda*—always in need of reform—we admit the importance of change. To refuse change is to stagnate; but to admit change is to prepare our souls for conflict and dissent.

If unity is our sole ideal, conflict is made a scandal. If our vision of the church requires paternal leaders to guide the passive children of God, then disagreement is always disloyal. But in a world of partners, dissent is an ordinary dynamic—one through which we purify our shared life and move toward God's future.

As Christians, we assent to God's privileged presence in Jesus Christ; we confess together the central place of Scripture in our lives; we acknowledge a common call to serve the reign of God. But amid this rich and constant agreement, we often disagree. Sometimes our priorities are at variance. On issues of justice, of sexuality, of authority, honest differences of interpretation emerge. If in these stressful times we can hold one another with respect, our conflicts may cleanse us and illumine our shared path of faith.

Jesus' life teaches us the religious value of dissent. The gospel records that, with some frequency, Jesus chose to disregard the established religious practice. Religious law prohibited harvesting corn on the Sabbath, yet Jesus and his friends did so (Matt. 12). Jesus healed a woman on the Sabbath, again breaking the law (Luke 13). Against the sanctioned custom for Jewish men of his day, Jesus spent much time with women—even foreign women and women of questionable reputation. In all these instances he acted in ways that contradicted established law: Jesus dissented. This disregard for law was neither casual nor selfish. His dissent discloses a deeper truth—that laws are meant to be servants of our life, not tyrannical masters.

Loyal Opposition

Jesus' example encourages us to examine religious dissent today. The question arises: Is there room in the church for a loyal opposition? Recent official actions give a negative response. Consider, for example, the Vatican's celebrated debate with Charles Curran, then a professor of moral theology at the Catholic University of America. In careful scholarship and pastoral writing for more than two decades, Curran has presented new convictions concerning human sexuality. His work provides a healing perspective on such troubling issues as masturbation, homosexuality, and contraception. This perspective, shared by most of his theologian peers, reflects a growing sense of the faithful throughout the United States and elsewhere. This emerging moral consensus questions some customary formulations of the Christian understanding of sexuality.

In 1986 the Vatican announced that Curran was no longer "suitable nor eligible to exercise the function of a professor of Catholic theology" and insisted that he be dismissed from his tenured position at the church-sponsored university. The Vatican's final judgment was directed more against Curran's right to disagree than against the substance of the disagreement. The official church seems to be saying that these complex questions of sexual morality are not open to discussion. No room exists for loyal opposition to official statements.

In the wake of Professor Curran's dismissal, moral theologian Richard McCormick has reviewed the issue of ecclesial dissent. He notes the tendency among some bishops to ignore the difference between the core of Christian faith and questions about its practical expression; all current teaching is placed on the same footing and an identical allegiance is demanded. McCormick also points out a tendency to isolate dissenters (as proponents of merely "private opinion") and to judge their motives (charging that they seek to set themselves up as rival authorities to the teaching church). In his characteristically careful and respectful style, McCormick raises the crucial question of reform: "When and through what mechanisms does authentic teaching cease to be authentic, that is, give way to a new formulation in the Church? And then more specifically, what is the position of the individual Catholic conscience during this transitional period?"

McCormick concludes his penetrating review in *Theological Studies* by listing the negative results of the official church's hostility toward dissent. Two of his conclusions are especially relevant to our discussion of partnership. First, although official teaching is often presented as the unanimous judgment of Catholic bishops throughout the world, very frequently bishops are not consulted prior to an important decision. Their consent is simply assumed. The implied rule of procedure is that a dissenting bishop will remain silent. "In such circumstances," McCormick concludes, "to read episcopal silence as unanimity is self-deceptive."

Official resistance to dissent also diminishes the laity. "Coercive insistence on official formulations tells the laity in no uncertain terms that their experience and reflection make little difference." McCormick then quotes the encouragement of Vatican II to the contrary: "Let it be recognized that all the faithful—clerical and lay—possess a lawful freedom of enquiry and of thought, and the freedom to express their minds humbly and courageously about those matters in which they enjoy competence" (*The Church in the Modern World*, par. 62). This vital participation in the community of faith depends on tolerance for dissent.

An Experiment in Partnership

The competence of the laity recalls the bold experiment that grew out of Vatican II. In the midst of the council, Pope Paul VI appointed a special commission to examine the question of birth control. At its first meeting in 1963 the commission was modest in size—three theologians and three lay men—and its membership confidential. In 1965 the group was expanded, first to fifteen members, then to fifty-five—including, for the first time, three married couples.

Adding these married people to the dialogue seemed safe enough: the two European couples conducted clinics in the church-approved rhythm method of restricting births, and the American couple, Patrick and Patricia Crowley, were chairpersons of the Christian Family Movement. The Crowleys greatly expanded the dialogue by soliciting the opinion of committed Catholic married people who were members of the Christian Family Movement. Patricia Crowley recounts that they expected the response to confirm the church's position about the effectiveness of the rhythm method. In fact, however, the result was just the opposite. Many couples testified that this method of periodic abstinence was not only ineffective in regulating births but spiritually destructive as well. The response to the Crowley questionnaire, drawn from 3,000 Catholic couples in eighteen countries, indicated that 63 percent found the rhythm method harmful to their marriages. Over the course of their meetings in

1965, the expanded commission developed a strong consensus. Of its nineteen theologians, fifteen judged that contraception was not, as the church had once determined, an intrinsic evil; of the fourteen cardinals and bishops, nine agreed with the theological majority. In their final report the Birth Control Commission recommended a significant change in church teaching.

Three years later Pope Paul VI set aside the judgment of this broad-based commission and, in the letter entitled *Humanae Vitae*, decreed that contraception was both unnatural and sinful. With this letter a noble experiment in partnership came to an end.

But something had changed. Catholics had been asked to participate, as responsible adults, in a church process. It had been suggested, for the first time, that lay Christians might be competent to make informed judgments about their own sexual responsibility. *Humanae Vitae* attempted to shut the door on this daring partnership in adult faith, but it was too late. Many married Catholics, often in the midst of raising large families, examined their consciences and found the official teaching inadequate. Obedience in their commitments to marriage and family led them to disregard this law. They did not leave the church, nor were they shamed into compliance. They simply went about their lives of faith, disregarding this rule.

Canon lawyers would remind us of the church's long-held conviction concerning the importance of the *reception* of the law—that is, the faith community's exercise of responsibility in accepting a law as authoritative in its life. This communal process is unconflicted, when a proposed law expresses what the community's experience has shown to be true. Sometimes, however, laws are crafted that do not represent the community's wisdom; the lawmakers are out of touch with the lively sense of faith in the body of Christ. Such laws tend to be ignored; they are not accepted within the community of faith as genuinely authoritative. And a law that is not "received" does not bind.

The furor generated among American Catholics by the 1968 statement against birth control exemplifies nonreception. If this instance of public disagreement has been painful, it has also reminded the faith community of its role in religious authority. We are partners in faith, sharing responsibility to either actively embrace official formulations or to testify to their inadequacy.

Rules of Engagement

Dissent draws us into conflict. Just as the military services set out rules of engagement to guide decisions made in conflict, the church needs guidelines for faithful dissent.

Loyal opposition presumes a mature witness of faith. To be trusted, a dissenting voice must be seasoned by years of discipleship. Protest merits special attention when it arises among those who live generous lives of faith. Their fidelity gives the church good reason to listen to their challenge. Charles Curran's well-earned reputation as faithful theologian and careful scholar, for example, makes his dissenting opinions more credible.

Faithful dissent's first rule of engagement is mutual respect, an essential of adult partnership. Christians in conflict must explore their differences with reverence for the tradition and for one another. Where and how Christians make public their dissent will be shaped by this respect. Mutual respect precludes anonymous letters to high ecclesiastical authorities; it prohibits unfounded accusations about our opponents' moral fiber; it prevents us from intentionally misrepresenting their opinions. These destructive behaviors sap the community's energy and cloud the controversy with mistrust.

A second rule of engagement is patience. The person who disagrees with a church teaching on some question must be open to responses and challenges, must be willing to pursue dialogue and seek further clarification. Official church leaders must also, of course, follow same guidelines. Concretely, this patience has been demonstrated by Leonardo Boff, Matthew Fox, and William Callahan, who have been willing to be silent for a period. Patience is a sign that one is willing to be part of a loyal opposition. But patience is not a synonym for submission. After patient self-scrutiny and a reexamination of their dissent, Christians will often be called to rejoin the struggle for purification.

A third rule of engagement prescribes a public process by which differing opinions can be tested and evaluated. The church sorely lacks such structures of open dialogue. Such a process would have to be genuinely adult, respecting all participants as partners in the process; it could not allow some information or accusers to remain anonymous, not permit a single authority to function as prosecutor, judge, and jury. Such a due process would establish a procedure that all participants would obey.

Partnership in ministry challenges us to this adult virtue: the ability to hold one another in conflict. And we begin to see that this embrace is part of our obedience. We are called, as partners, to take hold of the institutional church. We must be courageous enough to lay hands on the church, even in dissent and conflict, and not let it go. In this engagement our affection for the church will be buffeted by the conflicting emotions of anger and guilt and regret—painful stirrings that are part of most adult relationships. If we hold firm, attempting neither to control nor to flee, we will become mature partners in the purification and renewal of our wounded community of faith. The hope that sustains us in this struggle is for the dawning of a more graceful church.

Reflective Exercise

Recall a relationship that has been important to you for a long time. Revisit some of the disagreements that have been part of this enduring partnership. Select a particular conflict that turned out to be graceful. Spend time reflecting on the contribution that this conflict made to your relationship.

Is there an institution or organization that you presently hold in conflict? Perhaps your work site or parish; perhaps a larger institution—the nation, the church, the economic system. What feelings do you have about this painful embrace? How are you tempted—to flee, to control, to give in too quickly? In the midst of this institutional struggle, what is the grace for which you hope?

Additional Resources

Biblical scholar Gerhard von Rad provides insight into the story of Jacob wrestling with Yahweh in *Genesis: A Commentary* (Philadelphia: Westminster, 1961). We explore the provocative image of Jacob wrestling with God in several places: see *A Sense of Sexuality: Christian Love and Intimacy* (New York: Image Books/

Doubleday, 1990), chap. 15, and *Christian Life Patterns* (New York: Crossroad/Continuum Books, 1992). In these discussions, as here, we alter the translation to identify Jacob's adversary as "something" (rather than "a man," as in the Revised Standard Version), to better express the ambiguous mood of the nocturnal struggle.

The Vatican statement concerning Charles Curran appears in *Origins*, Aug. 28, 1986; quote taken from p. 203. Richard McCormick's excellent review of dissent in the church appears in his "Notes on Moral Theology: 1986," *Theological Studies*, Mar. 1987, pp. 87–105; quotes taken from pp. 99, 102, and 104. See also his article "L'Affaire Curran," *America* 154 (1986): 261–67 and "L'Affaire Curran II." *America* 163 (1990): 127–143, co-authored by Richard P. McBrien. For further important analyses of religious dissent, see Charles Curran, *Faithful Dissent* (Kansas City, MO: Sheed & Ward, 1986), and Ladislas Orsy, *The Church: Learning and Teaching* (Wilmington, DE: Glazier, 1987). For an instance of responsible dissent, see "The Cologne Declaration," *Commonweal*, Feb. 24, 1989, pp. 102–4.

Robert Blair Kaiser recounts the history of the papal commission on birth control in *The Politics of Sex and Religion* (Kansas City, MO: Leaven, 1985). Philip Kaufman provides a brief and insightful retelling of this event in *Why You Can Disagree and Remain a Faithful Catholic* (New York: Crossroad/Continuum, 1989). Theologian Yves Congar explores the notion of a community's reception of the law in "Reception as an Ecclesiastical Reality," in Giuseppe Alberigo and Anton Weiler, eds., *Election and Consensus in the Church; Concilium*, vol. 77 (New York: Herder & Herder, 1972), pp. 57–66.

Part Three

Transformations in
Leadership

9. Exploring the Leader's Task

> People must think of us as Christ's servants, stewards entrusted with the mysteries of God. What is expected of stewards is that each one should be found worthy of this trust.   (1 Cor. 4:1–2, JB)

Most traditional cultures give leaders an elevated status. Mounting the regal throne or ascending the high altar, the leader stands above the people, superior to them. Jesus urged his disciples to resist this interpretation of leadership and, in his own life, modeled an alternative: "The greatest among you must be your servant. Those who exalt themselves will be humbled, and those who humble themselves will be exalted" (adapted from Matt. 23:11–12, JB). His leadership reached its height in his paradoxical elevation on the cross.

From the outset the Christian community has stumbled in its efforts to live up to this extraordinary ideal of "servant leadership." We have often succumbed to cultural pressures to interpret leadership in the community of faith in terms of privilege and status (witness the titles "Your Eminence" and "Prince of the Church"). Popes through the Middle Ages invoked the title "servant of the servants of God" even as the papal office became increasingly authoritarian. Today, as the Christian body moves toward greater partnership in faith, our leaders come down from their pedestals; yet their ministry carries a special responsibility. How are we to describe the particular authority of our servant leaders?

Many people find the image of servant confusing. "Servant" too easily translates into slavery and servitude, while the service of leadership that Jesus demands arises not in a master/slave economy but among a community of disciples. Being a servant also implies powerlessness, but leaders must be powerful—strong enough to initiate action, to confront obstacles, to speak the truth, to console those in pain. How can we reconcile the image of servant with the demands of the leadership role? Another gospel image—stewardship—shows the way.

In the New Testament a steward is an authoritative servant. "Steward" is a translation of the Greek word *oikonomos:* the one who sees to the law *(nomos)* of the household *(oikos)*. The steward oversees the domestic order: the rhythms, rules, and agreements by which a household or community thrives. In the New Testament and elsewhere, stewardship describes a leadership position reserved for experienced, capable persons. Stewards exercise considerable authority, but not in their own name. Stewardship links power with service (of the community) and authority with dependence (on the Lord). These dynamics describe the exercise of leadership in the contemporary community of faith.

Stewards of the Group's Power

Christian leaders are stewards of God's power as it stirs in a community of believers. Leaders are not to *do* the group's work for it, nor are they single-handedly to *supply* the group's vision. They do not import a grace and power that is otherwise lacking here. Their role is to *support* the group's life in the Spirit. Their task is to foster the network of effective relationships through which members care for one another and pursue shared goals. When they do this, our leaders foster the fruitful flow of God's power among us.

"Common sense" tells us that leadership is the business solely of the person in charge, but organizational analysts question this assumption. Leadership involves more than the formal leader. In fact, preoccupation with the formal leader—the chairperson of a committee, the supervisor in a work group, the pastor in a parish—narrows our attention too quickly. Looking at one person, we miss the activity of the group as a whole.

Bringing the group to life and coordinating its power—this is leadership's core. Leadership—or better, *leading*—goes on in the give-and-take of the whole group. Watching this interplay helps us recognize leadership as a group process more than an individual possession—a process that encompasses all those activities that make a group effective. The formal leader is part of this larger process. Understanding leadership as a group process does not do away with the need for designated leaders. Seeing leadership in this wider view simply clarifies the task of the person in charge.

Theologian Annie Jaubert reminds us that in the earliest Christian communities leadership was seen as "the responsibility of all and the charge of some." What *is* the charge of the formal leadership role? How does the person "in charge" serve the broader leadership process? The leader's job description often differs from group to group, but common expectations emerge. Effective leaders act (1) to nurture commitment, (2) to enhance the group's power, and (3) to face the group toward its future.

Leaders Nurture Commitment

Commitment is an adult embrace. Sociologist Jacqueline Scherer calls it the active ingredient that links an individual to the group. To nurture commitment means to strengthen the emotional and intellectual bonds that hold the group together. Leaders nurture commitment by keeping the facts of our interdependence before us. Effective leaders reinforce the conviction that we need one another. By celebrating our successes and by recalling the dangers that we still face, leaders remind us that "we are in this together."

Effective leaders show us the benefits of belonging. Belonging means that I *feel included;* belonging also means that I *participate actively.* To participate actively, I must invest time and energy. But active participation gives me something significant in return—a richer sense of myself. When a group calls out the best in me, investing myself comes easy. Participating becomes a mirror reflecting my truest self. Then the demands of belonging are not burdensome. Rather, "what I have to do" and "what I want to do" coincide. And commitment flourishes.

Groups come alive as people invest themselves—both their talents and their needs. From people's talents a group draws the skills and experience that make it effective. But from members' needs a group draws an even more important resource—

commitment to common action. Effective leaders bring people's needs into common focus, then tap this energy for action.

James MacGregor Burns, an eminent historian of the American presidency, sees this as the genius of leadership: the ability to transform personal needs into collective goals. Burns speaks of the leadership process as an "education of needs." The Latin root *educare* means "to lead out." Leaders "educate" our needs by leading us beyond the isolation of our private interests. Our needs link us to other people, and effective leaders help us recognize this truth. Other people share our concerns, and they, too, want relief. A new realization dawns: by joining together, we may *all* achieve what *each* wants. Our private interests are not set aside; they become part of shared hopes. And shared hopes stimulate shared goals.

By shaping separate interests into shared goals, leaders craft the common good. Personal goals and group goals overlap. We interpret our own interests in new ways, seeing others not as competitors but as valued partners in a joint enterprise.

To help groups translate their shared hopes into practical goals, leaders must be at ease with conflict. A group's goals do not preexist, fully formed but hidden, like buried treasure waiting to be discovered. As theologian Bernard Loomer reminds us, the common good is an emergent good. Antagonism among members, disagreement over the right course of action, resistance to change, competing demands on the group's limited resources—these are the ferment in which common goals emerge. Leaders afraid of conflict try to avoid the messy compromises that diversity demands. In doing so, they cut the group off from the emotional roots that generate commitment.

Leaders Enhance the Group's Power

Good leaders release other people's power. The chairperson of a task force on affordable housing reminds new members of the valuable resources that they bring to the complex problem; a school principal initiates a faculty development program and encourages teachers to participate; the parish council's executive committee devises practical ways for parishioners to take on greater responsibility—these are leadership activities. Effective leaders invite people to recognize their own gifts and offer these to the common task.

Many successful leaders use the management role to develop the group's power. But managing and leading are not the same. Organizational consultant Tom Peters captures the distinction succinctly in his suggestion that management is about arranging, and leadership is about empowering. But effective managers make their administrative responsibilities a vehicle for leadership behavior.

Managing involves overseeing other people in their performance of tasks. The group has work to do; the person in charge monitors this joint effort. As manager, the leader supervises the group's use of its resources—time and talent, machines and money, property and personnel. But effective leaders do not just regulate resources; they make *more* of the group's resources.

How does this happen? Good managers make it easier for other people to do well: By staffing—getting the right person in the proper job. By recruiting—enlisting new members to share the group's tasks. By training—expanding people's skills so that they can do a better job. By evaluating—providing constructive feedback to help people improve their work.

Good managers help groups devise workable strategies—for making decisions, for setting goals, for resolving conflict, for keeping one another informed. When the work is well organized, members know how their differing responsibilities support the common effort. These practical procedures build the group's power, focusing its energy on shared tasks and common goals.

Managers also carry responsibility for control—monitoring performance to keep it up to par, evaluating progress to ensure that goals are met. Control includes bringing together a number of resources, keeping a complicated effort on track, and giving a sense of direction to a larger effort—all essential to effective collaboration. Lacking such control, groups easily become ineffective. Energy evaporates as decisions are delayed and resources wasted.

But many of us are uneasy with control. Bitter experience reminds us that management is often exercised in constraint and coercion. We have seen leadership positions abused, power used for private gain rather than the common good. We know that, without the safeguards of shared goals and mutual accountability, managerial control often masks manipulation.

To remind ourselves that the exercise of control is not always manipulative, we might recall the power of the conductor in an orchestra or the director in a play. Each role requires control—the ability to focus a group's energies, to channel diverse resources into an organic whole. For the group to be effective, the leader *must* exercise control. But the leader's control exists in context. Both the conductor and the musicians are accountable to the musical score. The goal of the joint effort—a successful performance—lies beyond the leader's singular ability and provides the criterion by which the leader's action can be judged. Both the group and the leader are accountable to something beyond individual preference: the script that they all follow. Both the conductor and the musicians know the score. When control is exercised in this way, in pursuit of a common goal and in the context of mutual accountability, the temptation toward manipulation can be resisted.

This ambivalence about control helps explain some of the tensions today around leadership in collaborative ministry. Religious leadership often includes responsibilities for organizational management and institutional control. We see an increasing reluctance to move into these roles, in large part because management seems a thankless task. It demands skills of initiation and restraint, assertion and accountability. Yet the very exercise of these control functions seems tainted. Group members are suspicious of any action that holds a hint of coercion, and in some religious settings managerial actions are interpreted as coercion. In the face of such suspicion, leaders may back away from the exercise of organizational control. But without the freedom to exercise control when it is necessary, the burdens of organizational leadership become overwhelming, even for experienced and generous ministers. Knowing that leadership positions deprived of the resources of control are doomed to failure, many talented people today refuse to take on this organizational role. When this happens, ministry suffers.

Many of us believe that we have good reason to be suspicious of organizational power. Yet there are hopeful signs that we are moving beyond this widespread suspicion of our leaders. Slowly, in our dioceses and parishes and religious houses, we recognize that without organization and management our corporate life suffers. We learn to distinguish control from coercion. When the actions of the person in charge remain accountable to the gospel and are in the service of the common good, control can be a graceful exercise of leadership. Maturity demands not an abandonment of our suspicions of control but their clarification. Without the control function, our efforts are weaker—personally and communally.

By nurturing competence and exercising control, good managers strengthen the group's power. As this happens, managing becomes a style of effective leadership. But managing and leading do not always go hand in hand. Management activities focus primarily on implementation: supervising people in the accomplishment of designated tasks; coordinating resources for the achievement of existing goals. Few organizations function well without this concentration on the task at hand. But management activities can have other effects as well.

In some groups the *implicit* goal of management becomes stability—maintaining the current patterns of organizational life. In pursuit of greater effectiveness and efficiency, good order and internal harmony are prized. The manager's job is to follow a plan already in place, not to encourage innovation. Conflict is to be avoided, change kept to a minimum. In an organizational setting like this, management and leadership are at odds.

Leaders Face the Group Toward Its Future

Both managing and leading involve influencing people in the pursuit of common goals. But important differences emerge between the two concepts. Leaders do more than supervise subordinates; they recruit people to construct the future together. Vital organizations acknowledge that the people in charge have this dual responsibility—administration and transformation. Administration supports organizational stability; transformation helps the group confront the demands of change. But some bureaucracies downplay the responsibility for change, defining the person in charge as essentially a guardian of the status quo.

Limiting the designated leader in this way erodes the whole group's effectiveness.

Transformation goes with the leader's job. Leadership moves beyond coordinating plans already in place to activating a vision adequate for the future. Effective leaders engage us not just in accomplishing tasks but in formulating this shared vision. But formulating vision is a complex and volatile undertaking. Previous convictions come under review; questions of the group's meaning and purpose arise; resources of imagination and hope, until now bruised or buried, come to life. Once begun, the process can seldom be held within the boundaries of "the way things are."

Effective leaders, aware that current arrangements may not be adequate for the future, encourage openness to change. Sometimes the change takes the shape of reform. As we come together to evaluate present procedures and policies, our intent is not to overturn our current vision but to find better ways to accomplish it. But sometimes a group's active participation has a more radical effect. As we come together in the dialogue about our values and needs, a new vision emerges—one that questions the adequacy not only of current procedures but of current goals as well.

Genuine leadership opens the door to structural change. Facing the future does not automatically demand an overthrow of the status quo. But in many organizational settings, any suggestion of change is viewed with suspicion. Subtle pressure builds for those in leadership roles to understand their responsibilities primarily—even exclusively—in terms of unity and stability. When this happens, leaders become immersed in the problems and tasks of organizational maintenance. While efforts to maintain the organization are worthy in themselves, these management tasks can so absorb the attention of the leader that the larger purposes of the group suffer.

Leaders empower groups for transformation. In pursuit of transformation, leadership supports structural change as well as organizational maintenance. Transformation does not repudiate the past simply because it is past, but it does hold a group open to new development. As James MacGregor Burns notes, unless a process of influence has a "function, however small, in changing an existing structure of interaction" it does not really qualify as leadership.

The Shape of the Leader's Stewardship

Leadership in today's church includes both management and transformation. While caring for the needs of the present, our leaders alert us to the demands of God's future. They struggle to balance service with authority. How shall we picture these authoritative servants?

The parable of the faithful steward, in the twelfth chapter of Luke's Gospel, shows us three characteristics of the Christian leader. First, a steward acts as a servant rather than an owner or master. Second, the steward's chief strength is a seasoned reliability: an inner authority, developed on the job, on which both the steward and the community can depend. Third, the steward operates in a context of absence, making responsible decisions while the owner is away. In his first letter to the Corinthians, Paul describes the same characteristics: the steward acts as a servant, is trustworthy, and exercises leadership "until the Lord comes" (1 Cor. 4:5, JB).

The position of servant deprives the steward of both independence and possessiveness. Stewardship is marked by a paradoxical realization: we are responsible for what we do not own. The objects of our care—people, values, work projects, natural resources—are not our possessions. A steward is, by definition, not an owner. When Christian faith takes root in us, we recognize that creation and all its fruits belong to the Lord. Yet adult responsibility calls us to be assertive and decisive in our care. The challenge is to be caring without controlling, to be decisive without becoming possessive.

The temptation that we experience here is one that accompanies any investment: when we care deeply for something, we often try to control it, to possess it. Parents learn this painful lesson of stewardship as they acknowledge that their children are not, in any final sense, "theirs." They are neither reproductions nor possessions. Pastors and principals are invited to this same discipline: "my" parish and "my" staff are not really "mine." Christian leadership demands a continuing purification of decisiveness and care.

The paradox of nonpossessive care, rooted in our most basic relationship with the Creator, has a long tradition among Jews and Christians. Psalm 39 expresses this relationship powerfully. Impressed with the brevity and fragility of human life, the psalmist writes: "I am your guest, and only for a time, a nomad like all my ancestors" (Ps. 39:12, JB). This "guest involvement" describes Christian leadership today. The exercise of authority is always a guest performance. Whatever our responsibilities, we are guest authorities—serving for a time, at the pleasure of the Lord, with persons and projects we do not own. That we fail at this extraordinary ideal more often than we succeed only reminds us that stewardship demands a severe maturity.

Generous Absence

Christian leaders are stewards in the Lord's absence. The absence of Jesus Christ, begun in his traumatic death and celebrated in his ascension, is the context of Christian stewardship. Jesus' death absented him from the community. "In a short time you will no longer see me" (John 16:16). This loss had startling results: Jesus' absence brought the Spirit into our midst, luring us into more authoritative roles in our shared life. When the Lord is present, we need only be good disciples; our dependence is complete. But Jesus' confusing and generous absence created a leadership vacuum among his first followers. In the upper room at Pentecost his friends asked the disciple's question: "What are we to do?" But now they were looking not at Jesus but at one another. This frightening absence ignited their own stewardship.

To be sure, Christ has not abandoned us. Through his enduring presence in the Spirit, we remain a community of disciples. But this is a mysterious presence, unlike his physical presence among the first Christians. To believe in the ascension and second coming of Christ, we must also believe in Jesus' mysterious absence.

Jesus' death teaches us a special lesson about the link between leadership and absence. His death was not a disruption of his giving but its final act; the letting go of his leadership was his final gift to us—a gift that bears fruit in our own exercise of leadership.

But we struggle, as Christian stewards, to embrace the connection between generosity and letting go. Accustomed to leadership and its perquisites, we find it difficult to give these up, to step aside and hand on responsibility to the next generation. We spend time defending our authority instead of grooming others to assume leadership. From the vantage point of our maturity, the next generation is always immature, unready for responsibility. They do not have our experience or our savvy or our plain good sense. Worst of all, they are not us! But they are the future. In the final maturing of our ministry, we are invited to be powerful enough to let go, to turn over our efforts and our authority to the future. We follow Christ in this abandonment, convinced that our stewardship finds its final fruitfulness in letting go.

Reflective Exercise

Look to your own experience of leaders. From your own life, bring to mind a person who stands as an example of a good leader. This may be someone from your past or a person currently in a leadership position. Choose a person who embodies many of the elements that you find most significant in the leader's role.

Now consider this leader in action. Recall concretely a single project or event that captures what is best about this person as a leader. Take some notes for yourself concerning the person's behavior and attitude, values and goals, as displayed in this particular leadership setting.

Then return to the themes of this chapter:

- Leaders nurture commitment.
- Leaders enhance the group's power.
- Leaders face the group toward its future.

Compare your notes on a particular leader with this model of the leader's task. In what ways does the person in your reflection fit this model? Are there ways in which the good leader you chose challenges the model?

Additional Resources

The Ministry of Governance, ed. James K. Mallet (Washington, DC: Canon Law Society of America, 1986), provides a valuable collection of articles on the leader's role in the community of faith; see especially the concluding chapter by James Provost. Theologian Annie Jaubert's discussion of the "mutual but asymmetrical dependence" that characterized the early Christian communities appears in "Les Épîtres de Paul: le fait communautaire," in Jean Delorme, ed., *Le Ministère et les Ministères Selon le Nouveau Testament* (Paris: Éditions de Seuil, 1974), pp. 16–33; quote taken from p. 25.

James MacGregor Burns's now classic formulation of the leader's role is found in *Leadership* (New York: Harper & Row, 1978); quote taken from p. 130. Noel M. Tichy and Mary Anne DeVanna expand his discussion in *The Transformational Leader* (New York: Wiley, 1986). Jacqueline Scherer discusses commitment in *Contemporary Community: Sociological Illusion or Reality?* (New York: Harper & Row, 1973). For discussion of the tasks of leadership in the current ecclesial setting, see John Coleman, "Dimensions of Leadership," pp. 223–28, and Helen Marie Burns, "Leadership in a Time of Transformation," pp. 228–32, available in *Origins* (Sept. 13, 1990).

Gerard Egan continues his important contribution to the understanding and practice of effective leadership; see, for example, his *Change Agent Skills in Helping and Human Service Settings* (Monterey, CA: Brooks/Cole, 1985) and his more recent two-volume series, *Change-Agent Skills A: Assessing and Designing Excellence* and *Change-Agent Skills B: Managing Innovation and Change* (San Diego, CA: University Associates, 1988). For more on the leader's role in change, see Rosabeth Moss Kanter, *The Change Masters* (New York: Simon & Schuster, 1983); Tom Peters, *Thriving on Chaos* (New York: Harper & Row, 1987); and David L. Kirkpatrick, *How to Manage Change Effectively* (San Francisco: Jossey-Bass, 1985).

In *The Management of Ministry: Building Leadership in a Changing World* (San Francisco: Harper & Row, 1989), James D. Anderson and Ezra Earl Jones call religious leaders to a gospel definition of their task. Bernard Loomer's analysis of power is found in "Two Kinds of Power," *Criterion* 15 (Winter 1976): 11–29. For an expanded discussion of stewardship as a religious image of leadership, see James D. Whitehead, "Stewardship: The Disciple Becomes a Leader," in Michael Cowan, ed., *Leadership Ministry in Community* (Liturgical Press, 1987), pp. 69–80.

10. Leaders and Power

> You will receive power when the Holy Spirit comes on you, and then you will be my witnesses not only in Jerusalem but throughout Judaea and Samaria, and indeed to the ends of the earth. (Acts 1:8, JB)

Our culture paints a heroic portrait of the leader. The American ideal values independence over collaboration, self-reliance above the ability to cooperate. In this vision the good leader, gifted with a strong personality, stands alone.

As we saw in chapter 9, both theology and organizational theory challenge this view. Christian leaders are charged with a special—but not unique—responsibility for God's power as it stirs among us. Our leaders do not possess religious power unavailable to others. Rather, they interact with the rest of us in the flow of God's power in the community of faith. Participating in the interplay of power, leaders sometimes initiate action and sometimes respond. Certain circumstances may demand that the leader act alone, but the normal work of leadership depends on coordination and consensus building. Successful leaders regularly rely on resources beyond their own: the group's considered decision, the expertise of the staff, the judgment of trusted colleagues. Their leadership style welcomes other people's power.

But not everyone finds "other people's power" friendly. Some of us see power as a zero-sum game in which other people gain power only at our expense. Many of us are ambivalent: we want powerful people on our side but resent being dependent on them. But some people, comfortable with their own power, are more at ease with the power of others. For them, being strong means more than physical force or social domination. They have moved beyond such narrow understandings toward a broader awareness of their own strength. Religious leadership depends on this expanded sense of personal power.

Transforming Personal Power

Questions of personal power arise throughout life: Can I make it on my own? Do I have enough strength to meet this challenge? To succeed, must I be stronger than anyone else? Developmental psychologists assure us that these nagging concerns are normal. Questions of personal adequacy arise not simply as signs of weakness. Power issues are perennial, awakened as often by our successes ("I didn't realize I was this strong!") as by our defeats. As we respond to these questions of power, we give shape to our sense of self.

In *The Experience of Power*, psychologist David McClelland examines four orientations toward personal power—four basic ways that adults experience themselves as strong. In an impressive cross-cultural study of both women and men, McClelland found a pattern among these experiences: as adults mature, they feel strong in new and different ways. Not abandoning earlier experiences, mature adults expand their sense of being strong. But movement through these levels of development is not guaranteed; personal wounds and cultural pressures can delay or defeat the maturing process. As adults, some people continue to identify their power only with its earliest expressions, feeling uncomfortable with more mature movements of personal strength. The community of faith flourishes when our religious leaders model the full range of power experiences. In the paragraphs that follow we explore four basic orientations toward personal power suggested by McClelland's work.

RECEIVING POWER

An original and basic experience of strength comes as power received. Childhood gives this gift to many of us. Our parents use their power to care for our real needs and to support our growing strength. When we are nurtured well as children, we learn to feel safe in the presence of others' power. Protected and encouraged by trustworthy adults, we have been empowered.

Feeling powerful this way continues in adult life. We are strengthened by the love of others and renewed by their support. In friendship and marriage, teamwork and collaboration, we learn to feel powerful in relying on other people. Religious experience deepens our appreciation of what we began to learn in childhood: God's power, utterly beyond us, shapes us and makes us strong. The mystic's awareness becomes our own: "I can do all things in God who strengthens me."

This sense of power matures into the strength of receptivity. I can depend on the resources of other people as well as my own. I do not possess alone all that brings meaning and joy and accomplishment to my life. There are strengths beyond my own that I need. To ask for and accept these resources does not demean me but opens me to the experience of power received.

Many forces conspire to frustrate our experience of receptivity as empowering. Some of us, growing up in troubled families, remember dependence as demeaning: other people used their power to "hold us back" or "hold us down." Growing up in an environment that was not safe taught us not to trust. When these bitter experiences bring us to adulthood deeply hesitant about depending on others, we have to learn that this energetic embrace can renew and empower us.

Adult experiences can also leave us cautious about depending on other people. A friend lets us down; a colleague fails to come through on an important project. We feel embarrassed and angry, vowing not to leave ourselves vulnerable again. American culture feeds this inclination, reminding us that independence is the ultimate virtue.

But the experience of power received returns again and again. We fall in love and learn anew how good it is to be held. Restored by a vacation, we delight once again in our dependence on nature and its beauty. After a long period of struggle in a relationship, reconciliation comes—unsolicited—surprising us with its power. Experiences like these remind us that receptivity makes us strong. We give thanks for the power that comes to nourish, to heal, to bring us delight.

ACHIEVING AUTONOMY

While receptivity opens us to the strength of others, autonomy helps us savor the strength we have on our own. This second sense of power celebrates self-reliance and self-sufficiency. We are eager to be in charge of ourselves, determined to develop the resources that we need to go it alone.

The activities that help us feel strong at this stage are those that develop our own abilities or give us control over our own life. McClelland found that some people high in this power orientation were exercise or body-building enthusiasts. Many were avid readers of self-help books and similar psychological literature, interested in knowing "what makes people tick"—especially themselves. Others worked diligently to master information in a particular area (nutrition, money management, home or automobile maintenance) so that they would not need to consult other people.

Autonomy is a positive achievement. Acting on my own behalf expands my sense of power: "I do some things well; I can count on my own resources to see me through." This sense of effectiveness gives us confidence to take on the responsibilities of adult life, both in love and work. Having a skill, mastering a difficult task, being able to bring a project to completion—each of these strengthens self-confidence. More than needy children or passive victims, we are agents in our own lives.

Psychologists remind us how much the sense that we can make it on our own if we have to contributes to mature interdependence. Collaboration requires that we rely on others and open ourselves to their influence. But without some basic confidence in our own resources, *real* collaboration escapes us. Instead, we become too dependent, leaning on other people because we feel inadequate on our own, expecting them to make up for the resources we lack. This lack of autonomy will undermine any partnership, whether in work or in faith or in friendship.

Achieving autonomy is not always easy. Factors in our personal history may frustrate efforts to develop this sense of power. A dominating parent may so manage our life that we are left with no sense of autonomous power. We are cared for, but we cannot shape our own world. Or poverty may educate us in impotence: we learn that we are too weak, too ineffectual to act on our own. Encouraged to see ourselves as victims, we express our strength only in self-destructive acts of violence.

Thus autonomy is a developmental achievement, but it is not the end of the journey. A mature sense of personal power must expand beyond a fascination with self-sufficiency. Refusing to move on condemns us to live out the American stereotype of the "self-made man." Cooperation and collaboration are difficult for people limited to this sense of personal power. To them, working closely with other people suggests that one's own resources are deficient. Receptivity is for them an alien stance: openness to outside influence feels too much like weakness.

EXPRESSING POWER

A third face of power turns us outward, as we begin to influence others and to have an impact on our world. Strengths that we have received from others and resources that we have developed in ourselves are now tested in a social arena. The experience comes as we speak up for the first time at a meeting or hesitantly make a suggestion at work. When others respond favorably, a new sense of power stirs: "I make a difference here." New self-awareness supports personal assertion—a willingness to express our ideas, to make demands of others, to assume responsibility, to take charge.

At this third stage, we feel strong when we influence the world beyond ourselves. Among the people McClelland studied, this orientation was prominent among those in organizational roles of management or supervision, among lawyers and journalists, and for many in the helping professions—teachers, social workers, counselors. Success in all these enterprises is dependent on being able to influence the attitudes and behavior of other people. Both the first-grade teacher and the president of the United States want to inspire people; both a pastoral minister and a corporate executive try to influence others' behavior.

When power means autonomy, the focus is on our own strength: "I can do something." When power means influence, we become involved with developing and directing other people's power. To assume leadership in a group, we must be able to generate and focus energies that go beyond our own. Caring for a family demands this same coordination of diverse and often conflicting energies. Any role of supervision—foreman, teacher, mentor—asks us to shape other people's power.

Personal assertion and social influence, the special resources of this power orientation, can be displayed in different ways. McClelland notes that he found two alternate experiences at this stage. Some people felt powerful primarily in the combative stance of one-on-one competition. To best an opponent, to come out on top, to win—that is what made them feel strong. This interest in personal dominance, which McClelland calls the "primitive power motive," may be useful beyond the arena of sports. The personally dominant leader, for example, can be effective in some settings—a teenage gang, a military unit in battle—where the ruling image of power is physical strength in face-to-face conflict. But a leader who feels powerful *only* in face-to-face dominance quickly becomes authoritarian: "My way is the only way."

Such a dictatorial stance seldom serves in positions of organizational leadership or in the helping role. Being effective in these settings depends on an experience of personal power that McClelland calls the "socialized power motive." He found that people in this stance *felt powerful* when involved in motivating other people, offering assistance, coordinating resources, and helping group efforts move toward completion.

People who feel strong in personal assertion are willing to take charge and exercise control. Dominance and control, the strengths of this stage of power, sometimes appear in their darker guises. Unchecked, the impulse toward self-assertion makes us intolerant of the ideas or needs of others. Control can become coercion, especially if buttressed by the conviction that "I know what is best for them." This shadow side of power is a temptation to which social workers and politicians, managers and ministers can fall victim.

SHARING POWER

At an early stage we feel powerful because others' energy nurtures us. The source of power is beyond us; depending on this outside source, we are empowered. Later, autonomy introduces us to the sources of power within, helping us to feel strong in our own resources. Family and career responsibilities teach us to feel powerful when our actions influence others. Yet maturity lures us toward still another power experience—feeling strong in power shared.

People who have reached this stage genuinely feel themselves to be strong, but their experience is complex. Personal power, they sense, is taken up in something more than "just me." Values larger than self-interest, goals more significant than personal benefit motivate them. Some higher power—the will of God, the call of duty, a commitment to some transforming vision—prompts their principled action. Caught up in the energy of this larger sense of purpose, they feel both powerful and empowered.

People at this stage welcome interdependence. Partnership in power—the ability to enjoy *mutual* influence and *mutual* empowerment—now becomes real. We feel strong not only in autonomous activity but in the collaborative pursuit of common goals. When we work together, your power does not diminish me or replace my own. Rather, the power we share increases and enhances my strength.

At this stage the sense of personal power does not depend solely on getting one's own way. We can genuinely feel strong when we let others influence us, when we accommodate our behavior to others' needs, when we merge our own objectives into the larger goals of a group. Deferring to other people does not compromise us. We can choose to give up personal control in some circumstances, because to do so does not automatically signal the loss of personal power. We become capable of true interdependence—the genuine interplay of both strengths and weaknesses that characterizes the adult exchange of power.

Psychologists describe this experience as the "we" of power. An example may help. A group to which I belong is working on an important planning task. Eager that my proposal be accepted, I spend a good deal of time preparing my presentation and anticipating other people's responses. My goal is to get my proposal through the meeting unscarred. In the meeting itself I resist additions, counter objections, dismiss alternatives. Carefully guiding my contribution through the thicket of other people's comments, I finally prevail. My plan wins out; my proposal is adopted. I leave the meeting satisfied and gratified, feeling the force of my own initiative and influence. This is the "I" of power.

But a meeting like this can yield a very different experience of power. I bring to the session a plan I have carefully prepared. As discussion progresses, someone adds an idea that strengthens the proposal considerably. Another warns of a potential problem that I had overlooked. As more people contribute, comments begin to build on one another; a colleague's suggestion sparks a new idea from me. Free-ranging discussion energizes the group, calling forth our creativity. Gradually I let go my determined hold on *my* plan. By the end of the meeting, a new plan has emerged. This one does not have my name on it, but I have not been diminished. I have experienced the "we" of power.

This second meeting generated abundance. Power is not in short supply after all. As I was able to let go my control, my own power was not abolished but expanded. My strength (epitomized in the plan that I brought to the meeting) was taken up into a shared effectiveness. My sense of personal power was not lost but transformed.

Religious Leaders and Power

The myth of leadership focuses our attention on the second and third faces of power. We expect our leaders to be strong persons who have undergone serious discipline—business school or military training or seminary education. They should be self-sufficient folk, able to rely on their own resources. The myth continues: leaders are those who have power over others. They must be able to control situations, to prevail in disputes, to demand the desired results. McClelland's exploration of mature power suggests another vision, especially for the religious leader—a vision that draws on all these experiences of power.

In ministry we experience many times when direct control and autonomous action are necessary. To be effective, we have to become competent—and confident—in this exercise of the "I" of power. We need, at times, to confront other people or to make difficult decisions; we must act forcefully to guide a project to completion. But to be trapped in this independent stance, not because the situation calls for it but because we cannot face the challenge of relying on other people—this is to be limited as a leader. By learning to depend on others, ministers open themselves to the "we" of power. This healthy interdependence is rooted in a basic religious insight—we are not the source of our own strength. As ministers, we draw power from God and from the people we serve. Letting go the heroic but distorted ideal of self-sufficiency, Christian leaders witness to the power that belongs only to the Spirit but can be experienced in the interplay of the community's life.

Gifted and called, ministers must also develop their own strengths. Autonomy makes us more resourceful. Knowing our own capabilities, we can confidently offer them to the group and its shared task. But if we feel capable and confident only when we act on our own, being in a group will feel constraining. In leadership positions, we are likely to assume the stance of the distant leader (preferring to act on our own, without consulting group members) or the "expert" leader (willing to provide our expertise to the group's task but not participating in its life).

INFLUENCE AND CONTROL

Religious leaders exercise influence and control. In ministry today the leader's role is not to replace other people but to recruit them—their charisms, their hopes, their ideas—for a shared task. For this challenging work, a sense of personal power that finds expression in motivating, facilitating, and coordinating the activities of other people is required. Leaders need some comfort with stage-three power: the ability to feel strong in influencing other people.

People whose main experience of power comes at the third stage feel comfortable in the highly visible administrative roles of leadership. In his study of successful leaders in large organizations, McClelland found two critical patterns—assertion and coordination. The most effective leaders were able to draw on both—the coordinating skills necessary to mobilize the group's diverse energies and the personal presence required to inspire the group's allegiance. Most leaders reported tensions as they worked out the balance between personal assertion and the exercise of a more group-centered style of leadership. Importantly, though, they were able to *feel* powerful in both these kinds of intervention. Therefore, they were at ease with both kinds of behavior in their role as leader.

Effective stage-three leaders feel strong when they exercise their power *for* others. These people prize assertion and control: they are eager to exercise *their* power, but the sense of conquest is more impersonal. They do not have to "take up all the space" in order to feel influential. Mature stage-three leaders can feel powerful in a more participatory approach—guiding group members through a planning process and holding the group accountable to goals that they have helped formulate. In ministry, too, stage-three leaders make effective collaborators. Exercising their power less through domination than through management and planning, they can help a group work together effectively to serve a shared ministry.

SHARING POWER

In a hierarchical church we expect our leaders to be especially adept in the second and third faces of power: strong individuals and capable executives. As the hope of mutuality transforms the community of faith, we look for leaders who are good partners in ministry.

But leaders whose primary experience of power comes in assertion and control may find partnership difficult. In pursuit of greater collaboration, they may try to set aside a dominant leadership style that helps them feel strong. But if these leaders cannot *feel* powerful in this more collaborative stance, partnership exacts a high toll. They may go through the motions of mutuality, but only at real personal cost: acting collaboratively will diminish their confidence and erode their sense of effectiveness. Over the long run, this solution seldom works. We cannot expect our leaders to act continually in ways that leave them personally diminished. Only when collaborative behavior enhances a sense of self can we expect it to be part of the minister's ongoing leadership style. If partnership is to flourish, we need religious leaders who have some comfort with stage-four power— that is, leaders who genuinely feel strong when power is shared.

What do stage-four leaders look like? Again, McClelland's

work offers some clues. Stage-four leaders respond to authority and conflict in characteristic ways. Most organizations reinforce the bureaucratic understanding that authority comes only through approved channels. Many stage-three managers operate comfortably within this hierarchical pattern—accepting direction from their organizational superiors and expecting to be obeyed by their subordinates. Stage-four leaders, on the other hand, are more open to influence from a variety of sources. Comfortable in the interplay of power, these leaders often prefer to become part of a working group. In the group, they operate as active members more than as guides, surrendering some of their autonomy and assertiveness to the demands of genuine participation and letting themselves be influenced by the group's lead. Stage-four leaders also make good use of outside experts and consultants. As McClelland put it, "Those high in [shared] power do not feel at all that they personally have to know everything or understand everything. . . . Rather, they show a willingness to follow the advice of whatever authority was appropriate to the task at hand." People working with these leaders report that their openness permeates the work scene. Co-workers feel less hemmed in by regulations and more responsible for their own contribution to the common effort.

These mature leaders are also less defensive about conflict. They view dissent not as the enemy of organizational effectiveness but as a valued resource. Differences are not resolved from the starting point that "my view must prevail." On the contrary, these leaders approach differences of opinion and strong disagreement as reservoirs of creativity, expecting them to generate new solutions. Stage-four leaders encourage risk-taking behavior, recognizing that creativity leaves room to fail.

Ministering to the "We" of Power

Effective religious leaders recognize that God's power is not in short supply, restricted to formal roles, or held captive in church services. Like the loaves and fishes in the gospel story, God's gracious power is abundant, blessing us with a surprising extravagance. This realization relieves leaders of the responsibility to provide an ever-scarce power. Instead, their role is to remind groups of their own extraordinary resources and to orchestrate the use of these gifts.

The Eucharist, our central experience of grace, instructs us constantly in these four faces of power. This sacrament comes to us as a gift. Its saving grace is not ours but God's, abiding in the vital community of faith rather than in single leaders. Our leaders can grow more effective in their guidance of this community celebration; through study, practice, and prayer, their service as presider and preacher can be enhanced. By welcoming community involvement and supporting the participation of other gifted Christians, religious leaders contribute to the sacrament's graceful performance. But in the end the sacrament celebrates the flow of God's power as it reconciles and nourishes us. We are taken up in a power that is both beyond and within us, making this group stronger for its mission of love and justice. As we experience the "we" of power, gratitude is our response.

Reflective Exercise

Consider the four expressions of power discussed in this chapter:

- Receiving power
- Achieving autonomy
- Exercising influence
- Sharing power

Look for examples of each of these expressions of power in your own life these days. Do not rush this reflection. Spend time allowing your memories of power to emerge. Then list several concrete instances of your experience of yourself as strong.

Now consider these questions:

- Which of these four expressions of power is most characteristic of you these days?
- Which expression of power is most difficult for you?
- Which expression of power brings you the most consolation?

Additional Resources

For a full account of the research findings upon which this developmental model depends, see David McClelland, *Power: The Inner Experience* (New York: Irvington, 1979); quote taken from p. 312. Hilary Lips examines the ways in which gender expectations shape the experience of personal power in *Women, Men, and the Psychology of Power* (New York: Prentice-Hall, 1981). In *Real Power: Stages of Personal Power in Organizations* (Minneapolis: Winston Press, 1984), Janet O. Hagberg provides an intriguing look at the interplay of personal power and leadership style. For further analysis of the exercise of personal power in the work setting, see Sherry Suib Cohen, *Tender Power* (Reading, MA: Addison-Wesley, 1989), and Rosabeth Moss Kanter, *Men and Women of the Corporation* (New York: Basic Books, 1976) and *The Change Masters* (New York: Simon & Schuster, 1983).

Organizational analysts today stress the significance and efficacy of the leader's ability to share power; see, for example, C. C. Manz and H. P. Sims, Jr., *Superleadership: Leading People to Lead Themselves* (Englewood Cliffs, NJ: Prentice-Hall, 1988) and Diane Tracy, *The Power Pyramid: How to Get Power by Giving It Away* (New York: Morrow, 1990).

Robert Greenleaf draws on both biblical images and corporate examples in his *Servant Leadership: A Journey into the Nature of Legitimate Power and Greatness* (New York: Paulist Press, 1977), a book that continues to provide both solace and challenge for many in ministry. In *Strength of the Weak* (Philadelphia: Westminster Press, 1984), Dorothee Soelle brings together political theory, feminist psychology, and liberation theology in an evocative critique of contemporary understandings of power. Donna Schaper discusses the dynamics of power in *Common Sense About Men and Women in the Ministry* (Washington, DC: Alban Institute Publications, 1990).

For a comprehensive look at the current analysis of leadership among social scientists, see Martin M. Chemers and Roya Ayman, *Leadership Theory and Research* (New York: Academic Press, 1992).

11. The Symbolic Role of the Leader

> As he prayed, the aspect of his face was changed and his clothing became brilliant as lightning. . . . A cloud came and covered them with shadow; and when they went into the cloud the disciples were afraid. And a voice came from the cloud saying, "This is my Son, the Chosen One. Listen to him." And after the voice had spoken, Jesus was found alone. (Luke 9:29, 34–35, JB)

The first Christians struggled with the paradox of Jesus: he was like them in so many ways, a friend with whom they spoke and ate; but he was also much more. God's power and mercy became palpable in his words and touch. In the gospel story that Christians call the transfiguration, Jesus' friends were given a sudden glimpse into the Christ, the chosen one. For a moment they saw him in a new light; they recognized in this ordinary person God's extraordinary presence. Then, after this revelation, "Jesus was found alone."

This paradox continues in the church's life today. Christian leaders guide the community's life of faith and worship. Our leaders are believers like us, yet they are different. We have asked them to represent our shared faith and to remind us, day in and day out, of God's continuing presence among us.

Sacraments and Symbols

Religious leaders serve as symbolic persons in the community of faith. They stand at the center of many privileged moments of our encounter with God. A priest officiates at our wedding and later presides over the Baptism of our children; a beloved pastor anoints our dying parent. But these sacramental moments do not exhaust the mystery of God's presence among us. Jews and

Christians have always believed that our God is not a distant deity but a power that stirs in every part of life. In the Incarnation Christians confess that God has entered our flesh; now no place is exempt from God's healing touch.

But how does God's grace become visible and tangible among us? If we recognize God's splendor in sunsets and storms, we most often feel God's touch in our contact with one another. Frightened by a nightmare, a small child screams out in the night. Her mother rushes into the bedroom to calm her. Cradling her sweaty, distressed infant in her arms, she repeatedly assures her, "It's all right. It's all right." Gradually the child's fear subsides, and soon she is fast asleep. In this common experience God's care reaches through a parent's voice and touch to console a troubled child. The world is not really a nightmare; despite all the frightening events of life, "It's all right."

> I, Yahweh, your God,
> I am holding you by the right hand;
> I tell you, "Do not be afraid,
> I will help you."
> (Isa. 41:13, JB)

The mother returns to the living room and the magazine she was reading. She smiles ruefully, thinking, "Who am I to say, 'It's all right'? My own life is filled with confusion, and I'm telling my daughter, 'It's all right!'" But the deed is done: her parental instincts have witnessed to a religious faith she herself struggles to believe. How is the child to hear God's assurance if not through a parent's voice? The mother's words are more than her own, because they represent a larger conviction; they symbolize and witness to an optimism that she cannot individually guarantee.

This homey experience reminds us of a special mystery in human life: we are more than ourselves. A caring touch or generous gesture may have an impact that reaches beyond our intention. Even when we do not plan it, our actions say more than we intend. A friend who has been overly busy and distracted, for example, may notice your quiet, reflective attitude. Your composure evokes in her an almost-forgotten hope for some personal calm. Your peaceful demeanor—without intending to—

symbolizes and reawakens a fragile value in your friend's life. We are all symbolic persons: our actions—of affection or compassion or patience—remind others of God's presence. We all stand for more than just ourselves.

If, as individuals, we are symbols of God's healing presence, so are we in our shared life. At Pentecost the Spirit of God aroused the first Christians to a sense of power. This new energy generated a way of living together that caused others to exclaim, "See how they love one another!" This group of believers became a sign of God's grace in the world. In the community's compassion, our invisible God was made visible. In the group's just action, our hidden God became more real. This is what we mean when we say that the church is a sacrament—a symbol of God's grace and presence in the world.

This is, of course, a high ideal. Communities, like individuals, frequently fall away from their potential. Mired in selfishness or injustice or apathy, they become countersigns, convincing evidence that religion is an illusion or, at best, an opiate. But the ideal survives: communities and individuals alive with an energy that makes present to us hopes we had almost abandoned.

Only in this incarnational context can we properly understand the symbolic role of the religious leader. The people of God comprise a sacramental community. The church is Christ's body—a continuing sign of God's loving presence among us. A sacramental community is vital only when its many members make God's presence tangible in their actions of love and justice. Baptism invites all of us to become sacraments and signs of God's healing presence. As theologian Bernard Cooke observes, "Most specific to one's Christianity is the *power to act sacramentally*" (italics added). This call, which "points to the presence of the divine saving power in any Christian individual or community whose actions flow from faith and discipleship," is rooted in our Baptism, not in ordination to a formal leadership role.

Leaders assume their symbolic role within such a group. Their responsibility is to *serve* this presence of God, not *provide* it. Religious leaders are by profession what every Christian is by vocation. The designated leader guides the community's actions of forgiving, healing, and nourishing one another in the Eucharist. But the religious leader does not accomplish these actions because others *cannot*. On the contrary, in these sacraments the leader acts to remind all of us that we perform these actions too. In our daily lives, as we forgive, heal, and nourish one another, we make Christ visible and tangible. We act as symbolic persons. Our formal sacramental celebrations are meant to remind us—not relieve us—of our own sacramental vocation.

Yet leaders continue to play a special role in the community. We have selected them to represent our faith and to remind us of God's enduring presence. When the ordained minister reads the gospel before the community, God's words become audible. In a rite of reconciliation, the priest's voice announces God's forgiveness. The leader's style of presiding can encourage others to participate or can exclude them from their sacramental calling. We can recognize these different styles of presiding in the ritual of anointing, as illustrated in the examples below.

Two Styles of Leadership

A family has gathered around the hospital bed of a dying father. As the various members of the family speak quietly with one another, the chaplain enters the room. After a few moments of conversation, he addresses the group: "If you will all step back, I will now anoint William." The leader, as representative of both God and the larger church, steps forward to anoint the dying person. He, and he alone, performs this service. The members of the family watch as this sacramental, symbolic activity takes place.

This first example portrays the leader as powerful and the community as weak. The leader replaces the community as the symbolic focus of God's presence. As God's representative, he is expected to provide for all our spiritual needs. In such a vision the leader prays and heals in ways the rest of us cannot. We may even be grateful to be relieved of this responsibility ourselves.

Quite a different scenario takes place in many hospitals today. As the family gathers around a dying member, the chaplain arrives and speaks some words of consolation to those gathered. After a brief explanation of the ritual that is to follow, the chaplain says, "If you will all step forward, we will now anoint William." The chaplain still exercises considerable leadership: inviting the members forward, explaining the ritual of anointing, guiding this shared exercise. But this leader's actions convey a very different message than those of the first leader. As an official representative of the church, the chaplain invites family members to step forward rather than to step back. They are actively to invoke God's blessing on William at the time of his death. The leader generates and guides this symbolic action of a community instead of simply supplying it.

In this scenario the religious leader is not separate from the community, invested with powers that other Christians utterly lack. The leader's actions do not replace our own; rather, they remind us of our responsibility.

When Christians gather to invoke God's blessing, our leaders guide our petitions. Picturing our leaders as already *possessing* these gifts of God, which they can then dispense to the community, leads us astray. When ordained leaders alone function in community ceremonies, the community comes to imagine that priests have an exclusive right to dispense God's blessings. We fall into a commercial mentality, acting as though God's graces had been handed over to the institutional church at wholesale for its clergy to distribute at retail.

To believe that only the institutional church can allot God's blessings is to invent a world of scarcity. In this environment the religious leader's genuine symbolic role is significantly altered. The leader no longer represents the community's faith that God will bless us (in however unpredictable a fashion). Now the leader uniquely *represents* God: in rituals he dispenses, in God's name, healing and nourishment. He performs in the community of faith not as a leader of our petitions but as a provider of scarce grace.

When we act as though only the ordained leader has power to announce the gospel, we imagine a scarcity of power. We make God's abundant grace captive to institutional control. In such a worldview, we judge that only the priest can preach; no other baptized persons share this symbolic power to formally speak about God's word. We judge that a lay person, directing a prayer service in church, must not sit in the official presider's chair; this place is reserved for the ordained as the unique representative of God and the church. The power to act symbolically in God's name is seen as being in short supply.

When we acknowledge that *every* Christian mediates God's blessing and forgiveness, we remember that power is abundant. We are all called to extend blessings—though a well-trained, designated leader will ordinarily guide such formal rituals as baptizing and anointing. Any prepared and faithful Christian can preach the Good News—though a designated presider ordinarily oversees this important service and guarantees its authenticity. In this understanding, the leader neither absorbs the community's power to act symbolically nor supplies such power to an underprivileged group of believers. Instead, the designated leader calls others to exercise their own symbolic power to bless, anoint, forgive, and preach. Such a leader generates power in a community instead of jealously guarding against its usurpation.

The Leader as Mediator

Religious leaders occupy precarious terrain as mediators between God and the community. Communities of faith come in touch with God in part through the mediation of their leaders. We express our petitions and our gratitude to God through them. We ask them to carry our religious hopes and anxieties. Their sermons and pastoral decisions represent the community's aspirations. Yet better understanding the dynamics of human community, we recognize the group's role even here. Leaders do not merely assume our burdens; we actively invest them with our group's ambitions and dreads. Leaders carry these weighty values of the community. This confusing dynamic makes religious leadership a dangerous and exhausting occupation.

A community of faith designates its leader as a mediator—one who stands between. *Mediator* is an enduring image in Christian life, but it survives today only by being transformed. The role of mediator changes as our view of our religious world shifts. In a hierarchical world we pictured God as transcendently beyond and above us. Such a worldview elevates our leaders, placing them above the community, between God and the rest of us.

In the world of mutuality that Christians are reclaiming these days, we understand mediation differently. No longer living in a vertical world, we do not picture our leaders above us. Leaders are our partners in faith, not our parents or rulers. But even in a world of partners, leaders remain mediators.

In his comprehensive studies of the Christian liturgy, theologian Edward Kilmartin analyzes the priest's role as mediator in the Eucharist. Catholics have traditionally emphasized that the priest represents Christ to the community. Kilmartin reminds us that this mediation of Christ to the group is possible only because the leader first represents the community's own faith. This correction locates the leader firmly within the community. The priestly leader is not solely a representative of God or the institutional church; such a person also represents the faith of the community.

THE LEADER IN THE EUCHARIST

The symbolic role of the leader takes on a special importance in the community's celebration of the Eucharist. For many centuries the focus of this sacrament was the breaking of the bread. In their common prayer Christians remembered not only Jesus at the Last Supper but the event at Emmaus, when the disciples recognized Jesus "in the breaking of the bread" (Luke 24:31). Sharing food and drink in this holy setting, Christians expected the extraordinary nourishment of Christ's presence among them. In these privileged gatherings, their faith grew; they felt more hope; they were renewed in their resolve to be loving and just. Their breaking and sharing of bread signaled and caused this communal nourishment. In this sacramental action the leader brought the community's petitions, voiced their faith, and, as Jesus did at the Last Supper, presided over the breaking of the bread.

In the early Middle Ages the symbolic role of the leader at the Eucharist took a fateful turn. Focus shifted from the breaking of bread to the consecration, as Christian piety emphasized the transformation of the sacramental bread and wine into the body and blood of Jesus Christ. The holiest part of the Mass became the priest's announcement, "This is my body," and later, the elevation of the host. Jesus' presence, *preserved* for our personal veneration, replaced the traditional focus of Christ's presence in bread *consumed* in common. This nourishing bread was taken out of the hands of the community and entrusted solely to the hands of the leader. (Many other changes in the ritual of the Mass contributed to this major shift. The offertory procession was dropped, and with it the offering of bread by the community. Small unleavened wafers replaced a common loaf and the need to "break bread" disappeared.)

In this shift the symbolic role of the liturgical leader took on new importance. The priest's words alone transformed the bread into Christ's body; his hands alone held this sacred host. Suddenly the leader occupied center stage: the Eucharist became *his* to perform, while a passive community "heard Mass." Christ's priesthood seemed fully expressed in his symbolic leadership, and the priestliness of the community was forgotten.

In the liturgical reforms of the last half-century, Catholics have been returning to an earlier style of celebrating the Eucharist. Again we gather in confidence that, breaking bread together, we avail ourselves of extraordinary nourishment. The focus of our shared meal shifts from the priest's unique actions at the consecration to the community's sharing of this blessed bread and wine. Once more, everyone is encouraged to hold this bread, the sign of Christ's nourishing presence. The liturgical leader presides at this communal celebration rather than providing for a passive community. Although his role is less heroic, the priest still acts as a mediator in the Eucharist, reminding the whole community of its priestliness.

MEDIATING GOD'S BLESSINGS

Two small but significant shifts in Christian prayer illustrate the changing role of the minister as mediator. Traditionally the presiding priest would recite this prayer: "May God *bless you*, in the name of the Father, the Son, and the Holy Spirit." The leader, speaking in God's name, mediates this blessing to the group. More commonly today a presider will pray, "May God *bless us*, in the name of the Father, the Son, and the Holy Spirit." The leader still mediates God's blessing, pronouncing the prayer in the group's name. But this small shift in vocabularly relocates the leader in the community. Now the leader speaks, not as if standing at God's side and addressing the rest of us, but invoking God's blessing on *us* all. In this prayer the leader stands with the community, as one of us. The role of mediator in prayer endures, but the nuance is very different.

This shift in the leader's relation to the community is repeated in the prayer that concludes the eucharistic liturgy. Traditionally the presider would pray, "Go in peace; the Mass is ended." Today many eucharistic ministers pray, "*Let us* go in peace, to praise and serve the Lord." Again the shift is small but significant. In the traditional form, the leader sides with God and tells the people it is time for them to leave. The implication seems to be, "I'm staying." The leader lives here, in the sanctuary, in the church; this is where a sacred minister belongs. Other members of the community return to a secular world where they live and work. In the new form of the concluding prayer, the leader identifies with the community: "Let *us* go! We all live in both the church and the world. So we go out from the Eucharist together." Again mediation is necessary; somebody must say this prayer that concludes the liturgy. But it is said not by someone who is profoundly different from us but by someone who goes with us "to praise and serve the Lord."

These simple prayers are examples of a larger change in liturgical leadership. The second-century theologian Justin Martyr described the leader of the liturgy as "president." Presiding, like mediating, is a style of leadership that survives by changing. If we picture the ordained leader as the only sacramental actor in the community, we assume that the presider does it all. The president of the liturgical assembly says the prayers, gives the homily, prepares and distributes the host and chalice, blesses the community. Made different from us by ordination, the liturgical leader is equipped to do what we cannot.

In a world of adult partners in faith we look at the presider in another light. The president of the liturgy sees that the liturgy is celebrated properly. This person is the symbolic center of the celebration—but as servant, not hero. The presider does not have to do it all—to sing, no matter how poor a voice; to preach, no matter how ungifted. As presider, a leader orchestrates the celebration to which many members contribute. The leadership role is not abandoned but transformed.

The role of mediator is also changing in the teaching ministry of the bishop. In the Catholic community, the bishop suffered the most dire effects of our heroic image of the leader. He was expected to live apart, often in a palatial residence. When he did appear in public, it was often for an extraordinary occasion, dressed in unusual garb. His secret selection left us to imagine him in semimagical terms. Envisioning the bishop as extraordinarily holy and wise and prudent, the community exiled him in this exotic role of aloof "man of God." We pictured the bishop as being privy to special information—about the gospel, revelation, and the church. The teaching documents of the bishops appeared in finished form for our obedience, not our discussion. But this is changing.

In the past decade the American Catholic bishops have prepared three special teaching letters—on nuclear armaments, on American economic life, and on women in the church. In these letters the bishops have attempted to mediate gospel values to daily life. But the style of preparation of these letters signals an important change in the bishops' symbolic role in the community. The bishops did not prepare these documents in secret, nor did they release them as finished teachings. They did not present these texts "from on high," as befits superiors in a hierarchy. Instead, they repeatedly consulted the community of faith. Sharing a rough draft of the documents, they asked our suggestions. This is not the behavior of parents but of partners!

This mutual style of leadership has offended some. "Bishops are supposed to know what they're doing! Let them make their authoritative statement (and then we may or may not obey)." The style of collaboration that they demonstrated looked to some like weakness. These people were disappointed and angered; their parents had let them down.

The bishops are modeling to the community of faith a new style of leadership. They show us that they do not have privileged access to God's will. They do have an imperative to witness to the gospel and to mediate the church's best hopes for human life today. But in this they act as our brothers, not as our parents. They need the advice and help of others in the community. They are fulfilling their role as mediators, but now from a very different symbolic position in the community.

Symbolic Persons

Religious leaders are symbolic persons. The imagery of an icon can help us avoid the temptations that surround this perilous, if necessary, role. Gazing at an icon, believers look toward an invisible God; handling an icon, believers come in touch with an intangible God. Leaders, as icons, direct our eyes toward God. Their symbolic service fails when they *distract* believers from God, when our gaze stops at the leader.

Using another set of images: leaders are channels, not vessels, of God's power. God's grace and blessings flow into the community through these special channels. But leaders do not possess or contain this mysterious power. They are not repositories of grace from which they may dispense or withhold blessings. As symbolic persons, religious leaders do not absorb our responsibility but give it focus. Through their formal ministry of forgiving, nurturing, and preaching, leaders remind us of these necessary dynamics in our own lives. Their symbolic role is effective when the community of faith becomes a more powerful sign of God's presence in the world.

Reflective Exercise

Spend time in reflection on the symbolic quality of your own experience.

First, recall a time when someone's action moved you deeply. This may have been an act of kindness or patience, or a homily or letter that communicated "something extra" to you. Try to feel again how that action represented to you God's goodness.

Now call to mind a group that especially impresses you. It might be a parish, a family, a group committed to social action. How does this group represent or symbolize "something extra" to you? What feelings of faith or confidence do they arouse in you?

Is there a religious figure about whom you have strong feelings? This may be a local person (for example, a pastor or spiritual director in your own life) or a more public figure (Mother Teresa, Martin Luther King, Jr., or Pope John XXIII, for example). Reflect on the range of feelings that this person evokes in you. How does this person represent "something extra" to you?

Additional Resources

Edward Kilmartin explores the priest's symbolic role in the sacraments in *Christian Liturgy: Theology and Practice* (Kansas City, MO: Sheed & Ward, 1988); see p. 173 for his reminder that ritual prayers are petitions and p. 324 for his brief discussion of the liturgical leader's relationship to the believing community. For a brief and clear outline of the historical changes in the liturgy of the Eucharist, see J. D. Crichton's *Short History of the Mass* (London: Catholic Truth Society, 1983).

For two excellent discussions of the distinction between clergy and laity, see Alexandre Faivre, *The Emergence of the Laity in the Early Church* (New York: Paulist Press, 1990), and Bernard Cooke, "Obstacles to Lay Involvement," in J. Metz and E. Schillebeeckx, eds., *The Teaching Authority of Believers; Concilium*, vol. 180 (New York: T. & T. Clark, 1985), pp. 63–70; quote taken from p. 68.

In *The Emerging Laity: Returning Leadership to the Community of Faith* (New York: Image Books/Doubleday, 1988), chap. 6, we undertake an initial examination of the symbolic role of the religious leader. For an analysis of the complex dynamics of projection in religious leadership, see Bruce Reed, *The Dynamics of Religion* (London: Darton, Longman & Todd, 1978).

In *That They Might Live: Power, Empowerment and Leadership* (New York: Crossroad/Continuum Books, 1991), Michael Downey draws together a range of contributors to discuss the foundations of leadership in the community of faith.

12. Prophetic Leadership Today

> Behold, I am doing a new thing: now it springs forth, do you not perceive it?   (Isa. 43:19, RSV)

We live at a momentous time in the church. Renewal quickens our faith and arouses our generosity, and we perceive God's presence in the changes that spring forth. But these events confuse us as well. So much has changed!·Have we not lost important parts of our Christian heritage? The distress that we experience is as old as the Psalms: "This is the cause of my grief, that the ways of the Most High have changed" (adapted from Ps. 77:10, RSV). The transformations of the past twenty-five years have brought us to grief.

This peculiar mix of hope and loss recalls the ancient gift of prophecy. In our distant religious past, prophets appeared in times of distressing change to show God's people which direction to take. The great prophet Moses led his people out of servitude and through a hostile desert. Nathan challenged King David's leadership; Jeremiah accused Jerusalem of being deaf to God. In periods of stagnation or infidelity, prophets called the community to change—to let go old ways and renew their commitment to God. This revolutionary gift challenged our ancestors to recognize signs of God amid the chaos of change.

Prophecy was still vibrant during Jesus' time. John the Baptist played the role of prophet as he called people to conversion. And Jesus' own life was essentially that of a prophet: wandering from town to town, interpreting the Scriptures, challenging his listeners to live in justice and love. In the earliest Christian communities this ministry continued to flourish. Paul recognized prophecy as one of the gifts given to a faith community (1 Cor. 12:10); the author of Acts listed the prophets and teachers active in Antioch (Acts 13:1); the writer of the book of Revelation described himself as a prophet (Rev. 1:3).

For 200 years after the death and resurrection of Jesus, the gift of prophecy remained strong among Christians. Often serving as itinerant ministers, prophets would visit Christian communities, celebrating the Eucharist and preaching conversion and renewal. During the third century, however, this special ministry withered and seemed to disappear.

Whatever happened to prophecy? As the church expanded, concern mounted about orthodoxy and heresy. We wanted to be faithful to our past, not seduced by every new wind of doctrine or belief. In such a climate, prophecy seemed like a luxury we could not afford. Fearful of the prophet's fertile imagination, with its puzzling insights and insistent claims, the church turned away from this dangerous gift. Prophecy did not die, of course. As Edward Schillebeeckx observes in his *The Church with a Human Face*, bishops began to interpret this calling as part of their ministry: "The earlier prophetic authority of all believers now becomes a property of the office of the bishop." While the annexing of prophecy to the ministry of the bishop helped to prevent its abuse, it did little to foster its growth. The bishop, as chief administrator of a diocese, was frequently more concerned with stability than with new and potentially disruptive interpretations of Christian faith.

As an enduring gift of the Spirit, this revolutionary ability to see and challenge went underground. The active imaginations of religious mystics (and heretics) were fertile ground for this gift. Later, monasteries and religious orders would provide shelter for this fragile strength as the imaginations of Christians continued to envision the confusing movement of God among us.

As the ministry of prophecy waned, Christians began to portray this power in an ever more exotic light. Prophets (we told ourselves) were people gifted with an extraordinary capacity to see hundreds of years into the future. Describing prophecy as exceptional reinforced the prejudice that its power was absent in our own time. Because none of us possessed such an extraordinary vision, surely the ministry of prophecy no longer existed.

But our present period of upheaval invites us to envision

prophecy in a new light. Perhaps prophecy does not entail only seeing the distant future; it may refer to the ability to see clearly what is happening right now. Prophecy may not be so exotic or bizarre as we thought; this gift may be available—and required—in Christians today.

Prophecy is the ability *to show the church God's future*. The prophet's gift is less a vision of the distant future than a recognition of a future impinging on our life today. This understanding of prophecy acknowledges the gap between the church and the reign of God. As servant of God, the church struggles to discern God's initiative and faithfully to follow this direction. The church is a community in pilgrimage; on the way, we sometimes lose sight of God's action. Bogged down in busywork and every kind of distraction, we forget that "the ways of the Most High" can change. When the community drifts toward stagnation, God stirs the imagination of some of its members to see anew, to recognize again the need for conversion.

Seeing Through the Present

In *The Prophetic Imagination*, Walter Brueggeman sketches the shape of the prophet's role. Prophets help the community *see through* the present, to recognize God's action breaking into our life. The difficulty of this ministry is rooted in the nature of the present—all the duties, delights, and distractions that fill our day. The present absorbs our attention: the good we are doing and the troubles we are avoiding conspire to consume us.

The disciples on the road to Emmaus (Luke 24:13–35) were absorbed by the present. Staggered by the loss of Jesus, engulfed in grief, they forgot the central message of his preaching: by dying we come to life. Their immediate distress spiraled them into amnesia. Appearing in the guise of a stranger, Jesus pulled them out of their stupor. Recalling the words of the ancient prophets, Jesus challenged them to remember the pattern of God's power, which can transform failure and even death.

The Emmaus story reminds us of the power of the present to capture our attention. Absorbed in our daily life, we easily forget the past, with its salutary lessons, and we neglect the future, with its rightful claims. Encircled by the familiar demands of the present, we feel protected from unpleasant surprises and the need to change. We may complain about the pace of our hectic schedule, but we are secretly grateful for this defense against what the future holds.

Our daily duties, faithfully repeated, become the status quo. "This is how we do it around here" becomes "This is the *only* way to do things," which finally becomes "This is God's divine will for us." Brueggeman describes our religious ancestors' confusion of the status quo with God's will in the ominous phrase "the royal consciousness." Whether in ancient Jerusalem or the contemporary church, religious leaders are tempted to identify the established way of doing things with God's unchanging will. Gradually we replace God's surprising presence with predictable patterns and institutional procedures.

Prophets among us call attention to the royal arrangements in the church that seem to block the Spirit's movement. Clergy and laity are divided into two kinds of Christians, women are prevented from serving as sacramental leaders. The royal arrangement sponsors an international synod on the laity and fails to invite the laity as full participants. In such royal arrangements, the present way of doing things gains a sacred aura and becomes very difficult to challenge. But prophets encourage us to see through these arrangements and recognize God's surprising future.

A second gift that God gives to prophets is the ability to ask what time it is. Royal arrangements seek to build an orthodoxy that will be untouched by the winds of human time; they aspire to an eternally valid correctness. Brueggeman gives us two examples from Israel's history of the prophetic challenge to recognize a time for change.

Jeremiah exercised his ministry of prophecy in Jerusalem shortly before Israel was driven into exile in Babylon. The people of God had fallen into every kind of infidelity and injustice. The worship of false gods replaced their fidelity to Yahweh, and their ignoring of the poor compromised their commitment to justice. Jeremiah's imagination saw where this unfaithfulness would lead; he recognized the immediate future that was dawning on the nation. He draped a yoke around his neck and paraded through the city streets to dramatize what was in store for Israel (Jer. 27, JB). His unusual behavior cried out, "Now is time for us to change our ways!"

Jeremiah complained that Israel could not recognize the signs of the times:

> Even the stork in the heavens knows her times;
> And the turtledove, swallow, and crane
> Keep the time of their coming;
> But my people know not the ordinance of the Lord.
>
> (Jer. 8:7, RSV)

Being alert to time makes us vulnerable to loss. Time is about change; as Brueggeman reminds us, time is always an end-time—some part of our life coming to an end. Time is always an enemy of the royal arrangement.

Jeremiah's pleas went unheeded. The people of Jerusalem could not imagine what he was talking about; they could not guess what time it was. And so it became a time to go into exile, to wear the yoke of prisoners in a foreign land.

A generation later the Israelites found themselves immersed in a period of imprisonment. Living as captives in Babylon, they despaired of ever returning to their own home. In this mood of sorrow, the voice of Second Isaiah announced another surprising change: it was time to return to Jerusalem! God was about to rescue them and return them home (Isa. 40). Disheartened by their long exile, the people of God could not imagine such a change. The revolutionary voice of Second Isaiah told the people what time it was: "Remember not the former things, nor consider things of old. Behold, I am doing a new thing; now it springs forth, do you not perceive it?" (Isa. 43:18–19, RSV).

Vatican II challenged Catholics to recognize "the signs of the times"—signals of God's presence among us, signals of what time it is. Prophets among us listen to the changes happening in the church. They point out transformations in the human community's sense of women's dignity and the variety of their gifts. They remind us of the many ways in which our sexual love becomes fruitful. They have us acknowledge the depletions in the numbers of priests and vowed religious. Then the prophet sounds the unsettling question: What time is it?

We make prophets too heroic if we insist that they *know* what time it is. Perhaps their gift is the boldness to raise the question. In the midst of change, we do not need to see clairvoyantly into the distant future. We need only the courage and patience to ask of ourselves: What time is it?

But the ability to ask this threatening question demands a special discipline. Many of us, absorbed by the demands of our ministry and the needs of our community, do not have the leisure to watch for the signs of the times. We are much too busy. The noise of the present does not permit us to hear the subtle sound of the future. Prophets are those folk among us who dare to do less. They are willing to be less devoted to good work, less consumed by the legitimate demands of the present day. Their peculiar discipline is to stop the busyness and, in the ensuing stillness, to listen. Only as the absorbing and distracting demands of the present are stilled will we hear the sounds of the future. This is a considerable risk. The good we are doing now not only fills our day but tells us who we are. In our work we find our worth. Busyness is proof of our importance. Without it, who would we be? What if we quiet our hearts and then hear nothing? Despite this threat, prophets invite us to greater silence so that we may hear the subtle murmurs of God's Spirit. These sounds alone can tell us what time it is.

Coming to Grief

Prophecy is a two-edged sword. It announces God's future breaking into our present, and it warns us of an end to the royal arrangement. Prophecy arouses us to hope and also brings us to grief: "This is the cause of my grief, that the ways of the Most High have changed."

In a time of renewal our excitement about new possibilities at first distracts us from the other dynamic of change: we must let go parts of our religious life that we thought were essential. Only gradually do we realize, in the words of our colleague J. Gordon Myers, that "every beginning starts with an ending"; new journeys commence with farewells. The prophets among us teach us to say good-bye.

Acknowledging our losses and letting them go requires us to grieve. But to many Americans, grieving is a sign of weakness, a shameful submission to emotion and tears. Our culture instructs us to cut our losses, put our troubles behind us, and get on with life. Remember: big boys don't cry. These imperatives lead us to deny our distress and mask our mourning. But the tradition we share as Jews and Christians holds a different legacy about grieving: it is an honorable action and a necessary virtue. To taste these emotions that we would rather just swallow, courage and patience are required.

Prophets help a community to grieve by bringing private pain to public expression. Very often the pain of a transition is first experienced in private. A woman feels great sorrow that she cannot serve the church as a priest. A gay Christian regrets that his committed love for his partner of many years must remain hidden from public view. A priest's trouble with alcohol seems to be only a matter of personal weakness. This individual distress, arising repeatedly throughout the church, suggests a pattern of *shared* pain; yet an organization resolutely committed to defending the royal arrangement must keep this pain private. If we can isolate individuals in their pain, our institutional arrangements will never have to change.

Prophets see this widespread distress in another light. By bringing private experiences to public expression, prophets invite us to hear these complaints in unison. What if this is more than personal pain? What if these sounds of distress are signs of God's immediate future breaking into our defended present?

Bringing private pain to public expression has both a psychological and religious effect. Removing this pain from its isolation, we discover how many others carry a similar distress. We are not alone! This woman's sorrow is joined to the grief that many women feel over their treatment in the church. This gay man's regret is reinforced by many Christians who find official statements about sexuality at odds with their own conscientious experience. This priest's alcoholism is a symptom shared by many other ministers. There is solidarity in this shared pain. A common grief empowers us to question the royal arrangement. The terrible threat, and power, of grieving is the public admission that things are not fine. In Brueggeman's words, "Real criticism begins in the capacity to grieve because that is the most visceral announcement that things are not right."

Religiously, we rescue our pain from privacy by giving grief a voice. As long as distress remains isolated in our hearts, it remains mute. When we pronounce our pain together as Christians, we turn our distress into prayer. Our complaint becomes a public lamentation. We lift up our voice in anger, regret, and even blame to a God that we do not understand. We complain and question and reproach God. Jews and Christians have a rich tradition of such grieving. In the Hebrew Scriptures Job cries out,

> Since I have lost all taste for life,
> I will give free rein to my complaints;
> I shall let my embittered soul speak out.
> I shall say to God, "Do not condemn me,
> But tell me the reason for your assault."
>
> (Job 10:1-2, JB)

This style of prayer flourishes in the Psalms as well:

> I am worn out with groaning,
> Every night I drench my pillow
> And soak my bed with tears;
> My eye is wasted with grief,
> I have grown old with enemies all around me.
>
> (Ps. 6:6-7, JB)

These groans and accusations are our untidy prayer in a time of grief. With these messy laments we reach out to a mysterious God.

FROM DEPRESSION TO DESOLATION

Turning our pain into prayer transforms our emotions. Instead of denying them, we hold them up for God's inspection. We hand our pain to God and demand some attention. Our religious memory assures us that this strategy works: "I have seen the affliction of my people who are in Egypt, and have heard their cry because of their taskmasters; I know their sufferings, and I have come down to deliver them out of the hand of the Egyptians" (Exod. 3:7-8, RSV).

This healthy grieving begins our healing. As theologian David Power has observed, "That which is remembered in grief is redeemed, made whole, renewed." In prayer we acknowledge our pain and ask God to do something about it. This daring exercise transforms our depression into desolation.

Depression is a complex mood that arises as we fail to face an emotion such as shame, loneliness, or anger. If we cannot acknowledge our anger toward our parents, this neglected feeling may transform itself into the fatigue of depression. When we refuse to face a significant fear, this emotion may turn into a pervasive mood of defeat. As Maggie Scarf observes in *Unfinished Business*, depression is a "hybrid emotion" generated by our denial of some other distressing feeling. The exhaustion and fatigue of depression come from our effort to keep this pain hidden and this sorrow private.

The experience of desolation is very different. In the Jewish-Christian tradition desolation is a noisy sorrow. The author of Lamentations cries out in desolation:

> All you who pass this way, look and see:
> Is any sorrow like the sorrow that afflicts me,
> With which Yahweh has struck me
> On the day of his burning anger?
>
> (1:12, JB)

This style of prayer is a blend of anger and pleading: "You cannot mean to forget us forever? You cannot mean to abandon us for good?" (5:20, JB).

In this mood we publicly voice our distress, loudly lament our loss. We both disperse some of our pent-up energy and try to get God's attention. Desolation is an unhappy mood, but it does not wreak the interior destruction of depression.

A troubled family finally agreeing to seek therapy is characteristically depressed. Anger, regret, blame—these emotions, unaddressed and unhealed, churn through the family. Exhaustion and fatigue envelop the members. In therapy the family learns to turn its depression into desolation. By naming the pain and searching out its causes, the family voices its distress. No longer mute, family members learn to communicate their pain. Blame and abuse give way to sorrow and regret. A mood of desolation ensues as they acknowledge the havoc that they have wrought and the hard work ahead, but this somber mood is very different from a crippling sense of depression.

Similar experiences multiply in today's church. The Woman's Ordination Conference, for example, challenges the royal arrangement that prohibits women from ministering as sacramental leaders in the Catholic church. Members of this group bring their individual pain out of its privacy; they join their distress together in a single, focused lament. Desolation abounds, but without the destructive results of depression.

Several years ago Vatican officials censured Archbishop Hunthausen of Seattle for a number of his leadership decisions. Many members of the diocese were distressed and angered by the punitive nature of this censure. Had these many Christians kept their sorrow to themselves, a mood of depression would surely have descended on the diocese. Instead, they came together to pray about their distress. In public discussions and liturgies, they raised their voices in lament. They brought their private pain to public expression. In so doing, they turned their potential depression into desolation. Lamentation became this diocese's mode of prayer. Observers, seeing this community in distress, recognized their grieving as both healthy and holy.

HOLY WEEK

As Catholics today, we lament the loss of a cherished vision of the priesthood. Sudden and profound changes alarm both the community and priests themselves. A sharp decline in the number of priests provokes concern. What does it mean that so few are choosing this way of life? But the transformation goes beyond statistics to touch the identity of priesthood. The priest is no longer the "special person" he once was, whose sacred hands alone were worthy to touch the body of Christ in the Eucharist. The reasons justifying required celibacy no longer convince many priests. Few Catholics—priests or lay people—give weight to the theological view that ordination makes the priest ontologically different from other Christians.

Those who work closely with priests report a deepening malaise. Priests and the rest of us, trying to make sense of this pervasive mood, often focus on personal reasons. An individual priest muses, "If I were a more generous person, I would not have these questions. If I would only work harder or pray more, these debilitating doubts would go away." But in this individual distress the prophet hears a shared lament: the priesthood is dying.

In the decline in numbers, in the erosion of a once-clear identity, in the loss of a privileged status in the community, priesthood as we have known it is coming to an end. This cruel fact is hardly admissible among us. Every step is taken to deny it: we assure ourselves that the downswing in vocations is only temporary; we explain that troubled priests suffer simply from personal problems. When denial no longer works, we slip into anger and blame, hoping to allay our confusion by finding someone at fault.

A prophetic community, rather than looking for a scapegoat, struggles to name its pain. The metaphor of Holy Week supports us in this struggle. This religious image gives our shared pain both a context and a direction. As Jesus prepared to go to Jerusalem the final time, his friends objected. The time is not right, Peter protested. Jesus, in one of his rare outbursts of anger, responded, "Get behind me Satan!" (Mark 8:33, JB). Approaching his death, Jesus experienced doubt and confusion. He resisted the abrupt and unfair end to his life; he begged the Father to take this cup of suffering from him. Finally he gave himself to a rhythm he did not understand. With sorrow and regret he let go his plans and hopes and even his life, trusting in a power that was stronger than death.

The Catholic priesthood follows Jesus as it enters its Holy Week. Confusion and threat are in the air. Denial abounds. In Rome, Peter's successor still protests. But despite the denials and resistance, the church is drawn along God's path. The institution of priesthood, as we have known it over the past several hundred years, is moving toward its death. But the journey of Jesus rescues this mortal loss from absurdity and from annihilation.

Priesthood is on a painful journey of purification. As a continuing gift of God to the faith community, priesthood will not be lost; but it will be radically transformed. Its Good Friday will bring an end to a royal arrangement: a priesthood restricted to unmarried men, a priesthood encumbered by clerical status. Following Jesus into death, priesthood will be brought to new life.

By dying we come to life—this is Christianity's central conviction. Today it dawns on the church that this pattern is true for priesthood itself. The Catholic community cannot flee the pain that we feel at this approaching death, but we can grieve our loss. We can come together in lamentation, voicing our complaint. We can acknowledge the cause of our grief: that the ways of the Most High have changed. This communal mourning will transform our depression into desolation and our grief into shared lament. In Holy Week, this is how we pray.

God invites us to a future that does not include all of our past. But we are slow to see what is happening. Mixed feelings surround this transformation, exciting the long-dormant power of prophecy among us. Today, as always, prophets help us see through the present with its royal arrangements. They urge us to ask what time it is. And, reminding us that new beginnings include painful farewells, they help us grieve. Prophets incite us to turn our confusion into lamentation, trusting that what is remembered in grief is redeemed and made whole.

Reflective Exercise

Select a community that is important to you—your family or neighborhood, a parish or small faith community, a working group or ministry team. Reflect on the group's energy these days; recall its hopes or its distresses, its enthusiasm or its apathy.

Then ask the prophet's question: *For this group, what time is it?* Spend time with the question, alert to the images and insights that arise. Then take some notes on your response.

Now look for signs of grieving in this group. Does it struggle to face some loss, to let go some part of its past that is no longer useful?

Finally, consider how you might help the grieving process. What actions or rituals might assist the group to mourn its losses and purify itself for the future?

Additional Resources

Walter Brueggeman offers an excellent analysis of prophecy in ancient Israel and in the church today in *The Prophetic Imagina-*

tion (Philadelphia: Fortress Press, 1978); quote taken from p. 20. We discuss prophecy as a dynamic of change in *The Emerging Laity: Returning Leadership to the Community of Faith* (New York: Image Books/Doubleday, 1988), chap. 12, and in "The Gift of Prophecy," *Spirituality Today,* Winter 1989, pp. 292–304.

Edward Schillebeeckx's observation about prophecy in the early church appears in *The Church with a Human Face* (New York: Crossroads, 1985); quote taken from p. 71. David Power's remarks on the power of grieving can be found in "Households of Faith in the Coming Church," *Worship,* May 1983, pp. 237–54; quote taken from p. 254.

J. Gordon Myers examines the role of grieving in institutional growth in "Organizational Grieving: The Path to Newness," *Journal of the International Association of Conference Center Administrators,* Fall 1989. Maggie Scarf examines depression in the lives of women in *Unfinished Business: Pressure Points in the Lives of Women* (New York: Doubleday, 1980). Peter Homans explores the dynamic of grieving in *The Ability to Mourn* (Chicago: Univ. of Chicago Press, 1989).

In *The Political Meaning of Christianity* (San Francisco: HarperSanFrancisco, 1991), Glenn Tinder reflects on the prophetic stance required of all followers of Jesus. T. Richard Snyder calls the people of God to look at their social responsibility in *Once You Were No People: The Church and the Transformation of Society* (New York: Crossroad/Contiuum Books, 1990). In *Living No Longer for Ourselves* (Collegeville, MN: Liturgical Press, 1992), Kathleen Hughes, Mark Francis, and their associates reaffirm the intrinsic relationship between worship and justice in the faith community.

Part Four

The Rigors of
Partnership

13. Acknowledging Our Needs

> God put all the separate parts into the body on purpose. If all
> the parts were the same, how could it be a body? As it is, the
> parts are many but the body is one. The eye cannot say to the
> hand, "I do not need you," nor can the head say to the feet, "I
> do not need you." (1 Cor. 12:18–21, JB)

Partners in ministry have need of one another. The work of a
parish staff, for example, often overlaps. To accomplish my goals
in ministry, I need your active support and sometimes your formal approval. In turn, my projects affect yours: an agreement to
expand my young adult ministry may mean that your budget for
child-care services has to be cut. Frequently we have to coordinate our work schedules or negotiate how we will share limited
resources—the parish hall or staff car, my address book of generous donors, your phone list of eager parish volunteers.

To work together well, we must be able to talk about what we
need from one another at these practical levels. Those of us who
work together in parish teams and diocesan staffs today benefit
from organizational strategies that strengthen collaboration. By
clarifying job descriptions and developing long-range plans, for
example, we become more comfortable with the discussion of
what we need from one another to do our jobs well. As a result
of such strategies, coordinated action and shared decision making characterize the pastoral practice of many dioceses and
deaneries.

But partnership in ministry requires that our discussion of
collaboration go deeper, to include what we need from one
another personally. As we work together—ordained and lay,

155

women and men, professionals and volunteers—what do we need from each other beyond the roles and rules of our organization arrangement? Consider these examples:

- A lay woman serving as adult ministry coordinator asks, "What do I need from the priests on the staff to know that I am genuinely accepted as a member of the ministry team?"

- A pastor in a parish with active lay leadership wonders, "What do I need from the parish council to know that my role is appreciated and my contribution welcomed?"

- When a new director joins an agency, how do staff members raise their concerns about the loss of the previous, much-loved director?

- As the youngest member of the ministry team, how does the youth minister ask colleagues to stop treating him like "the new kid on the block" and start taking his work seriously?

Our concerns here go well beyond job descriptions. These demanding questions raise deeper vulnerabilities, because more than professional competence is at stake. This conversation focuses on "you and me" more than on the job.

Partnership raises questions: What is our relationship to be? What can we confidently expect from one another? No automatic right answer comforts us here. A small group of people who share a strong value commitment—advocacy for the homeless or hospice ministry for people with AIDS—may develop strong ties of emotional support. A group that is more highly structured and more diverse in values—say, a university faculty or hospital staff—may display cooler patterns of cooperation and concern. Neither one of these is necessarily the right pattern for collaboration. But in every ministry setting *some* pattern will develop, whether by choice and negotiation or by default.

Effective collaboration does not mean that co-workers must be close friends. Deep friendship and devoted personal love are special relationships, necessarily rare. Sometimes colleagues become friends, but friendship is seldom the best model for shared ministry. Partnership in ministry requires that we be available to one another and that we speak the truth. A lack of mutual accessibility and candor compromises collaboration from the start.

Expectations of closeness and collaboration have to be worked out in particular settings as we take into consideration the persons involved, the scope of our commitments, and the larger values we hold. But to work out these answers requires that we be able to talk—directly and without manipulation—about what we need from one another personally in order that our common work go well.

A Risky Conversation

Discussing our interdependence is risky, because the issues involved have emotional weight. Hope and expectation, loyalty and mistrust, affection and devotion, hurt and forgiveness—these topics seem somehow unprofessional. I fear that letting you know that I need something gives you power over me while accepting something from you leaves me in your debt. To discuss these concerns with colleagues makes me feel embarrassed, even vulnerable. These feelings seem especially inappropriate if I am in a leadership position: surely a leader should be able to go it alone!

Because the emotions are so threatening, groups sometimes conspire to avoid discussing interdependence. "We're here to do a job. It's a waste of time to be talking so much about ourselves. This kind of navel-gazing has no place in a group committed to the gospel; we have more important things to do." Statements such as these, for all their ring of hard-headed realism, often signal a group in flight from the demands of partnership. The goal is to silence and shame anyone foolhardy enough to raise issues of interdependence. And often the strategy succeeds.

A Crucial Gender Difference

A conversation about our emotional expectations, difficult for us all, generates special tension between women and men colleagues. Considerable evidence today suggests that women and men respond differently in discussing emotions. This is not true, of course, for every man and every woman. But the work of Nancy Chodorow, Carol Gilligan, and other students of gender differences notes a strong cultural trend. Many women learn early to be aware of their emotions. By adulthood, most women have developed a working vocabulary that helps them identify what they feel. This awareness makes many women, if not always comfortable with their feelings, at least alert to the emotional dimensions of what happens around them. Their sensitivity has implications for collaboration. Most women want to know where they stand emotionally as they work out the other practical details of effective collaboration.

Many men bring a very different history to a partnership in ministry. Most North American men report an upbringing and education that urged them to downplay or deny their emotions, especially those judged to be "womanly"—fear, dependence, tenderness, affection, appreciation. As a result, some men come to adulthood with limited awareness of their emotional lives and little vocabulary for identifying how they feel. A man will say, "I know when I feel good and when I feel bad, but beyond that I'm at a loss for words!" These men are often at a disadvantage in discussions of emotions. Beyond that, they have been socialized to see such discussions as irrelevant or as signs of weakness. Neither attitude is likely to put a man at ease in a conversation about what we have a right to expect of one another as we work together.

For many women, exploring issues of interdependence early in a working relationship is important. In team ministry or other collaborative settings, then, a woman often initiates the discussion about "who we are for one another here," because she sees clarification of this question as the *foundation* of genuine partnership.

For many men, on the other hand, this discussion is not the foundation but the *fruit* of partnership. Any discussion of "what we need from one another" seems out of place in the early stages of collaboration. These men are comfortable in such a potentially threatening discussion only if a tested atmosphere of trust and acceptance already exists. Practically, then, many men find the conversation about personal needs to be appropriate—if at all— only after a period of effective collaboration. Other men would say that such a discussion is *never* appropriate in the work setting.

Men and women, then, have a different sense of timing. A woman expects to discuss interdependence early on, because she appreciates knowing where people stand with one another. The discussion challenges her (as it does a man), but she considers it necessary. After an honest look at mutual needs, she more willingly invests herself in the practical demands of collaboration. Without this opportunity to clarify expectations, she may remain uncertain about her role and uneasy in her working relationships. This uncertainty eventually dissipates her energy, eroding her commitment to the common endeavor.

Following a different rhythm, her male colleague may consider any early discussion of partnership premature. He expects such a conversation—accepts it, feels up to it—only later. For him, a working relationship does not *start* here; co-workers have to *earn* the right to this kind of self-disclosure. A woman colleague introducing this discussion early in a work relationship with him meets resistance and confusion. He may misinterpret her request for dialogue, seeing it as a need for reassurance ("She's a weak woman") or as an inappropriate demand that they become emotionally involved. He may even consider her request a sexual advance. The woman, in her turn, interprets his resistance as defensiveness ("As a man he is, of course, frightened of his feelings") or indifference ("After all, most men just don't care").

None of these responses supports our efforts at partnership. Instead, we must be aware that, as women and men, we may be interpreting the situation between us differently. We have to be willing to explore these differences and be open to the conversation about what we need from one another.

Skills for the Conversation

Discussing what we need from one another becomes easier when we know how to communicate well. A warm and direct approach comes naturally to some people, but many of us have to learn this effective behavior. The communication skills most needed in collaboration include self-disclosure, empathy, and confrontation.

Skills of self-disclosure help us share ourselves in appropriate ways. As we have seen, partnership does not demand the intimacy of close friends, but it does require that we be able to share our vision, explain our ideas, and tell one another what we think and how we feel about issues that touch our common ministry. Self-disclosure depends on (1) knowing our own ideas and needs and feelings and (2) expressing these in ways that fit the situation. For effective self-disclosure, we need both confidence that what we have to say is worthwhile and flexibility to determine the best way to express ourselves.

Skills of self-disclosure help us initiate well; skills of empathy help us listen. To listen is to pay attention. It requires a receptive, but not a passive, stance. If we cannot pay attention, we do not hear; if we do not listen, we cannot understand. To listen well is to listen actively, alert to the full meaning. Listening well helps us understand another person from within that person's frame of reference.

Empathy begins in this openness. We set aside our own concerns and turn toward others. But openness may not be enough: we must show the other person that we understand not only their words but what they hold significant. Empathy does not demand that we always agree with or simply accept one another's ideas unchallenged. It *does* demand that, before we evaluate, we take the time to understand another person's ideas and feelings from his or her point of view. Evaluation is not secondary, but it is subsequent.

Confrontation is a third skill of collaboration—but not in the term's narrow connotation as interpersonal conflict. Confrontation involves the ability to give and receive emotionally significant information in ways that lead to further exploration rather than to self-defense. Many collaborative efforts require confrontative behavior.

Consider these examples. A diocesan task force meets with chancery officials to recommend a new plan for collegial decision making, one that calls into question current patterns of leadership. A member of the local house of religious sisters challenges the community to a deeper commitment to simplicity in life-style. Uncomfortable with a growing sense of polarization on the pastoral team, the pastor plans a special meeting to explore some troublesome issues. Dealing effectively with each of these situations requires courage as well as skill. But a ministry group unable to face situations of this kind, through fear of disagreement or controversy, will not long function as an effective force in ministry.

Confrontation, then, is a skill essential to partnership. To confront effectively, we need to communicate in nonjudgmental ways, to deal with anger in ourselves and one another, and to offer emotional support even as we disagree. Such skillful confrontation, as we shall see in chapter 15, supports a virtuous response in conflict.

Heroic Leaders

Poor communication complicates collaboration. But heroic expectations of our leaders jeopardize our shared ministry even more. American culture celebrates the business executive who works eighteen-hour days, the political leader who does not bend under pressure, the entrepreneur who succeeds against the odds. Fascinated with celebrities—the Trumps and Iacoccas of the world—we expect our leaders to be different from the rest of us. These larger-than-life figures may satisfy our need for heroes, but they are unlikely models of partnership.

In chapter 3 we saw the damage that the image of the heroic leader can do, leading us to treat those in authority as *not like us*. Expecting our leaders to be different—wiser, holier, more generous—we assume that they have no needs. Ministry ideals often reinforce these unreal expectations. The priest, for example, learns that he must be a man for others—universally available, able to give without counting the cost, willing to serve others without asking anything in return. Generosity like this does not leave much room for personal needs! When a priest finds that his strength and virtue do not match this ideal, he tends to blame himself. Rather than questioning the distorted cultural image, the priest punishes himself for falling short. Feeling inadequate, he is likely to resist any conversation about needs.

In the first place, the discussion frightens him. Admitting that he needs anything from those he serves—or even from those with whom he works—contradicts the heroic image of priesthood. These needs make him "less" than he wants to be. Beyond that, many priests sense—accurately—that the conversation about what the leader needs is frightening for others as well. Some people want their leaders to be strong and autonomous, there to lean on without asking anything in return except obedience and awe. For priests to admit that they are not self-sufficient, that they need something from the community, would shatter the community's fantasy about its heroic leaders. Not surprisingly, then, some religious groups avoid the conversation about mutual needs and thus collude in support the illusion of heroic leaders.

In our efforts to sustain the conversation about our mutual needs, we taste another bitter fruit of our heroic expectations about leaders: sometimes we have to live with needs unmet. Many of us have learned that, as ministers and leaders, our job is to satisfy other people's needs. If a need arises, our duty is to respond. This heroic expectation is rooted in a distorted picture of the community: parental ministers exist to meet the children's needs. In such a world, ministers are trained to please the community, to keep everybody happy.

If other people's needs carry this extraordinary weight—"It's my job to meet them"—then any conversation about needs can only bring new burdens. No wonder, then, that we avoid this honest discussion! But maturity teaches us that not all needs will be met. Sometimes the conversation about mutual needs reveals areas where resolution is easy: "Now that I know what you want from me, I'm willing to modify my behavior." But this kind of resolution is not always possible. Clarifying what we expect of one another does not guarantee satisfaction. Letting you know what I need does not automatically put you under obligation to meet those needs. Frequently the conversation will have to move toward negotiation, as we attempt to work out a compromise that is mutually satisfying (or at least mutually acceptable).

Each of us comes to collaborative ministry with legitimate needs. But even genuine needs can go unmet; this is a fact of our creatureliness. Reality is not set up to provide all-powerful leaders or all-caring colleagues whose role it is to care for our needs. The rigors of maturity challenge us to purify our expectations of one another. Letting go romantic illusions about our leaders, we can participate as partners in the conversation about our needs.

Heroes and Partners

We cannot do without heroes. Martin Luther King, Jr., Mother Teresa, John F. Kennedy—these larger-than-life figures enrich our lives. But in the daily arena of shared faith, heroic expectations overburden our religious leaders and defeat the partnership of adult faith.

If heroic visions of leadership have shaped the priesthood, they have also influenced the ministry of the bishop. In recent centuries the bishop lived in isolation (sometimes splendid isolation), venturing into the community only on special ritual occasions. We came to assume that this extraordinary person was above human needs. When a prelate did experience illness or moral failure, the secret was kept from the community. Secrecy's goal was to avoid scandal, but its effect was to reinforce the illusion of the religious leader immune from the human condition. In recent years Catholic bishops have struggled to dismantle this unhealthy image. Public announcement of a bishop's sabbatical leave for reasons of fatigue and another's treatment for alcoholism have come as grace to the community of faith, forcing us to confront our unrealistic expectations.

The ideal of the heroic leader reaches its peak in the papacy. Vatican press releases fuel this image: the pope publishes a staggering volume of instruction each year (with the help of hidden staff writers); his travels suggest an indefatigable servant of the church. Here, certainly, we have a heroic leader, unlike us in our needs and limitations.

The Christian ideal of the heroic leader finds its roots in a classic philosophical image of God. Thomas Aquinas and other theologians were much taken with Aristotle's picture of the source of all reality: an unmoved mover. Aristotle reasoned that at the beginning of all movement must rest a force that is the cause of all activity but is itself unmoved. Christian theologians saw in this cosmology an inviting picture of what God must be like. God moves all things, first in creation and then in compassion and redemption. But this source of all life is itself unmoved; this eternal power must remain free of any lack, untouched by all longing or desire. Our God is not needy!

This portrait is, of course, less a theological truth than a masculine fantasy. What more exalted ideal than to influence others without being influenced by them! Christian leaders, aspiring to imitate this invulnerable deity, set out to care for all people without needing their support in return. This ideal exalts leaders, placing them securely beyond need. But heroes make poor partners in ministry.

Gradually we are abandoning this ancient picture of a religious leader. Returning to the passionate portraits of God in the Hebrew Scriptures, we again celebrate our Creator as a God of desire. Ours is not a God of control—dispassionate, distant from our emotions and needs. Our God, enfleshed in Jesus, shares our world of feeling and failure and need. Following this passionate and vulnerable God, our leaders can enter more thoroughly into the continuing conversation about needs.

Reflective Exercise

Be present to an experience of shared ministry in your own life right now—in a small faith community or ministry task force, as a member of a parish committee or the pastoral staff. Spend a few moments with the experience, recalling the ministry group and your participation in its life. Then consider the following questions.

How comfortable is this group with the conversation about interdependence—an honest and nonmanipulative discussion of what people need from one another in order to minister well? Be concrete, giving examples from your own experience.

In this setting, what factors (in you, in the group, in the work) support this discussion of mutual needs?

As you see it, what are the chief obstacles to this direct discussion of what people need from one another here?

What practical next step would you suggest to support the group's ongoing conversation about interdependence?

Additional Resources

Fran Ferder and John Heagle provide perspective and practical assistance for interdependence in *Partnership: Women and Men in Ministry* (Notre Dame, IN: Ave Maria Press, 1989). In *Intimate Strangers: Men and Women Together* (New York: Harper & Row, 1984), sociologist Lillian B. Rubin draws upon both case material and psychological theory to explore the sources of differences between women and men that can lead to strain in partnership. Anne Marie Nuechterlein and Celia Allison Hahn reflect on the interaction of women and men in ministry in *The Male-Female Church Staff: Celebrating the Gifts, Confronting the Challenges* (Washington, DC: Alban Institute Publications, 1990).

Nancy Chodorow's influential reinterpretation of the dynamics of gender differences is found in *The Reproduction of Mothering: Psychoanalysis and the Sociology of Gender* (Los Angeles: Univ. of California Press, 1978). Carol Gilligan advances this discussion in *In a Different Voice: Psychological Theory and Women's Development* (Cambridge, MA: Harvard University Press, 1982). For a comprehensive and readable review of "where things stand" in current research on gender differences, see Carol Tavris and Carole Wade, *The Longest War: Sex Differences in Perspective* (San Diego, CA: Harcourt Brace Jovanovich, 1989).

Organizational analyst Marvin R. Weisbord describes the hunger for interdependence in the work setting in *Productive Workplaces: Organizing and Managing for Dignity, Meaning, and Community* (San Francisco: Jossey-Bass, 1987). Patricia Gundry offers an incisive appraisal of women's experience in ministry in *Neither Slave Nor Free: Helping Women Answer the Call to Church Leadership* (San Francisco: Harper & Row, 1988).

Deborah Tannen provides clues for understanding the different communication styles of men and women in *You Just Don't Understand: Women and Men in Conversation* (New York: Ballantine, 1990). See also Cecilia Allison Hahn, *Sexual Paradox: Creative Tensions in Our Lives and in Our Congregations* (New York: Pilgrim Press, 1991) and Carol Tavris, *The Mismeasure of Women* (New York: Simon & Schuster, 1992).

14. Learning to Share Power

> The faithful all lived together and owned everything in common; they sold their goods and possessions and shared out the proceeds among themselves according to what each one needed. They went as a body to the Temple every day but met in their homes for the breaking of bread; they shared their food gladly and generously; they praised God and were looked up to by everyone.   (Acts 2:44–47, JB)

The accounts in Acts give our earliest glimpses into Christian partnership. Holding goods and food and possessions in common, these early communities learned to share power. Today, as then, sharing power strengthens our common life. A religious group, a ministry team, a marriage matures as we look directly at how influence and control will be shared. But for many of us, *power* is a dirty word. Troubled memories conjure up the bosses and bullies of our past; these negative encounters leave a residue of anger and hurt. We have seen power used to humiliate people and destroy relationships. So—especially in religious settings— we avoid any conversation about how power operates among us.

Recognizing how volatile power is, we will use the word here in an inclusive sense. Among social scientists, for example, power refers *first* to activities—the ways people initiate action and influence one another. To offer suggestions, to invite people to get involved, to initiate a plan of action, to try to persuade other people—these are power activities.

Power refers *second* to structures—the roles and rules a group sets in place to get things done. How we divide the work, the way we establish the budget, who sets the agenda—these are questions of power. The way we make decisions, when information is shared, how we deal with conflict and dissent—these are issues of power. As partners, we have to raise these questions explicitly and discuss them openly.

The conversation about power brings established procedures under review. Looking for ways to strengthen the group's life, we examine our current behavior. This public discussion does not set out to destroy the power structure but to examine it more closely, to say "out loud" what is really going on among us. The goal, as sociologist Richard Sennett notes, is to make the power structure "visible and legible."

To feel the force of this metaphor, we have to return to grade school, where penmanship is a priority issue. The goal of first grade is to make our penmanship *visible:* we learn to make the letters, to stay within the lines, to avoid too many smudges on the page. The goal of second grade is to make our penmanship *legible,* so that a person of ordinary good will and eyesight, looking at the marks we have made visible, can decipher the message we want to convey. Our penmanship is visible when it can be seen, legible when it can accurately be read.

And how does that metaphor apply to the issue of power? The power structure is *visible* when we can see what is going on, when we are explicit with one another about how influence and control actually function among us. The power structure is *legible* when we can "read" it properly, when we know what it means, when we can trace the connections between the procedures in effect and the larger values and purposes that they are supposed to serve.

Let us take an example. For most of us as Catholics, the procedures that produce our leaders—bishops and pastors—are neither visible nor legible. Recognizing that these selections do not just happen by chance, we sense that some process must be at work. But to the vast majority in the faith community the process is invisible. Secrecy and confidentiality surround the appointment of our religious leaders. Most of us recognize that there are circumstances in which confidentiality is not only politically astute but morally virtuous, but the secrecy that covers this leadership selection seems excessive. "Who are they keeping the secret from?" we wonder. And secret procedures, however justified, ensure that leadership selection remains invisible.

An invisible process also remains illegible. There is no way to read its meaning. We are unable to trace the connections between our current procedures of leadership selection and the gospel values of servant leadership. That our procedures practice what the gospel preaches is not immediately evident.

Recognizing that these procedures are not visible does not necessarily suggest that they are wrong. But when our patterns of leadership selection are invisible, the community of faith is at a loss. We cannot be edified by the witness of a procedure that explicitly reflects the gospel; we cannot hold accountable to the gospel a process that falls short of this goal.

These hidden processes of leadership selection are being challenged today. Scholars familiar with the first centuries of Christian life remind us that communities played a vocal part in the selection of their bishops and pastors. In *Archbishop: Inside the Power Structure of the American Catholic Church,* Jesuit political analyst Thomas Reese describes the current procedures for the selection of bishops as "a complex process shrouded in secrecy with the participants bound by pontifical secret about the names under consideration." In discussing many of the details of this process, Reese make the process visible and invites a greater accountability.

Questions about power are unnerving. Using the admittedly volatile example of leadership selection may suggest that the public discussion of power is of interest only to people whose motives are tainted by anticlericalism. The recent efforts by U.S. Catholic bishops to transform patterns of ecclesial power may help put that suspicion to rest.

In September 1986, Archbishop Raymond Hunthausen of Seattle made public the details of an ecclesiastical investigation of his ministry. The archbishop acknowledged that his earlier compliance with Vatican insistence on secrecy had been wrong. He informed the community of faith of the charges that had been made against him, the procedures through which his ministry had been reviewed, the findings of this review, and the action that followed. He made power visible.

This commitment to visibility was reiterated by the special commission of U.S. bishops appointed to review the Hunthausen case. Reporting to their fellow bishops on the procedures used in their assessment, Cardinal Joseph Bernadin from Chicago, Cardinal John O'Connor from New York, and Archbishop John Quinn from San Francisco noted that "the commission further agreed internally that it would base its conclusions only on documents seen by Archbishop Hunthausen and on discussions with persons designated by him or consulted with his knowledge and concurrence. Each person interviewed was free to share with Archbishop Hunthausen everything discussed with the commission and the archbishop was free to seek any such information from any person interviewed by the commission."

Another example: In 1986 an international group of cardinals gathered in Rome to discuss what could be done to relieve the Vatican's financial deficit. Cardinal John Krol, archbishop of Philadelphia at the time, insisted that the Vatican's plea to dioceses throughout the world for additional funds to offset this deficit be accompanied by a more complete report of its budget. This was a request to make power legible—to make clear the connections between the call for generous financial support of the saving mission of Jesus Christ and the way that monies collected would actually be spent.

And this request generated a response. In March 1988 a Vatican financial report for the year 1986 was published in *Origins,* the documentary service of the National Conference of Catholic Bishops in Washington. The U.S. bishops noted that this was the first time that the Vatican had permitted public release of such information. The extent of the information actually disclosed was modest, and the financial categories displayed were quite general—but the budget moved into public view. And once visible, that budget was open to discussion. Public discussion builds pressure for public accountability. The community of faith still has little say in Vatican financial disbursements; but the more we know about patterns of church finance, the more effective we will eventually be in making our voices heard.

As these examples remind us, the public discussion of power supports its purification. Making power visible uncovers discrepancies between our rhetoric (with its stress on servant leadership) and our practice (which often links leadership with privilege). Making power legible confronts us with the gap between the values we proclaim (the essential equality of women and men in creation and in Baptism) and the structures that are in place among us (policies that systematically exclude women from sacramental roles and institutional leadership). The conversation about power challenges us, as the church, to reexamine our organizational life and to strengthen the links between ecclesiastical power and the gospel vision we serve.

This open discussion of power is a hallmark of democracy. Vatican sources admonish Catholics in the United States that the church is not a democracy. Accepting this instruction in good faith would be easier for most of us if the statement did not end that quickly. "The church is not a democracy in the sense that no political arrangement can be equated with the body of Christ," as Margaret Steinfels has noted. By the same token, she continues, "the church is not a roman state or a medieval monarchy or a Renaissance kingdom or a modern bureaucracy." But across Christian history we have adapted elements of each of these political forms to carry on the corporate affairs of the faith community. Biblical scholar Letty Russell reminds us that in the body of Christ, no one of these particular patterns of power has authority of itself. "It is the connection of that pattern with the divine self-revelation of God that gives it authority and limits its claims. For Christians, an important criterion is consistency with the exercise of authority in Jesus' ministry."

Power Structure, Power Struggle

Many groups start out with a sense that power belongs to the person in charge. And a strong leader bolsters the group at this early stage: welcoming new members and helping them feel safe, encouraging people to participate, modeling effective behavior. Relying on the leader is normal at this point, but a group founders if its dependence continues too long. Then both leader and members fall victim to the illusion that the group's power resides in the leader.

When this happens, the demands on the person in charge increase dramatically. Consumed by the group's continuing need for answers and assurance, the leader feels overwhelmed by and finally alienated from these needy followers. Group members grow resentful as well. Their bond with the leader, experienced earlier as gratitude, now reminds them that they are powerless. The leader's dominance, which once allayed anxiety, now fosters frustration.

To grow into an effective group, members have to question the assumption that power resides in the leader alone. Some groups work toward new understandings of power by discussing goals and expectations. Other groups modify the current roles and rules, broadening participation so that more people share responsibility. Through these negotiations, members come to a better sense of how the power structure works and where they fit in. An experienced leader takes the lead in this effort to move the group beyond its early dependence.

But sometimes the power struggle lives up to its name. Some groups, aware that the pattern of dominant leader and dependent members no longer fits, respond with active resistance. Trying to dismantle the earlier pattern, members insist on an enforced equality: "We're all adults here. No one is more in charge than anyone else." Or the preferred solution may be substitution: we move "our choice" into the designated leader's slot, leaving the patterns of unequal dependence intact. With the dynamics of leadership left unchanged, it is not long before "our choice" becomes "the enemy" and another coup is called for.

This disruptive behavior seeks the same goal as more orderly negotiation—to test the pattern of power and to find one's place in it. The way out of this vicious cycle is not to attack the leader but to examine the patterns of leadership. Where power exists and how power functions must be reinterpreted. The formal leader is only part of the interplay of power. Efforts at reform that miss this basic insight risk turning the leader into a scapegoat or a demagogue.

LOOKING AT THE LEADER

In many groups, then, the discussion of power starts with a look at the leader. Team members question the leader's motives; the ministry staff finds fault with the pastor's management style. Analysts urge us to see this distress in a good light, as a sign that the group is maturing. But for the leader, holding on to that perspective is difficult! These heated discussions of power feel like a personal attack: "It's *my* influence that the group seems intent on redistributing; it's the adequacy of *my* way of doing things that's being publicly evaluated." If a leader responds to all questioning as a personal challenge, the battle is joined and emotions run high. Feeling threatened, the leader may look for someone to blame and turn against the apparent troublemaker. Or the leader may become emotionally isolated or practically withdrawn from the group. Other people then feel pressured to take sides. Some rush to protect the leader; others unite in a shaky coalition against the person in charge. In this scenario the stakes are high in the process of change.

Leaders who respond less defensively model a different vision. Their message is that power need not be interpreted as a personal possession and jealously guarded from attack. Rather, it is a resource that needs to—and can—be examined, accounted for, and exercised in new ways.

The conversation about power signals that a group has begun to mature. The leader's management style, the group's practical priorities, the way that decisions are made on this team—most analysts agree that if, over the course of a year's time, these issues do not become explicit topics of discussion and negotiation, inhibiting forces are at work. And those inhibiting forces are not always the leader's fault. Often a group resists the leader's effort to share power, preferring the diminished but more defended role of passive participants. Nevertheless, a religious group—a parish council, a ministry team, a diocesan staff—that cannot or will not take up the power discussion is headed for stagnation. The group may continue to function, but it is unlikely to move toward effective collaboration.

RENEGOTIATING POWER

Discussing our current experience of power—who has it, how it is being used—helps us recognize both what helps and what hinders collaboration. We can reaffirm arrangements that already serve us well: an effective way of dividing responsibilities, a decision-making strategy that works, a proven procedure for dealing with conflict. We can adjust procedures that have become problematic: an outdated personnel policy, a process of supervision that has broken down, an unwieldy chain of command. This direct discussion does not mean that now—at last—things will finally go "my way," but the power conversation at least makes room for renegotiation.

In a genuine conversation, the parties not only have their say but each stands open to the possibility of change—even conversion. For some, this openness to negotiation itself can feel like an erosion of the leader's power. In fact, however, as John Harris observes in his *Stress, Power, and Ministry*, the authority of the religious leader comes "not chiefly from canonical law or religious belief, as it did fifty years ago, but much more from a reciprocal understanding . . . about the tasks of the Church and the framework of expectations in which both [leaders and other members] will work together."

Renegotiating power does not mean denying the differences among us, whether these are differences in ability, in experience, or in sphere of responsibility. The goal, rather, is to reinforce our awareness of mutuality. In mutuality, as we saw earlier, the giving and the receiving go both ways. Because both parties contribute something of importance, both have some say in how things turn out. Each has some control over the outcome—not necessarily *equal* control, but genuine influence.

Shared Power and the Structures of Partnership

Collaboration begins in an appreciation that we need one another and are good for one another. But for collaboration to thrive, this appreciation must be reflected in our patterns of power—the roles and rules, laws and customs that shape our life together. Partnership is a communal process in which domination of one over the other is explicitly rejected. As we saw in chapter 5, partnership is not limited to "one right way": several organizational styles can protect shared ministry from the perils of domination. Being partners does not force a strict mathematical equality into our relationship; rather, partnership asks that influence and control be *shared*.

As new hopes for partnership enliven the community of faith, these must be translated into new structures of shared influence. These expectations do not require that the leader give up all control. In fact, canon law and diocesan policy make that option untenable. Organizational theory and common sense suggest that it would be foolish as well. The future of partnership lies neither in disenfranchising our leaders nor in an exclusive commitment to consensus decision making. What is required, at the local level but especially at broader levels in the church, is further exploration and testing of fresh forms of shared control.

In many places in the church today, collaboration thrives because of the sensitivity and initiative of the person in charge. But real partnership—the give and take of reciprocal influence and shared control—must be safeguarded by procedures that go beyond the good will of particular leaders. Our commitment to collaboration must find expression in the formal arrangements that shape the community of faith. This demands a transformation of structures.

Concretely, what are the structures of partnership? Let us look at three: processes that expand dialogue, processes that extend decision making, and processes that enlarge mutual accountability.

Since Vatican II there have been many efforts to expand the structures of dialogue. The U.S. Catholic bishops have led the way in modeling a commitment to dialogue, soliciting comments from the broad community in their preparation of national pastoral letters. Chancery offices and diocesan agencies have been reorganized into secretariats and deaneries, to ensure better communication. Pastoral synods and ministry assemblies have been convened at the diocesan level; parish councils and school boards are active on the local scene. Partnership is enhanced by policies that ensure that lay women and men are regularly included in these settings (in numbers that go beyond tokenism), to reflect their involvement in the life of the church and their commitment to Jesus' larger mission.

Second, partnership is enhanced by broadening the participation of the faith community in decision making. In a report on the collegial structures set in place since Vatican II, J. Gordon Myers and Richard Schoenherr have shown that the American church has been more successful in sharing pastoral responsibility than in sharing organizational power. The past two decades have seen a dramatic increase in the range of administrative and ministerial responsibilities carried out by those who are not priests. In diocesan marriage tribunals, for example, women canon lawyers, along with deacons and other married Catholics, play active roles in a crucial ministry once restricted to priests.

But those who are not ordained are not well represented in the councils of decision making, where organizational power is at work. Partnership in ministry demands a further broadening of decision making. Our church is still structured so that men make most of the decisions affecting women, and clergy make most of the decisions affecting lay persons. As long as that imbalance continues, partnership will be frustrated.

Formal processes of accountability in ministry require expansion as well. Most institutions develop structures of vertical accountability; in other words, leaders must report only to those higher in the organization. This is still the dominant pattern in the church as well. The priest is accountable to the local bishop; it is the bishop to whom he must give an account of the exercise of his ministry. In turn, parish staff members are accountable to the pastor, in his management role as organizational leader. These structures of vertical accountability are necessary and often useful, but they do not promote partnership.

Partnership requires structures of *mutual* accountability. Partnership respects the fundamental interplay of power—the giving and receiving that go both ways. This interplay must be evident as those in ministry are held accountable in their work. Where partnership is at play, colleagues are accountable to one another as well as to those higher in the chain of command. These structures of mutual accountability are beginning to function in some places within the church. In ministry teams and agency staffs, co-workers are devising ways to keep one another better informed and are learning how to comment constructively on one another's work. These processes are the harbinger of more formal structures of mutual accountability.

For our expectations of mutual accountability to be more than rhetoric among us, as Catholics we will have to set in place effective procedures to include the community in the evaluation of ordained ministers. Formal processes of evaluation are, to be sure, risky business. Where there is insufficient trust, the formal review becomes a defensive standoff. Where there is insufficient maturity, the evaluation process can become a pawn in a wider play for power. But when planned as part of a larger process of dialogue, and when carried out with competence and care, a program of performance review can be gracious—a true moment of grace, an exchange that contributes to the growth of the priest as well as to the vitality of the community. This broadening of evaluation reinforces the essential truth that priesthood is responsible *to* as well as *for* the local community of faith.

The promise of partnership stands as a challenge to us all. Personal transformation will be required as we open ourselves to the requirements of genuine interdependence. Structural transformation will be demanded as we bring our roles and rules into greater congruence with our deepest values. Through these transformations we will confirm again in our own time that ancient-yet-new image of the church: we are a priestly people called to be partners in the mission of Jesus Christ.

Reflective Exercise

Return once more to a recent experience of collaboration in ministry. Select a group setting with which you are quite familiar, so that your reflection will be fruitful. After you have made your selection, turn to these considerations.

Identify one "pattern of power" (perhaps an established procedure, a decision-making process, a system of accountability, or a characteristic way of conducting meetings) that influences your ministry in this setting. Briefly describe this pattern.

Has this pattern of power come up for discussion in your ministry group? With what results? Be concrete, offering examples from your experience in this group.

What practical steps might be taken to support the conversation about power in this ministry setting? Again be as concrete as you can; give examples.

Additional Resources

Richard Sennett discusses "visible and legible" power in *Authority* (New York: Vintage Books, 1981); see especially chapter 5. Elisabeth Schüssler Fiorenza offers a challenging analysis of the ecclesial dynamics that undercut "a discipleship of equals" in *In Memory of Her* (New York: Crossroad/Continuum, 1983). John C.

Harris examines the dynamics of power and leadership in his *Stress, Power, and Ministry* (Washington, DC: Alban Institute Publications, 1983); quote taken from p. 23.

Thomas Reese discusses the process of selection for new bishops in *Archbishop: Inside the Power Structure of the American Catholic Church* (San Francisco: Harper & Row, 1989), chap. 1; quote taken from p. 2. See also Bernard Cooke, ed., *The Papacy and the Church in the United States* (New York: Paulist Press, 1989). The text of the report of the special commission reviewing the case of Archbishop Raymond Hunthausen of Seattle appeared in *Origins* (June 4, 1987): 40–44; quote taken from p. 40.

In *The Future of Partnership* (Philadelphia: Westminster Press, 1979), Letty Russell examines the images and structures of the Christian tradition that both enliven and frustrate the gospel imperative of mutuality; quote taken from p. 24. She continues the discussion in *Growth in Partnership* (Philadelphia: Westminster Press, 1981). Margaret Steinfels's address, "The Church and Its Public Life," was published in *America* 160 (1989): 550–58; quote taken from p. 557.

J. Gordon Myers and Richard Schoenherr report on collegial structures in the U.S. Catholic Church in "The Baptism of Power," *New Catholic World*, Sept./Oct. 1980, pp. 217–20. Kennon L. Callahan explores a new model for pastoral leadership and the organizational structures that support its implementation in *Effective Church Leadership* (San Francisco: Harper & Row, 1990). Robert G. Duch examines the possibilities of shared power in *Successful Parish Leadership: Nurturing the Animated Parish* (Kansas City, MO: Sheed & Ward, 1990).

15. Managing Conflict

> After Paul and Barnabas had had a long argument with these persons it was arranged that Paul and Barnabas and others of the church should go up to Jerusalem and discuss the problem with the apostles and elders.   (Adapted from Acts 15:2, JB)

Conflict has a bad reputation, especially when associated with the church. Our religious heritage has often connected controversy with sin, conflict with disobedience, dissent with disloyalty. Some of us carry wounds from the dysfunctional families that taught us to link conflict with blame and shame. Common sense concludes that conflict feels bad and has bad results. But even as we nod in assent, most of us recognize that this negative judgment does not tell the whole truth. Our lives reveal a broader wisdom. By the time we have reached our thirties or our forties, we can look back on personal experiences in which struggle strengthened us. We can recall friendships in which a conflict faced deepened a relationship while a dispute covered over had disastrous results.

Effective leaders acknowledge this broader truth about conflict. James MacGregor Burns reminds us that "leaders, whatever their profession of harmony, do not shun conflict; they confront it, exploit it, ultimately embody it."

Conflict Defined

Conflict is the emotional and intellectual arousal we feel in the face of discrepancy. Conflict alerts us that a gap exists. The gap may be in interpretation: looking at the same event, we see different meanings or motives. Or the discrepancy may appear in missed expectations: things do not turn out as I expected; you act different-ly than I thought we had agreed you would. Or the struggle takes shape in disagreement over goals: we approach a situation with different needs, so the results we want are different.

In many religious groups we find three different responses to conflict. A small percentage of people actually enjoy controversy. For them, conflict is a tonic, energizing their involvement in the group's life. A somewhat larger group dislikes conflict intensely and will go to any lengths to avoid it. The rest of us, usually the largest portion of the group, actively dislike conflict but—under sufficient pressure or with compelling reason—can summon our courage to face it. These three responses exist simultaneously in a group and clash as that group comes into conflict.

Conflict signals discrepancy. As a signal of discrepancy, it gets our attention. The tension that we feel can function as an early-warning system—inviting us to deal with the discrepancy immediately, before it becomes a barrier between us. But if this arousal is not managed well, tension escalates. Then conflict be-comes a stop sign, bringing our group effort to a halt.

The Benefits of Conflict

In this chapter we explore the benefits of conflict—how conflict serves a group's growth. We then describe a pattern of escalation that makes conflict dangerous and finally examine an emerging Christian virtue of facing conflict. First, conflict's benefits.

CONFLICT REVEALS VALUES

What we fight about points to what we care about. To under-stand a group we must appreciate not only its goals but its battle history. Often a group's core values—those deep convictions that actually sustain its life—can be tracked more clearly in its ongoing struggles than in its mission statements. By revealing what is important enough to fight about, controversy shows us what is really significant on this scene. Finding ourselves in heated disagreement—in a parish planning meeting, for example—sometimes gives the first clue that deeply held values are at stake. Many of us know this from our personal lives: "Not until I got angry did I realize that I cared."

Values are our patterns of care become conscious. As philosopher Susanne Langer reminds us, "Values exist only where there is consciousness. Where nothing is felt, nothing matters." Looking with respect at the conflicts that characteristically arise among us, we can discover *what* our values are—or, perhaps better, *where* our values are.

Philosopher Alisdair MacIntyre argues for this intimate connection of conflict and value. "Traditions, when vital, embody continuities of conflict." Every enduring institution is constituted, in part, by a continuous argument about its purpose and values. "A living tradition, then, is an historically extended, socially embodied argument, and an argument precisely in part about the goods which constitute that tradition." Deprived of vital conflicts, a tradition withers and dies.

Conflict reveals values, and it can also teach values. Conflict stimulates moral development. Psychologists Lawrence Kohlberg and Carol Gilligan and their colleagues have demonstrated that ethical maturity involves a process of expanding our moral perspective as we come up against the limits of our current moral stance. Experiencing conflict is one of the ways we become aware of the boundaries of our own moral stance. In a diocesan meeting, for example, other people contradict our opinions, dispute our claims, question our convictions. Challenged in this way, we can turn our efforts simply to self-defense. But staying open to the give-and-take of the confrontation may show us both the strengths and the limits of our current position. A community's moral perspective broadens as we learn to welcome alternate views and appreciate plural values. And many of us learn this best in the crucible of conflict.

CONFLICT AROUSES COMMITMENT

Conflict generates energy—always heat, sometimes light. Often its energy seems simply destructive. But this negative view is shortsighted. Conflict disrupts—but it also galvanizes a group, renewing commitment and energizing participation. As any beleaguered parish minister knows, indifference is a greater enemy than is conflict. Apathy defeats us more often than does controversy. The more important the issues are that bring us together, the more likely conflict will arise—because the level of our investment is so high.

A group that has no conflict has no life. Better, a group that refuses to acknowledge its conflict risks stagnation. To deny the disagreements among us takes real effort. And even when we deny them, they seldom go away. More and more effort goes into looking away from the growing disruption. We start to deal with one another gingerly. Our relationships move to a superficial level, so as not to threaten this uneasy peace. These attempts to mask differences and cover over conflict sap the group's energy. Participation falls off or becomes simply a matter of routine.

CONFLICT ACCOMPANIES CHANGE

Genuine leaders, as we saw in chapter 9, do more than administration. Effective leaders empower groups for transformation. And in service of transformation, conflict is not only inevitable but an ally. Organizational renewal and institutional reform provoke controversy, bringing differences to light. For the leader who interprets differences only in dualistic categories of right or wrong, conflict will be a threat—a sign of failure or bad will. But the leader who can tolerate differences finds controversy a friend.

Planning for change clashes with parts of the past. Conflict questions the status quo, exposing the gap between what is and what could be. Pragmatically, then, leaders have good reason to welcome the clash of differing perspectives. Better plans result—more creative, more comprehensive. Again we hear from James MacGregor Burns: "Planning leaders must perceive that consensus in planning would be deceptive and dangerous, that advocacy and conflict must be built into the planning process."

Well attended, conflict channels our rich diversity into a richer future for us all. Alisdair MacIntyre offers an example from history. The twelfth and thirteenth centuries were a time of upheaval in Europe. Population shifted from rural to urban settings; universities replaced monasteries as chief centers of learning; national vernaculars competed with the previously universal language of Latin. How did a vibrant new culture emerge from such chaos? MacIntyre describes a process that is as relevant to our time as to medieval Europe: "Part of the answer is: by generating just the right kinds of tension and even conflict" between these competing forces—conflict that proved to be "creative rather than destructive."

Effective leaders learn to accept conflict as a necessary and even valued companion of transformation. Whatever our native hesitancies, we can learn better ways to welcome conflict's energy, harness its power, focus its purpose, and discern its contribution to the future we share.

Patterns of Escalation

Controversy can illumine our values and motivate our commitment. But conflict's energy easily goes awry. Consultant Speed Leas and his associates at the Alban Institute in Washington, D.C., have studied the dynamic of conflict in religious settings. They find that religious groups facing conflict often experience a negative pattern of escalation—a process of intellectual distortion and emotional withdrawal that defeats collaboration. Leas identifies several stages in this deteriorating spiral. To determine where a group stands, he suggests examining the goals that people have in facing disagreement and the language that they use with one another.

At an early stage, we become aware of some discrepancy among us: misunderstanding between members, disagreement over a plan of action, a difference of opinion on an important issue, some disappointment over unmet expectations. The group is then in a state of arousal. Intellectually, people want to understand the problem, so they talk things over, ask questions, seek explanations, look for clarification. Emotionally, too, people are eager to heal the gap. But religious groups, wanting to calm the waters and avoid hurt feelings, often encourage conformity as a way to affirm solidarity.

At this early point, people in the group feel challenged but not panicked. Their goal is to solve the problem. People use language to communicate—state opinions, seek information, ask clarification, offer solutions—not to defend themselves or distort their opponent's position. The group feels that "we should be able to handle this. We have the resources we need to deal with the problem."

The most effective intervention at this stage comes from the group itself—sometimes from the official leader, sometimes from other members. Intervention's goal is to support collaboration, reminding us that everybody's perspective is welcome and everybody's contribution is needed. The leader can introduce a workable process of group problem solving, for example. Perhaps a task force can be established, broadening the practical skills and political scope of the group working on the problem. Strategies can be adopted to focus attention on issues rather than on personalities. To keep communication clear, for example, we might agree to hold ourselves to basic guidelines: get the facts, seek additional information as needed, stop rumors early. And we keep communication direct, so that people who disagree remain in contact with one another.

When a group lacks this commitment to continuing contact, conflict moves into a second stage. Members withdraw from one another, feeling the need to protect themselves and defend their position. The group's arousal, no longer channeled into creative problem solving and effective action, finds another focus. The issues that divide us become more personalized. Solving the problem remains a goal, but it is not quite as important as protecting ourselves—from being misunderstood, from being taken advantage of, from being excluded, from looking foolish.

At this stage, we grow suspicious of other people's motives and sensitive to personal affront. Language becomes more general; discussions become more vague. Members urge one another to greater "trust" or complain about "lack of openness" in the group. The group's mood suggests that much is at stake, but people hesitate to talk about their concerns. Instead, they communicate by innuendo. Emotions run high, but their sources remain murky.

Even at this stage, effective intervention usually comes from within the group. Reversing the distortions creeping into our relationships is now the priority. Early on, a gripe session may clear the air. A meeting like this—caringly and carefully planned, operating within clear guidelines, with an opportunity for genuine reconciliation—encourages members to voice their concerns to one another. People can dispel rumors, clarify motives, explain actions. When it works, the session strengthens ties by putting members back in touch with one another and with the larger values they share. But publicly airing our complaints can be tricky. Without a climate of mutual respect and accountability, complaints become accusations, making matters worse.

Other strategies can help as well. Often it is not too late to introduce a formal process of group problem solving. Working together on a common problem can refocus the group's energy and reestablish trust. A group at this stage, aware that dealing with one another has become difficult, may welcome training in communication and confrontational skills. With these more effective communication patterns in place, some of the emotional static will be resolved. These strategies of collaboration work better at the first stage, of course—before the emotional climate heats up. Religious groups are under extra pressure in the second stage, as the volatile personal agenda rivals the public task.

In many groups an outside facilitator is not yet welcome at the second stage. Some people hesitate to air the group's dirty laundry in front of a stranger. Others suspect a political motive: "Whose side will this outsider take?" And most members, while confused and uneasy, are still not in enough pain to recognize that the group needs help.

But if help does not come, from within the group or without, matters are likely to get worse. Factions form as members mobilize to ensure that *their* position prevails. As the group moves beyond the vague uneasiness of the second stage, its energy once again finds focus. Our sense of purpose shifts: defending our view is not enough; we must win out over our opponents. The problem that originally confronted the group recedes into the background. Our primary goal is that we carry the day—because "we're right and they're not."

In this emotional atmosphere, dichotomies thrive. We see the world in terms of "us" and "them"—and "they" are now the enemy. A mild paranoia settles in, distorting thought. Group members seem convinced that situations are not as they seem; innocent events are scrutinized for hidden machinations. Inside our own factions we give ourselves over to mind-reading, finding evil intentions and malicious motives behind whatever the other side does. Firmly mired in our own misperceptions, we see no need to check them out. Rumors are accepted as fact, at least so long as they confirm our own worst suspicions.

Opposing factions, now no longer really communicating, quickly reach a stalemate. Thus intervention, by the time a group reaches this stage, cannot begin with shared problem solving. Not enough trust exists to sustain collaboration. Approaches based on negotiation and compromise hold more hope of success. In his influential books *Getting to Yes* and *Getting Together: Building a Relationship That Gets to Yes,* Roger Fisher and his associates outline practical strategies for negotiating fair and mutually acceptable agreements between parties divided by antagonism and mistrust. Their approach, proven successful in international disputes and within multinational corporations, is being applied successfully in ministry settings as well.

An outside facilitator can be most effective for a group at this stage. Group leaders, caught up in the internal polarization (or at least seen by other members as taking sides), can no longer play a mediating role. And members, now aware that the group is in trouble, are more open to outside help.

But if help is not available, conflict deteriorates further. Tensions escalate as members separate themselves from "those others" and seek retribution. At this level of conflict, the group's goals and language change again. Winning is not enough. We must get rid of our opponents—dissolve the parish council, remove the pastor, fire the superintendent of schools, discredit the justice ministry task force. At this point of polarization, many religious groups appeal to higher authority. The pastor or the bishop or the Vatican is then brought into the fray, to act as parent or policeman in punishing "those others."

Our vendetta may even grow into a religious crusade. Not only do we have to get rid of these miscreants, we have to warn others about them! We circulate petitions, place ads in the diocesan paper, picket the chancery office. We have to make sure that the next parish knows how dangerous this pastoral associate is; it is up to us to ensure that the culprit theologian never teaches in this diocese again.

Intervening at this level of escalation is hard. Distortion this extreme makes resolution difficult. What usually happens, even when intervention is attempted, is further deterioration—people who are involved leave or are dismissed, outside forces take over the situation, reputations fall, relationships collapse. All that is left to remind us of what happened is a heritage of hurt.

This sorry state of affairs is where some of us begin our involvement with a conflicted group, either assigned as a new leader or coming in as an outside consultant. The challenge at this point is less to solve the original problem than to start a process of reconciliation. The process is a delicate one, fraught with difficulty. But if the group is going to recover, the process must begin. A leader on the scene, charged with developing structures of reconciliation, usually needs critical outside support—access to a professional in the field or a savvy colleague who can serve as a sounding board. The details of reconciliation are particular to every group, but several general themes need to be respected.

Establishing ways for people to talk to one another across the lines of polarization comes first. Creating a safe climate—one in which people feel free from personal attack—is critical. Only then can people relax the defensive posture that has become their ordinary way of dealing with one another.

Developing ways for people to tell their stories, including their painful experience of the recent conflict, comes next. The story-telling process has to be guided carefully, so that people do not just rehearse all the old ills. But *some* expression is necessary. Refusing to acknowledge the pain, in the hope of "putting it all behind us" or "not dragging up the bitter past," more often deepens alienation. Listening to one another's personal history reinforces the links among us: our similar journeys, the religious values we still hold in common, the goals we continue to share. These bonds go beyond what currently separates us to affirm a larger context of shared meaning and hope.

Inviting the group to learn from this conflict experience sometimes helps make sense of the pain. Our distress is real, and its results have been negative. But the experience need not be *just* a disaster. Facing what has happened, we can learn something about ourselves and one another. We will then approach our next controversy wiser for our wounds.

Finally, we can explore together the reality of forgiveness. Religious groups at this advanced stage of conflict should not be pushed into rituals of reconciliation. While recognizing that self-transcendence always remains a possibility, we must honor the fact that genuine reconciliation cannot be forced. Leaders should take care not to move too quickly toward expressions of forgiveness just because "that's the Christian thing to do." A better strategy is to give people the opportunity to discuss together what forgiveness would actually demand of this group, what shape reconciliation could practically take. "Concretely, what would it mean for me to extend forgiveness to you? What would it mean for me to accept your forgiveness?" Responding to these questions readies us for reconciliation. Now we can develop meaningful rituals: opportunities for prayer, confession, and thanksgiving, with one another and for one another.

As a sacramental people, we know that reconciliation cannot be rushed, that forgiveness cannot be forced. There are times when it seems that we cannot talk enough or explain enough or regret enough to bring us back together. The harm seems too heavy, the distance between us too great to be bridged. At this point we realize the power of forgiveness as more than a personal achievement. It is a gift and a grace that, spent by our conflict, we must await in hope.

A Christian Virtue of Facing Conflict

Fifty years from now Christians will have available a clearly defined virtue for confronting conflict. This strength will help us face discrepancy and focus its energy toward the common good. Today such a virtue does not yet exist. But its building blocks are present among us: vision, patience, courage, reconciliation.

Virtue combines vision and practice. We must first develop a vision that appreciates conflict's meaning and recognizes its potential. Then we must develop the strategies, the practical skills, to make this vision real.

As heirs of a rich religious tradition, our vision is always shaped by remembering—*anamnesis*. Recalling the fierce debate between Paul and the authorities in Jerusalem helps us heal our vision of conflict. In the long argument between Paul and the leaders in Jerusalem, a new insight was born. It dawned on us as a people of faith that the Christian way was not just a reform of Judaism but a path for all peoples. This controversy, more than a scandal, turned out to be graceful. Conflict helped us see God's future.

Examining more recent history continues to heal our vision of conflict. Over the past twenty-five years, many religious congregations have begun the careful and critical study of the lives of their founders. Pious biographies of previous years cloaked these founding figures in saintliness and overlooked their peculiarities. Now, under a more honest gaze, their lives reveal conflict as a constant companion. These founders were innovators, people restless with the status quo. History shows that their special gifts and ambitions placed them in conflict with both the church and their society. Their efforts to start new movements of service and piety set them at odds with local bishops and other authorities. But they persevered, due in part to their determination and their tolerance for conflict. This memory illumines a central dynamic of church growth: conflict is a partner of change and a necessary companion of renewal.

Our *anamnesis* can have a more immediate focus. Personal experience supports a more positive vision of controversy. We all have horror stories of conflict; these we remember and retell. But each of us has other experiences as well—experiences in which dealing with a conflict deepened a relationship or released creativity in a group. Our own lives proclaim that crisis is sometimes graceful.

These exercises in religious memory help us see conflict in a friendlier light. When we reclaim these memories, we rescue Christian faith from amnesia—a forgetfulness of our past. The pain of disagreements and struggles leads us to "forget" them, to place them out of sight. But when we do this, we also bury our memories of graceful conflict. In such amnesia, we falsify our past.

Strategies for Facing Conflict

A renewed vision of conflict encourages us to develop patience and courage. Patience's sometimes feeble reputation comes from being too often associated with passivity and docility. But patience is not always pious forbearance; it does not automatically excuse our refusal to act. Patience is an ability to tolerate disruption. This virtue guides our attempts to name the disturbances in our heart and to acknowledge the conflicts in our community.

With patience we dare to examine our current style of facing controversy. "What do I bring to a conflict? Does my personal history help me face disagreements, or has it given rise to a pattern of avoidance or hostile silence?" Recognizing what triggers conflict—the hot topics and sensitive issues that make us angry or defensive—is the first step in healing these wounds. The virtue of facing conflict begins in the patient awareness of the strengths and sensitivities that I bring to any dispute.

Patience helps us learn from conflict by raising questions in our distress. "What is this conflict about? Is this a battle worth having?" Many disagreements do not merit our sustained attention. As individuals and as communities, we must develop criteria for discerning what is worth fighting about.

Virtuous attention to our disagreements helps us decide *when* to have a conflict. Is this the proper time and place? Do circumstances here give hope that we will be able to resolve the disagreement? Maturity makes us aware of our own limits: feeling tired or vulnerable, we take steps to avoid a conflictual meeting today. But to be *virtuous*, this prudent choice must be accompanied by a decision to confront this conflict later.

The virtue of facing conflict is shaped by courage as well as patience. Courage is the ability to face anger, to challenge the status quo, to risk the embrace of conflict. Like patience, courage builds on specific skills: the ability to state our convictions clearly and to challenge others with respect.

Leaders nurture the virtue of facing conflict by offering people opportunities to expand their communication and confrontational skills. This skill training can be especially effective, as we saw in chapter 13, when group members participate together. What is demanded of us as we hold one another in conflict? How do we survive this severe embrace without giving or receiving injury? Skills of assertion and confrontation rescue virtue from rhetoric, giving our courage practical shape.

Another strategy supports a virtuous response to conflict. In unheated times leaders can help groups establish ground rules for disagreement. Most groups are not explicit about how conflict or dissent should be handled. Some communities muddle through, guided by hunches of what might work and hopes that controversy will just go away. Other groups operate with the unspoken expectation that resolving conflict is the leader's job. If disagreement arises between members, we ask the leader to step in. As tension mounts in our meetings, we politely wait for the leader to do something about it. Some leaders succumb to this heroic expectation, but the smart ones do not. An effective leader sees to it that the group has an effective procedure of conflict management in place *before* conflict arises and that the group holds itself—individually and collectively—accountable to the process when conflicts actually occur. In many settings the group members themselves develop the procedure that works best. The group should at least understand what the guidelines are and be willing to follow them. When the group understands and accepts a procedure for dealing with conflict, the process becomes a trustworthy ally in times of distress.

Vision, patience, courage—to these elements of a virtue of healing conflict we now add the strength of reconciliation. In heated debate, we often offend one another. We push our point too fiercely; we fail to listen as respectfully as we might. A community that comes through a conflicted period needs time and space for forgiveness. Gifted with a tradition of reconciliation, a Christian community can anticipate this need for communal healing and thus support the exercise of this new virtue.

Christian ministry these days is a contact sport. Trying to learn the new rules of adult faith, we bump into one another. We strain to stay in the conversation that partnership demands. In *Plurality and Ambiguity,* theologian David Tracy reminds us of the challenge of genuine communication: "Conversation is a game with some hard rules; say only what you mean; say it as accurately as you can; listen to and respect what the other says, however different or other; be willing to correct or defend your opinions if challenged by the conversation partner; be willing to argue if necessary, to confront if demanded, to endure necessary conflict, to change your mind if the evidence suggests it."

The Christian tradition of the future will include a practical virtue for facing conflict only if this generation of believers has the courage and the ingenuity to craft such a virtue. By linking vision, patience, courage, and reconciliation, we forge a virtue that is both ancient and new. This strength will be our vital gift for those who follow us in faith and in conflict in the body of Christ.

Reflective Exercise

Bring to mind a group important in your personal life or ministry. Spend time with your memories of this group: the people with you, your history together, the group's focus and goals.

Now recall a significant experience of conflict that recently confronted this group. Identify what seemed to trigger the dispute, how the group responded, and what kind of resolution was achieved. Take note of your own thoughts and feelings during the group's conflict.

After some time in recollection, consider the following three questions.

- What values did this conflict reveal for the group and for you personally?
- How did this experience of conflict affect the group's commitment? Was your own sense of involvement influenced in any way?
- What changes accompanied this conflict? Which of these changes would you evaluate as losses? Which seem to you to be gains for the group? Which are gains for you personally?

Additional Resources

Speed Leas provides practical assistance for understanding and managing conflict in religious groups in *Discover Your Conflict Management Style* (Washington, DC: Alban Institute Publications, 1985) and *Moving Your Church Through Conflict* (Washington, DC: Alban Institute Publications, 1988). See also George Parsons, *Intervening in a Church Fight: A Manual for Internal Consultants* (Washington, DC: Alban Institute Publications, 1990).

Roger Fisher and William Ury have contributed significantly to the development of skills and strategies for dealing with conflict; see *Getting to Yes: Negotiating Agreement Without Giving In* (New York: Penguin, 1981). Other important works in this area include Roger Fisher and Scott Brown's *Getting Together: Building a Relationship That Gets to Yes* (New York: Houghton Mifflin, 1988), and William Ury, Jeanne M. Brett, and Stephen B. Goldberg's *Getting Disputes Resolved: Designing Systems to Cut the Costs of Conflict* (San Francisco: Jossey-Bass, 1990). In *Managing Conflict: Interpersonal Dialogue and Third-Party Roles* (Reading, MA: Addison-Wesley, 1987), Richard Walton discusses the leader's role in fostering diversity and managing differences in the work setting. Hugh Halverstadt provides practical ground rules for dealing effectively with conflict in religious groups in *Managing Church Conflict* (Philadelphia: Westminster, 1991).

In *Putting Forgiveness into Practice* (Nashville: Abingdon Press, 1986), Doris Donnelly gives graceful insight into the tasks of personal and social reconciliation; see also her "Binding Up Wounds in a Healing Community," in Michael J. Henchal, ed., *Repentance and Reconciliation in the Church* (Collegeville, MN: Liturgical Press, 1987). Jim Forest reflects on the gospel challenge of reconciliation in *Making Friends of Enemies* (New York: Crossroad/Continuum, 1989). We discuss themes of power and conflict resolution in an audiotape series, *Power and Conflict in the Church* (Kansas City, MO: Credence Cassettes, 1990).

Alisdair MacIntyre discusses the links between conflict and values in *After Virtue* (Notre Dame, IN: Notre Dame Press, 1981); quotes taken from pp. 206 and 160. In *People Skills: How to Assert Yourself, Listen to Others, and Resolve Conflict* (New York: Touchstone Books, 1986), Robert Bolton examines the skills of effective communication. David Tracy comments on the discipline of communication in *Plurality and Ambiguity* (San Francisco: Harper & Row, 1988); quote taken from p. 19.

James MacGregor Burns quotes Susanne Langer's description of the emotional roots of values on p. 44 of his *Leadership* (New York: Harper & Row, 1978); the words of Burns that we quote in this chapter are taken from pp. 39 and 420.

16. Obeying as Partners

Although he was Son, he learned to obey through suffering; but
having been made perfect, he became for all who obey him the
source of eternal salvation.   (Heb. 5:8-9, JB)

The rules of obedience change as we mature. In healthy families
time transforms the child's obedience to her parents into their
mutual commitment as adults. So it is in the life of faith: youthful virtues survive by being transformed. Our obedience to God
and to one another deepens as it develops. When obedience does
not mature, its bonds turn into bondage. How do we purify obedience so that it expresses our adult faith? We will trace this
transformation by examining three facets of obedience: the core
experience of this bond; the different worlds of obedience; and
connections between obedience and discernment.

The Heart of Obedience

Obedience is one of the ways we hold one another. We are born
into a complex network of bonds: family and faith and culture
embrace us in ways that both protect and constrain. To mature,
we must sort out these vital links, separating healthy bonds from
those that lead to bondage. As adults we must choose the links
that sustain our deepest values. In this way we discern the shape
of our obedience.

LINKING LIVES

Obedience is about belonging. When we obey, we bind ourselves to people and commit ourselves to shared values. We
belong only if we are able to link our lives in these enduring

ways. And obedience is about integration: through sustained commitments, we integrate ourselves into a community and its best hopes. We forge the loyalties that bind us, willingly, to this group. Without these practical commitments, our hopes and goals remain untethered. Our values, pursued in private, languish for lack of contact.

To mature is to learn obedience. Only gradually do we perceive the price of our commitments. The New Testament shows us that Jesus' experience was like our own: slowly he came to see the implications of his life choices. His energetic pursuit of the reign of God led him into trouble. The letter to the Hebrews tells us that "he learned to obey through suffering" (5:8). In the weeks before his violent death, Jesus began to recognize where his commitments were leading. The night before his death he fought this fate, resisting what seemed to signal the frustration of his dreams and hopes. But he finally found strength to face the consequences of his choices. "He became obedient unto death, even death on a cross" (Phil. 2:8, RSV).

Jesus was obedient to his death because he was obedient to his life. His exercise of this virtue was not the servile obedience of a victim. He did not submit to a fate that humiliated him but consented to a vocation that he did not fully understand. Karl Rahner has defined obedience as "a free acceptance of what is necessary or of what in a particular situation is inevitable." Jesus' commitments led him to an inevitable place. Accepting his life and death, Jesus learned obedience.

So it is with us. As we make commitments of love and work, we do not grasp their many implications. As we live these commitments, we learn about hidden challenges and unexpected strengths. We are amazed at the endurance and care it takes to love other people well. Ministry taxes our talent in ways we never would have guessed. The church—our religious heritage and home—disappoints us with its flaws. But we want to belong—to these companions, this congregation, this church—and so we pledge ourselves again. In these adult demands of fidelity, our obedience matures.

REALLY LISTENING

The root of the word *obedience* is "to listen to." Where we read "obey" in the English New Testament, the Greek text simply says "listen." The Letter to the Hebrews, in its original form, did not say that Jesus "learned to obey through suffering" but that he "learned to listen through suffering." Obedience is the ability to pay close attention. Conversely, disobedience is a refusal to listen: we turn our attention away.

Neither easy nor spontaneous, listening well is a learned discipline. Psychologists remind us that accurately hearing what another person says is difficult. Often while someone else speaks, we busily rehearse our response or construct our defense. Eager to have our plan prevail at a meeting, for example, we pay little attention to competing proposals. Thus learning to listen well is the beginning of obedience. Only with effort can we become genuinely attuned to others; only gradually do we learn to attend to the stirrings of our own heart. These daily disciplines make it possible to obey as adults.

Leaders likewise obey by listening. The Greek word for obedience in the New Testament, *akouein*, survives in the word "acoustics." A task of leadership is to see to the acoustics—the conditions that make listening and obedience possible. Rembert Weakland, the archbishop of Milwaukee, has given the church a splendid example of obedience. In the Spring of 1990 Bishop Weakland and a number of churchwomen in the archdiocese designed a series of listening sessions on abortion. In these gatherings church leaders listened as women spoke of their concerns and experiences. In these courageous exercises Bishop Weakland showed the church how a leader obeys.

Worlds of Obedience

Christians have traditionally learned obedience as members of a hierarchical family. We have pictured ourselves as children of God, obeying a loving and authoritative father. Our religious leaders, as representatives of God, acted as surrogate parents and deserved our docility.

Political metaphors complemented the family imagery of the Christian community. As followers of Christ, we were subjects in the Lord's kingdom. Religious leaders governed the city of God, and we owed them the obedience of faithful subjects. In a world guided by these images—family and kingdom—we pictured obedience as a dynamic of *command and submission.* Rulers

command the obedience of their subjects; children submit to
their parents' demands. For centuries, this was the feel of Christian obedience.

As we become an adult community of faith, this vision of
obedience is overturned. We no longer inhabit a hierarchical
world in which religious leaders are pictured exclusively as parents or rulers. This vertical image of superior/inferior betrays
our religious experience. Partners in Baptism, we follow a common vision. Though we remain children of God, we must become adults in the church, balancing a personal calling with our
communal responsibilities. In this new environment, the metaphor of command and submission no longer shapes our
obedience.

CALL AND COMMITMENT

In a world of adult faith, God's command comes as a call. God
calls us to daily fidelities and to exceptional acts of courage and
compassion. This call is more than a polite invitation, more than
the mere echo of our own preferences. Obedient, we respond to
God's call not in submission but by commitment. As our relationship with God matures, our style of obedience to religious
leaders must also change. The religious virtue of obedience survives only by being transformed.

Though we no longer picture our religious leaders as princes
or parents, we do not inhabit a romantic world in which every
social distinction is abolished. In the community of faith, we recognize the leader's responsibility to keep before us the imperatives and invitations of the gospel. We give authority to these
leaders, supporting their initiative and influence in the community and accepting the challenge that their responsibilities
bring. But our commitment is not a blind submission to their
royal or parental commands. Together we *all* obey the gospel,
with each of us accountable to the community.

This vision of an adult community changes the rules for obedience. In such a community leadership becomes, in the happy
phrase of theologian Annie Jaubert, "the responsibility of all
and the charge of some." Charging some among us with the spe-

cial task of leadership, we pledge our support to them. We obey by being attentive and by welcoming their efforts to shape and challenge our shared religious commitments. Our obedience is not submission to their commands but openness to their influence.

FROM OBEDIENCE TO BONDAGE

As we learn about adult obedience, we recognize a special danger in this religious bond. Both families and churches are tempted to block the maturing of their children. Both groups are charmed by the simplicity of the parent/infant relationship. In this simplified world the child has only to obey the parent, who in turn obeys God. In infancy the child lacks a formed conscience, a reliable interior authority to shape its judgments. The child also lacks the charisms or matured strengths that would guide its decisions. Thus it rightly submits to parental authority.

Institutions—both the family and the church—are tempted to defend such an appealing arrangement. The stresses of raising infants (with their tantrums and pouting) seem preferable to later difficulties (negotiating with teenagers, facing conflict with adult children). To avoid the trauma of maturing, a family or a religious group might coax its young to remain dependent and subservient. In such a milieu, we raise up obedience as the premier virtue; we discourage other strengths, such as courage and creativity. An inflexible, hierarchical world is imposed—one in which parishioners obey the pastor, who obeys the bishop, who obeys the pope. In this vertical world, obedience ascends and authority descends. Rigid formulas of faith replace personal and group decision making. Orthodoxy is reduced to the litmus test of loyalty. A servile obedience replaces individual conscience and adult commitment.

When an institution succumbs to this temptation, it degenerates into a dysfunctional system. In *Facing Shame*, family therapists Merle Fossum and Marilyn Mason trace the dynamics of dysfunctional families. A family's distress may originate in the overt violence of alcoholism or sexual abuse, or in a more subtle but compulsive ambition to be the ideal family. Whatever the genesis of their troubles, dysfunctional families display the same symptoms. A conspiracy develops to keep a secret from themselves (such as a parent's incest or a grandparent's suicide); its members have great difficulty with communication, especially about emotions; and the parents employ shaming as the dominant discipline to enforce obedience.

In such a system—whether this is a family, a parish, or a diocese—bonds of obedience unavoidably bend into bondage. Leaders do not welcome a free flow of communication, especially around the emotion-arousing area of conflict. They allow unsigned letters and anonymous complaints to circulate without a call for responsibility and mutuality. Leaders invoke confidentiality more out of defense than prudence. If members of a dysfunctional family or group challenge the system, leaders are tempted to shame them into silence. The silencing of Catholic theologians Leonardo Boff and Matthew Fox illustrates that this method of enforcing obedience is not dead. Adult obedience demands that we really listen and stay in the conversation. In these instances of disagreement, church leaders might demand, "We need to talk about this." Instead, the response is sometimes one of shaming: "Be silent!"—as if we were children scolded and made to stand in the corner. Such a method of enforcing obedience is even less effective with adults than with children.

When an institution resorts to shaming as a way to elicit obedience, it appeals to the wounded child that survives in many of us. Children in a family beset by abuse or other upheavals quickly learn that they cannot trust themselves or their parents. Their spontaneous laughter may ignite their father's rage; their minor failings are linked, in the child's psyche, with their mother's drinking. Made unsure of themselves, the children of such a family become extremely eager to please. They want to fit in and belong; they do not want to cause trouble. They become extremely docile children, and exemplars of obedience. In adulthood they bring to their parish and workplace a constant smile and a ready obedience. This is not an adult virtue, however, but the compulsive residue of a severely wounded childhood.

Only recently have we recognized the epidemic nature of this malady. Sharing our journeys of faith and doubt, we learn about clergy and religious and laity who have learned to become "people pleasers." Terrified of conflict, eager to comply, these believers have been crippled in their ability to obey as free adults. Instead, they have been entrapped in a servile, unholy obedience. For church leaders to take advantage of such woundedness to enforce conformity is both cruel and sinful.

When adult children of dysfunctional families begin to confront and heal their wounds, they are suddenly faced with their feelings about "obedience": to obey is to be diminished! Their youthful submissions were instigated by shame and performed in humiliation. Such persons remember obedience as degrading, as part of their illness. Little wonder that the adult child of a dysfunctional family doubts authority and distrusts obedience. To heal these wounds, many adults feel that they must leave a religious institution that employs shame to enforce obedience.

In a dysfunctional family or parish, conflict looms as a sign of disobedience and disloyalty. Leaders encourage us to submit as loyal sons and daughters. Conflicts are avoided or kept secret to avoid scandalizing "the children." In such an atmosphere any disagreement bears the scent of sin. What such an institution rightly senses is that a conflict could break up the arrangement of powerful parents and obedient children. Frightened of conflict and a loss of control, such an institution fights against change. Yet only by facing these wounds around shame and control can we heal both our church and our own lives.

HOW PARTNERS OBEY

In a world of adult faith we find ourselves among many authorities. We must stay in the conversation with the gospel, with religious leaders, with our communities of faith, and with our own conscience. All of these have a claim on our life and demand our attention. Balancing our many adult commitments, we may long for the idyllic world of the child—a world in which obeying parental leaders guaranteed our virtue. Yet the simple, one-way path of obeying our parents has been replaced by a bewildering intersection of multiple responsibilities. In this new terrain, how do adult Christians learn obedience?

The great gifts of our religious adulthood are conscience and charisms. Lacking these resources in childhood, our obedience was necessarily a simple and uncritical submission. But as adults we can obey only because we have a conscience—that acute, trust-worthy ear that permits us to really listen. With our conscience we recognize the difference between our just anger and petulance; we are able to distinguish between holy ambitions and compulsions; we can tell the difference between genuine commitments and servile bonds. This interior resource keeps us tuned to our conversation with God and authorizes our obedience.

Yet even with an insightful conscience, we would not be strong enough to carry out these commitments without our charisms. These personal strengths (ranging from a specific ability such as teaching to a virtue such as courage) make our obedience possible. Without these God-given strengths, we could not perform what our conscience bids us do. We would *see* what to do but would not have either the nerve or the strength to carry it out. A person who lacks conscience or charism can obey only as a child obeys.

Adult Christians learn that obedience is flexible fidelity to their commitments. This virtue begins in the ability to commit ourselves; without such commitments we may conform to others' expectations, but we cannot obey as adults. The virtue continues as we make our commitments endure: this is fidelity. We pledge ourselves to the future, promising to do whatever it takes to make our commitments endure. But our commitments are not guaranteed links with God. Some stagnate and die; others are found to be driven by unholy motives. If our fidelity to such commitments is not flexible, we will adhere to them even when they are destructive. Unable to change, we turn our fidelity into rigidity.

But how do partners in faith exercise the virtue of obedience in their daily lives? One place to look for clues is Christian marriage. Early Christians naturally saw marriage as a hierarchical institution: the husband was the head of the family, superior to his wife (Eph. 6). In their marriage vows, only the wife pledged obedience. Marriage imitated the simplified world of parent/ child: if the wife obeyed the husband, he would obey God; all would be well. Today fewer Christian couples inhabit that traditional world. Marriage has become a more mutual commitment. We do not obey each other as much as we obey our common pledge. Together we obey the covenant and promise we have made. Even the famous teaching of Ephesians begins with this mutuality: "Give way to one another in obedience to Christ" (5:21, JB). Together we obey Christ, and we do this by "giving way to one another." This commitment is our way of following the gospel. In and through our marriage we obey God.

The everyday struggles of marriage bring us down to earth. From the high-flying romance of our first years, we come down to the daily demands of love. Our disagreements teach us to compromise; our children instruct us in the art of sacrifice. In these strenuous fidelities, we learn about obedience and we humble ourselves.

But such humbling is very different from humiliation. Both words share the root "earth" (humus), but each puts us in touch with the earth in a very different fashion. Obedience, when enforced by shame in an effort to coerce, is humiliating. We are urged to submit—to bend down to the ground. When we are humiliated, we are diminished. But when we are humbled by the daily discipline of a chosen commitment, we get a different taste of the earth. We are brought low—in both exhaustion and gratitude—but we are not demeaned. When we are humbled by the goodness and sacrifice of our shared life, the earth does not soil us; rather, it roots us and makes us firm.

Connections Between Obedience and Discernment

The virtue of obedience survives by changing. If we are to obey as partners in faith, we will need a shared process of discerning what and how we are to obey. Adult Christians today search for a clear and practical method of reflection that will guide and protect our obedience.

Discernment refers to the effort that we all face in making an important decision: Shall we have another child? Should I change jobs? Should our parish take on this new responsibility as a sanctuary for Latin American refugees? Theologian William Spohn defines discernment as "a graced ability to detect what is the appropriate response to the invitation of God." The first Christians were well aware of the need for this ability: "Beloved, do not believe every spirit, but test the spirits to see whether they are of God" (1 John 4:1, RSV). "The spirits" that the author is referring to are the impulses that urge us toward significant choices. Discernment is a disciplined listening to the hopes and convictions that surge through our hearts. Such careful listening leads to trustworthy decisions and makes our lives obedient.

A process of discernment allows us to see through a community's demand or a leader's request to the gospel value that it enshrines. Adult obedience is never blind; it needs to see what each imperative in our life has to do with the reign of God. Our parish must decide how to respond to hunger and homelessness in our city. Our business needs to determine how to share its profits justly. These decisions express our faith: they are how we follow Jesus and obey the gospel.

A process of discernment will include four elements. The first of these is embarrassing: discernment begins in ignorance. If we possess clear and unambiguous information, we do not need to discern. If we have infallible parents, we need no process of decision making. We gather to reflect only because we are ignorant. Theologian Jon Sobrino has observed that Jesus' own discerning was necessary because he was unsure of what to do. This can be a scandal if we picture Christ as a God pretending to be human. But if Jesus was like us in all things except sin, then he shared our ignorance. Ignorance can be a scandal if a church thinks it should always know the right answer, or if leaders are too uncomfortable with the vulnerability that accompanies ignorance. But ignorance can be seen as a fruitful kind of absence: our lack of knowledge can open us up and make us docile. In the humbling silence of our ignorance, we listen more intently to one another. This absence alerts us to the stirring of God among us; it helps us pay attention.

A second element of discernment concerns the public nature of the process. Obedience is more than a private virtue. As theologian Paul Philibert says, "The obedience of mature Christian adults is primarily a community listening carefully for the signs of the Spirit, rather than one individual submitting to another individual." A community obeys only by developing a public process by which it comes to important decisions. A discerning community makes clear how it reflects and decides and invites its members to participate in its deliberations. The processes of decision making are made visible to the whole community.

Many different models of problem solving and planning are available to us. Designated authorities may play a variety of roles in the planning process. After all, a communal discernment does not make everyone magically equal in insight or erase the roles of responsibility already assigned to our leaders. It need not insist on total consensus; it is not a surrender to popular opinion. But a public process does make clear how this group moves toward a decision. In such an understanding there are no secret arrangements, no confidential deals done apart from this process. When a group commits itself to such a process, this becomes its way of obeying. Authorities also obey the process; they are not exempt from it, nor can they ignore it at their whim.

Congregations of women and men religious have been crafting such processes over the past two decades. Some parishes and dioceses have tentatively begun the effort to forge public processes of decision making. If we are many years from the firm establishment of such procedures in our church, we have at least begun. Only with such methods of communal discernment will religious obedience mature into adulthood.

A third element of discernment is negotiation. This is the crux of any method of reflection, and several suppositions are necessary if it is to succeed. First, the Spirit is among us; if we discuss with honesty and respect, God will guide us in these deliberations. Petulance, manipulation, and coercion will block our ears from hearing God's call here. Second, our obedience demands that we stay in the conversation. We can state this conviction about God's dynamic presence among us another way: the good will emerge. We may not know the best solution to this problem, but if we honestly share our partial insights, we will come to see what we are to do. Third, we must allow some conflict in this challenging embrace of discernment. We rule out manipulation and verbal abuse, but we must learn to tolerate honest differences of opinion, disagreement, and challenge. A community must be robust enough to survive these adult embraces. We wrestle with one another, not to injure but to learn how to proceed.

The final element of Christian discernment is reconciliation. If we have struggled over an important question, we have almost certainly hurt one another. Energetically stating my conviction, I offended you; the leader, while reminding us of the official church's position, treated us paternalistically. After much struggle the community has come to a decision, but the process is not finished. We need time and prayer to heal the bruises that our wrestling has caused. Faith communities might develop simple rituals by which we can apologize and be reconciled with one another. During this final stage of the discernment, some part of the community will also be grieving the decision: our will did not prevail; we were sure that God wanted some other decision. Those grieving need time and support in dealing with this loss.

Walking with God

Two final images of faith fill out the picture of our maturing obedience. In his dictionary of theology, Xavier Léon Dufour defines obedience as our collaboration in God's plan of salvation. We pledge ourselves to obey God's scheme for healing the world. But this plan of salvation is described by St. Paul as "a great mystery." We are trying to obey a mystery! How does one stay in the conversation with a mystery? Adult obedience can never be a simple compliance, because we are listening to the greatest mystery of our life.

God invited Abraham to leave home and follow a new plan of salvation (Gen. 17). This call and commitment, in which Judeo-Christian obedience begins, was an invitation "to walk with God." We pledge ourselves as God's companions on a journey that we do not understand. We commit ourselves to a mobile God—one who leads us into deserts and oases, into good years and out of dead ends. This is a God who said through the prophet Nathan, "I have never stayed in a house from the day I brought the Israelites out of Egypt until today, but have always led a wanderer's life in a tent" (2 Sam. 7:6, JB).

Adhering to a rigid rule or an unchanging portrait of God, we become idolatrous, not obedient. We have committed ourselves to a moving God, and our obedience must be to all the turns that chart this journey.

Reflective Exercise

Consider the shape of adult obedience in your own life. Recall a difficult decision you have made—in regard to your work or a significant relationship or your life in the church. Bring to mind the circumstances of the decision. Remember again the struggle, perhaps even the pain, that accompanied the choice.

Then explore the ways that this decision is part of your adult obedience.

- How were you a listener in this process of decision?
- To what did this decision link you? From what did it separate you?
- What shape did your accountability take here?

Additional Resources

Karl Rahner discusses "Christ as the Exemplar of Clerical Obedience" in Karl Rahner and others, eds., *Obedience and the Church* (Washington, DC: Corpus Books, 1968), pp. 1–18; quote taken from p. 3. Sandra Schneiders analyzes the changing shape of obedience for vowed religious in "Religious Obedience: Journey from Law to Love," in *New Wineskins* (New York: Paulist Press, 1986). Paul Philibert explores the adult shape of obedience in "Readiness for Ritual: Psychological Aspects of Maturity in Christian Celebration" in Regis Duffy, ed., *Alternate Futures for Worship*, vol. 1 (Collegeville, MN: Liturgical Press, 1987); quote taken from p. 115. See also *Christian Obedience*, ed. Christian Duquoc and Casiano Floristan (New York: Seabury Press, 1980). Archbishop Weakland's report on the listening sessions on abortion appears in *Origins*, May 31, 1990, pp. 33–39.

Moral theologian William Spohn provides an excellent discussion of the affective elements of discernment in "The Reasoning Heart: An American Approach to Christian Discernment,"

Theological Studies 44 (1983): 30–52; quote taken from p. 30. Jon Sobrino's discussion of Jesus' ignorance appears in his "Following Jesus as Discernment," in Casiano Floristan and Christian Duquoc, eds., *Discernment of the Spirit and of Spirits; Councilium*, vol. 119 (New York: Seabury Press, 1979), pp. 14–23. Theologian Annie Jaubert explores the shared responsibility in the Christian community in "Les Épîtres de Paul: le fait communautaire," in *La Ministère et les Ministères Selon le Nouveau Testament*, edited by Jean Delorme (Paris: Éditions de Seuil, 1974), pp. 16–33; quote taken from p. 25.

Mary Benet McKinney offers a practical tool to assist religious groups in coming to adult decisions in *Sharing Wisdom: A Process for Group Decision Making* (Notre Dame, IN: Ave Maria Press, 1986); see also J. Gordon Myers and John Lawyer, *A Guidbook for Problem-Solving in Group Settings* (Kansas City, MO: Sheed & Ward, 1985). Family therapists Merle Fossum and Marilyn Mason give a clear and compelling description of the interaction of shame and control in the dysfunctional family in *Facing Shame* (New York: Norton, 1986). Sidney Callahan discusses the personal and social dimensions of conscience in *In Good Conscience: The Role of Reason, Emotion, and Intuition in Personal Morality* (San Francisco: HarperSanFrancisco 1991). In *Sharing Faith: A Comprehensive Approach to Religious Education and Pastoral Ministry* (San Francisco: HarperSanFrancisco, 1991), Thomas Groome develops a useful model for practical pastoral reflection.

Increasingly, Christians recognize that their religious obedience takes shape in the context of work and family; see, for example, Wendy M. Wright, *Sacred Dwelling: A Spirituality of Family Life* (New York: Crossroad/Continuum, 1989), John C. Haughey, *Converting 9 to 5: A Spirituality of Daily Work* (New York: Crossroad/Continuum, 1989), and William E. Diehl, *The Monday Connection: A Spirituality of Competence, Affirmation, and Support in the Workplace* (San Francisco: HarperSanFrancisco, 1991).

Conclusion
The Play of Partnership

[Sophia, the feminine voice of God, speaks:] I was by his side, a master crafter, delighting him day by day, ever at play in his presence, at play everywhere in the world, delighting to be with the children of humanity.   (Adapted from Prov. 8:30–31, JB)

The promise of partnership: women and men, lay and ordained longing for new ways to live and work together. Segregated by ancient barriers, Christians have learned to imagine their service toward one another as the work of individuals. Is it not more fruitful to picture Christian ministry as the play of partners?

The promise of partnership rings out of the portrait of Sophia and Yahweh found in the book of Proverbs: creation as an enjoyment too rich to be private, too delightful to be simply work. In this surprising vision, creation is not the achievement of a solitary God but the fruit of partners at play. The Christian doctrine of the Trinity celebrates a partnership *within* God. This ultimate, mysterious power must be greater than an individual, more than merely masculine. If Adam and Eve, those first partners, were created "in God's image," must not the divine image include some mutuality? Christians sense within their Creator the promise of partnership.

The Play of Creation

Our vision of creation shapes our expectations about Christian ministry. As God acted in creation—workmanlike or playfully, alone or in collaboration—so must we act in our care for the world. Following clues in the book of Genesis, Christians have developed a portrait of creation as the *work* of God's hands: God crafted the world during a six-day work week. On the Sabbath, the Creator rests. This is an industrial model of creation, picturing creation as serious business carried out by individual effort.

The memory of humanity's fall seemed to further disqualify play or pleasure in creation for our religious forebears. Life was now necessarily serious: we would work by the sweat of our brow and bear our children in pain. Obligations would replace playfulness; even sexuality was to be shared in terms of duties rather than delights.

Is there any other way for Christians to picture creation? Hidden in the Hebrew Scriptures lies another portrait—one that may allow us to appreciate creation not as work but as God's play; not as individual effort but as partnership. In the book of Proverbs, Sophia (or Wisdom)—the feminine form of God—is seen at play with the Creator. At the dawn of our world, Wisdom and the Creator take pleasure in a shared performance:

> When he established the heavens,
> I was there . . .
> When he marked out the foundations
> of the earth, then I was beside him,
> like a master crafter,
> and I was daily his delight,
> rejoicing before him always.
> (Prov. 8:27, 29–30, RSV)

This picture of creation strikes traditional Jews and Christians as strange. We are not accustomed to seeing the Creator playing with a partner in creation—especially a woman partner! But there are precedents for this surprising vision. Among the many Hindu myths of creation is the story of God inventing the world out of play *(lila)*. And the recent restoration of the ceiling of the Sistine Chapel gives us a new perspective on an old portrait. We see colors that we had not expected and, if we look closely, we see a scene that we had ignored. The most celebrated focus of the painting is, of course, the outstretched hands of God and Adam. The spark of creation is ignited in the touch of two muscular males. But a fresh look at the picture reveals a neglected part of the story: God's left arm embraces a woman—a companion in creation?

The picture of creation found in Proverbs is not about God's gender. Theological reflection reminds us that the Creator is beyond all our categories of gender, race, and age (though most Western Christians still picture God as a single, white male). This scriptural story is about God's exuberance in creation: a delight so great that it demanded to be shared.

Different visions of creation remind us that, having been made in God's image, we return the favor: we craft stories and metaphors that make God look much like us. We then give these metaphors authority in our life. If we see God as a sober and solitary male, we choose our religious leaders to match. But other portraits are available to us.

The image of Sophia in Proverbs encourages us to see creation as God's delight and pleasure. In such a world we act not only out of duty but with pleasure. We learn to perform our obligations but also to take delight in our life. If rational control is important, so is the heart's desire. This universe is less serious— a place where imagination, invention, and improvisation are prized. Perhaps God is still at play here, inviting us to enter into the drama. Then our world has more "play" in it, more flexibility and resilience. Seeing creation as the play of God, we may better recognize ministry as a performance of many partners.

The Drama of the Church

If we can imagine creation as play, we can see that the church's life is a drama. In this continuing play, each of us performs a role—our own vocation. As a parent or pastor, as a citizen and worker, we play ancient roles. Each of these roles has been performed many times before. Yet at this special time in the church's drama, we play our roles anew—differently, as they have never been done before. As a teacher or healer, we play a role that has been performed for many centuries. But in our own health care setting or school we perform this vocation in a slightly novel fashion. Ours is an old role but, in our life, a new creation; we play this role with new energy and challenge.

Playing out our vocations in the drama of Christian life, we follow many scripts. The central script is our Scriptures. And we have other guidelines: our job description, the rules of our religious congregation, the parish's mission statement. As we play our ancient roles, we are eager to be faithful to these scripts.

But as we play out the drama of the church today, we also hear the voice of the Prompter. From below the stage or behind the curtain, an unseen voice reminds us of forgotten lines. These may be lines that are in the Scriptures but were deleted from our job description or mission statement. And sometimes the voice of the Prompter urges us to improvise. Another actor has not entered on cue or the hero has lost his place. What are we to do?

Today many Christians hear the Prompter urging women to center stage. But this is not in the script! How do we remain faithful to the script and also faithful to this mysterious Prompter? At times the pace of the drama slows down: dutiful actors repeat their lines by rote, without enthusiasm, just playing a part. In the midst of such a drama, the audience grows restless or drifts away. In a time of stagnation, creative players begin to improvise, not abandoning the plot but enlivening it. Again we ask, How shall we be faithful to our holy script and also faithful to the improvisation urged by the Prompter?

We play our roles in the church's drama with many motives. We play for attention or the delight of performing; the child in us encourages us to take pleasure in the play. And we also play our part in order to get it right; the serious disciple in us is concerned with this aspect of the drama, and we want to do a good job. But, and most important, we play our part—both ancient and novel—in order to enact the next scene in the church's life. In the 1990s we are performing the next act in the drama that is the church. If this responsibility is awesome, it should also be exciting.

Performing in Concert

Two convictions can save the performers of Christian ministry from succumbing to panic or exhaustion. First, we remind ourselves that the drama is the Spirit's. We are neither its author nor its director. We participate with vigor and creativity, but the play is not finally ours. This conviction will relieve us of assuming too much responsibility, of becoming too self-serious or heroic. We are players in a drama vaster than we can imagine.

Because the play belongs to God, we can afford to take risks and even to fail. We will not ruin the drama; our part is not that important! We can also afford to leave the stage before the final act; we need not worry too much about how things turn out. The Author of creation will see to that.

The second conviction is that we play in concert with others. We belong to a long history of partnership, stretching back to the play of Wisdom and Yahweh in creation. We perform our vocations best when we are among companions and friends. Christian ministers do not thrive as soloists or prima donnas. The Lone Ranger model of ministry is disappearing. We are meant to play together in the bewildering but creative drama of Christian life.

Community, in its simplest terms, is a gathering of people who support one another's performance. When we blunder and fall, our partners are there to catch us, to hold us well until we are ready to play again. Community is the place where we learn how to hold one another. If the church is fundamentally about embraces, so is the performance of ministry. In this image of mutual embrace, our reflection begins and ends.

Bibliography

Abbott, Walter M., and Herbert Vorgrimler, eds. *The Documents of Vatican II and The Commentary of the Documents of Vatican II*. New 25th-anniversary ed. 6 vols. New York: Crossroad/Continuum, 1989.

Anderson, James D., and Ezra Earl Jones. *The Management of Ministry: Building Leadership in a Changing World*. San Francisco: Harper & Row, 1989.

Bacik, James. *The Challenge of Pastoral Leadership: Putting Theology into Practice*. Cincinnati: St. Anthony Messenger Audiocassettes, 1990.

Baranowski, Arthur. *Creating Small Faith Communities*. Cincinnati: St. Anthony Messenger Press, 1989.

Bausch, William. *The Hands-On Parish*. Mystic, CT: Twenty-Third Publications, 1989.

————. *The Pilgrim Church*. Rev. ed. Mystic, CT: Twenty-Third Publications, 1989.

Bolton, Robert. *People Skills: How to Assert Yourself, Listen to Others, and Resolve Conflicts*. New York: Touchstone Books, 1986.

Brennan, Patrick. *Re-Imagining the Parish*. New York: Crossroad/Continuum, 1990.

Brueggeman, Walter. *The Prophetic Imagination*. Philadelphia: Fortress Press, 1978.

Burns, Helen Marie. "Leadership in a Time of Transition." *Origins* (Sept. 13, 1990):228–32.

Burns, James MacGregor. *Leadership*. New York: Harper & Row, 1978.

Busch, Frederick. *Absent Friends*. New York: Knopf, 1989.

Callahan, Kennon L. *Effective Church Leadership*. San Francisco: Harper & Row, 1990.

Callahan, Sydney. *In Good Conscience: The Role of Reason, Emotion, and Intuition in Personal Morality*. San Francisco: HarperSanFrancisco, 1991.

Cardman, Francine, and others. "In Solidarity and Service: Reflections on the Problem of Clericalism in the Church." In David Fleming, ed., *Religious Life at the Crossroads*, pp. 65–87. New York: Paulist Press, 1985.

Chirico, Peter. *Infallibility: The Crossroads of Doctrine*. Wilmington, DE: Clazier, 1983.

Chodorow, Nancy. *The Reproduction of Mothering: Psychoanalysis and the Sociology of Gender*. Los Angeles: Univ. of California Press, 1978.

Clark, Keith. *The Skilled Participant: A Way to Effective Collaboration*. Notre Dame, IN: Ave Maria Press, 1988.

Cohen, Sherry Suib. *Tender Power*. Reading, MA: Addison-Wesley, 1989.

"The Cologne Declaration." *Commonweal* (Feb. 24, 1989): 102–4.

Coleman, James. "Dimensions of Leadership." *Origins* (Sept. 13, 1990) 223–280.

Congar, Yves. "Reception as an Ecclesiastical Reality." In Giuseppe Alberigo and Anton Weiler, eds., *Election and Consensus in the Church*, pp. 43–68. *Concilium*, vol. 77. New York: Herder & Herder, 1972.

Cooke, Bernard. "Obstacles to Lay Involvement." In J. Metz and E. Schillebeeckx, eds., *The Teaching Authority of Believers*, pp. 63–70. *Concilium*, vol. 180. New York: T. & T. Clark, 1985.

———, ed. *The Papacy and the Church in the United States*. New York: Paulist Press, 1989.

Cowan, Michael, ed. *Leadership Ministry in Community*. Alternative Futures for Worship Series, vol. 6. Collegeville, MN: Liturgical Press, 1987.

Crichton, J. D. *A Short History of the Mass*. London: Catholic Truth Society, 1983.

Crossan, John Dominic. *Cliffs of Fall*. New York: Crossroad/Continuum, 1980.

———. *The Dark Interval: Towards a Theology of Story*. Chicago: Argus Press, 1975.

Curran, Charles. *Faithful Dissent*. Kansas City, MO: Sheed & Ward, 1986.

Dale, Robert D. *Pastoral Leadership*. Nashville: Abingdon Press, 1986.

D'Antonio, William V., James D. Davidson, Dean R. Hoge, and Ruth A. Wallace. *American Catholic Laity in a Changing Church*. Kansas City, MO: Sheed & Ward, 1989.

DePree, Max. *Leadership Is an Art*. New York: Doubleday, 1989.

Diehl, William E. *The Monday Connection: A Spirituality of Competence, Affirmation, and Support in the Workplace*. San Francisco: HarperSanFrancisco, 1991.

Dolan, Jay P., R. Scott Appleby, Patricia Byrne, and Debra Campbell. *Transforming Parish Ministry: The Changing Roles of the Catholic Clergy, Laity, and Women Religious*. New York: Crossroads Books, 1989.

Donahue, John A. *The Gospel in Parable: Metaphor, Narrative and Theology in the Synoptic Gospels*, Philadelphia: Fortress, 1988.

Donnelly, Doris. "Binding Up Wounds in a Healing Community." In Michael J. Henchal, ed., *Repentance and Reconciliation in the Church*, pp. 11–31. Collegeville, MN: Liturgical Press, 1987.

———. *Putting Forgiveness into Practice*. 5th ed. Nashville: Abingdon Press, 1986.

Doohan, Leonard. *Grass Roots Pastors: A Handbook for Career Lay Ministers*. San Francisco: Harper & Row, 1989.

Duch, Robert G. *Successful Parish Leadership: Nurturing the Animated Parish*. Kansas City, MO: Sheed & Ward, 1990.

Dues, Greg. *Dealing with Diversity: A Guide for Parish Leaders.* Mystic, CT: Twenty-Third Publications, 1987.

Duquoc, Christian, and Casiano Floristan. *Christian Obedience. Concilium,* vol. 139. New York: Seabury Press, 1980.

Dyer, W. G. *Team Building: Issues and Alternatives,* 2nd ed., Reading, MA: Addison-Wesley, 1987.

Egan, Gerard. *Change-Agent Skills A: Assessing and Designing Excellence.* San Diego, CA: University Associates, 1988.

———. *Change-Agent Skills B: Managing Innovation and Change.* San Diego, CA: University Associates, 1988.

———. *Change Agent Skills in Helping and Human Service Settings.* Monterey, CA: Brooks/Cole, 1985.

Faivre, Alexandre. *The Emergence of the Laity in the Early Church.* New York: Paulist Press, 1990.

Ferder, Fran, and John Heagle. *Partnership: Women and Men in Ministry.* Notre Dame, IN: Ave Maria Press, 1989.

Fiorenza, Elisabeth Schüssler. *In Memory of Her.* New York: Crossroad/Continuum, 1983.

Fisher, Roger, and Scott Brown. *Getting Together: Building Relationships That Get to Yes.* Boston: Houghton Mifflin, 1988.

Fisher, Roger, and William Ury. *Getting to Yes: Negotiating Agreement Without Giving In.* New York: Penguin, 1981.

Fletcher, John C. *Religious Authenticity in the Clergy.* Washington, DC: Alban Institute Publications, 1978.

Forest, Jim. *Making Friends of Enemies.* New York: Crossroad/Continuum, 1989.

Fossum, Merle, and Marilyn Mason. *Facing Shame.* New York: Norton Press, 1986.

Gilligan, Carol. *In a Different Voice: Psychological Theory and Women's Development.* Cambridge, MA: Harvard Univ. Press, 1982.

Gilmour, Peter. *The Emerging Pastor.* Kansas City, MO: Sheed & Ward, 1986.

Greenleaf, Robert K. *Servant Leadership: A Journey into the Nature of Legitimate Power and Greatness.* New York: Paulist Press, 1977.

Gundry, Patricia. *Neither Slave nor Free: Helping Women Answer the Call to Church Leadership.* San Francisco: Harper & Row, 1988.

Hackman, J. R. *Groups That Work (and Those That Don't).* San Francisco: Jossey-Bass, 1989.

Hagberg, Janet O. *Real Power: Stages of Personal Power in Organizations.* Minneapolis: Winston Press, 1984.

Hahn, Cecilia A., and James R. Adams. *The Mystery of Clergy Authority.* Washington, DC: Alban Institute Publications, 1980.

Harris, John C. *Stress, Power, and Ministry.* Washington, D.C.: Alban Institute Publications, 1983.

Haughey, John. *Converting 9 to 5: A Spirituality of Daily Work.* New York: Crossroad/Continuum, 1989.

Hoffman, Virginia. *Birthing a Living Church.* New York: Crossroad/Continuum, 1989.

Hoge, Dean E. *The Future of Catholic Leadership: Responses to the Priest Shortage.* Kansas City, MO: Sheed & Ward, 1989.

Holmberg, Bengt. *Paul and Power: The Structure of Authority in the Primitive Church as Reflected in the Pauline Epistles.* Philadelphia: Fortress Press, 1978.

Homans, Peter. *The Ability to Mourn.* Chicago: Univ. of Chicago Press, 1989.

Janeway, Elizabeth. *Improper Behavior: When and How Misconduct Can Be Healthy for Society.* New York: Morrow, 1987.

———. *Powers of the Weak.* New York: Knopf, 1980.

Jaubert, Annie. "Les Épîtres de Paul: le fait communautaire." In Jean Delorme, ed., *Le Ministère et les Ministères Selon le Nouveau Testament,* pp. 16–33. Paris: Éditions de Seuil, 1974.

Kaiser, Robert Blair. *The Politics of Sex and Religion.* Kansas City, MO: Leaven Press, 1985.

Kanter, Rosabeth Moss. *The Change Masters.* New York: Simon & Schuster, 1983.

———. *Men and Women of the Corporation.* New York: Basic Books, 1976.

Kaufman, Philip S. *Why You Can Disagree and Remain a Faithful Catholic.* New York: Crossroad/Continuum, 1989.

Kennedy, Eugene. *Tomorrow's Catholics, Yesterday's Church: The Two Cultures of American Catholicism.* San Francisco: Harper & Row, 1988.

Kilmartin, Edward. *Christian Liturgy: Theology and Practice.* Kansas City, MO: Sheed & Ward, 1988.

Kirkpatrick, Donald L. *How to Manage Change Effectively.* San Francisco: Jossey-Bass, 1985.

Laborers for the Lord. Washington, DC: United States Catholic Conference, 1990.

Lauder, Robert. *The Priest as Person.* Mystic, CT: Twenty-Third Publications, 1988.

Leas, Speed. *Discover Your Conflict Management Style.* Washington, D.C.: Alban Institute Publications, 1985.

———. *Moving Your Church Through Conflict.* Washington, D.C.: Alban Institute Publications, 1988.

Lee, Bernard, and Michael Cowan. *Dangerous Memories: House Churches and Our American Story.* Kansas City, MO: Sheed & Ward, 1986.

Legrand, H. M. "The 'Indelible' Character and the Theology of Minis-
    try." In Hans Küng and Walter Kasper, eds., *The Plurality of Minis-
    tries*, pp. 54–62. *Concilium*, vol. 74. New York: Herder & Herder,
    1972.

Lips, Hilary. *Women, Men, and the Psychology of Power.* New York: Pren-
    tice-Hall, 1981.

Loomer, Bernard. "Two Kinds of Power." *Criterion* 15 (Winter 1976):
    11–29.

McClelland, David C. *Power: The Inner Experience.* New York: Irvington,
    1975.

McCormick, Richard. "L'Affaire Curran." *America* 154 (1986): 261–67.

———. "Notes on Moral Theology: 1986." *Theological Studies* (Mar. 1987):
    87–105.

———. and Richard P. McBrien. "L'Affaire Curran II." *America* 163
    (1990):127–43.

McKinney, Mary Benet. *Sharing Wisdom: A Process for Group Decision
    Making.* Allen, TX: Tabor Publishing, 1987.

MacIntyre, Alisdair. *After Virtue.* Notre Dame, IN: Notre Dame Press,
    1981.

Mallet, James, ed. *The Ministry of Governance.* Washington, DC: Canon
    Law Society of America, 1986.

Manz, C. C., and H. P. Sims, Jr. *Superleadership: Leading People to Lead
    Themselves.* Englewood Cliffs, N.J.: Prentice-Hall, 1988.

Marty, Martin. *A Cry of Absence.* San Francisco: Harper & Row, 1983.

Monette, Maurice L., ed. *Staffing Tomorrow's Parishes: Experiences and Is-
    sues in Evolving Forms of Pastoral Leadership.* Kansas City, MO: Sheed
    & Ward, 1990.

Murphy, Thomas. "The Host of Challenges Priests Face." *Origins* (Aug. 4,
    1988): 1–4.

Myers, J. Gordon. "Organizational Grieving: The Path to Newness."
    *Journal of the International Association of Conference Center Administra-
    tors* (Fall 1989)

Myers, J. Gordon, and John Lawyer. *A Guidebook for Problem-Solving in
    Group Settings.* Kansas City, MO: Sheed & Ward, 1985.

Myers, J. Gordon, and Richard Schoenherr. "The Baptism of Power."
    New Catholic World (Sept./Oct. 1980): 217–20.

National Pastoral Plan for Hispanic Ministry. Washington, DC: United
    States Catholic Conference, 1987.

Nouwen, Henri. *In the Name of Jesus: Reflections on Christian Leadership.*
    New York: Crossroads Books, 1989.

Nuechterlein, Anne Marie. *Improving Your Multiple Staff Ministry: How to
    Work Together More Effectively.* Minneapolis: Augsburg, 1989.

Nuechterlein, Anne Marie, and Celia Allison Hahn. *The Male-Female*

Church Staff: Celebrating the Gifts, Confronting the Challenges. Washington, DC: Alban Institute Publications, 1990.

Orsy, Ladislas. *The Church: Learning and Teaching.* Wilmington, DE: Glazier, 1987.

Osborne, Kenan. *Priesthood: A History of the Ordained Ministry in the Roman Catholic Church.* New York: Paulist Press, 1989.

Parent, Rémi. *A Church of the Baptized: Overcoming Tension Between the Clergy and the Laity.* Translated by Stephen W. Arndt. New York: Paulist Press, 1989.

Parsons, George. *Intervening in a Church Fight: A Manual for Internal Consultants.* Washington, DC: Alban Institute Publications, 1990.

Peters, Tom. *Thriving on Chaos.* New York: Harper & Row, 1987.

Pettigrew, A. M. "On Studying Organizational Cultures." *Administrative Science Quarterly* 24 (1979): 570-81.

Philibert, Paul. "Readiness for Ritual: Psychological Aspects of Maturity in Christian Celebration." In Regis Duffy, ed., *Alternative Futures for Worship,* pp. 63–121. Vol. 1. Collegeville, MN: Liturgical Press, 1987.

Pneuman, Roy W., and Margaret E. Bruehl. *Managing Conflict: A Complete Process-Centered Handbook.* New York: Spectrum, 1982.

Power, David. *Gifts That Differ: Lay Ministries Established and Unestablished.* New York: Pueblo, 1980.

———. "Households of Faith in the Coming Church." *Worship* (May 1983): 237–54.

Rahner, Karl. "Christ as the Exemplar of Clerical Obedience." In Karl Rahner and others, eds., *Obedience in the Church,* pp. 1–18. Washington, DC: Corpus Books, 1968.

Reed, Bruce. *The Dynamics of Religion.* London: Darton, Longman & Todd, 1978.

———. *The Task of the Church and the Role of Its Members.* Washington, DC: Alban Institute Publications, 1988.

Reese, Thomas J. *Archbishop: Inside the Power Structure of the American Catholic Church.* San Francisco: Harper & Row, 1989.

Rubin, Lillian B. *Intimate Strangers: Men and Women Together.* New York: Harper & Row, 1984.

Russell, Letty. *The Future of Partnership.* Philadelphia: Westminster Press, 1979.

———. *Growth in Partnership.* Philadelphia: Westminster Press, 1981.

———. *Household of Freedom: Authority in Feminist Theology.* Philadelphia: Westminster Press, 1987.

Scarf, Maggie. *Unfinished Business: Pressure Points in the Lives of Women.* New York: Doubleday, 1980.

Schaper, Donna. *Common Sense About Men and Women in the Ministry.* Washington, DC: Alban Institute Publications, 1990.

Scherer, Jacqueline. *Contemporary Community: Sociological Illusion or Reality?* New York: Harper & Row, 1973.

Schillebeeckx, Edward. *The Church with a Human Face.* New York: Crossroads Books, 1985.

Schneiders, Sandra. *New Wineskins.* New York: Paulist Press, 1986.

Schoenherr, Richard. "Study of U.S. Diocesan Priesthood Statistics: 1966–2005." *Origins* (Sept. 6, 1990): 206–8.

Schütz, John Howard. *Paul and the Anatomy of Apostolic Authority.* Cambridge: Cambridge Univ. Press, 1975.

Segundo, Juan Luis. *Theology and the Church.* Rev. ed. San Francisco: Harper & Row, 1985.

Sennett, Richard. *Authority.* New York: Vintage, 1981.

Smith, Kenwyn, and David N. Berg. *Paradoxes of Group Life: Understanding Conflict, Paralysis, and Movement in Group Dynamics.* San Francisco: Jossey-Bass, 1987.

Snow, John. *The Impossible Vocation: Ministry in the Mean Time.* Cambridge, MA: Cowley, 1988.

Sobrino, Jon. "Following Jesus as Discernment." In Casiano Floristan and Christian Duquoc, eds., *Discernment of the Spirit and of Spirits,* pp. 14–23. *Concilium,* vol. 119. New York: Seabury Press, 1979.

Soelle, Dorothee. *Strength of the Weak.* Philadelphia: Westminster Press, 1984.

Sofield, Loughlan, and Carrol Juliano. *Collaborative Ministry.* Notre Dame, IN: Ave Maria Press, 1987.

Spohn, William. "The Reasoning Heart: An American Approach to Christian Discernment." *Theological Studies* 44 (1983): 30–52.

Steinfels, Margaret. "The Church and Its Public Life." *America* 160 (1989): 550–58.

Sundstrom, Eric, Kenneth DeMeuse, and David Futrell. "Work Teams: Applications and Effectiveness." *American Psychologist* (Feb. 1990): 120–33.

Swain, Bernard. *Liberating Leadership: Practical Styles for Pastoral Ministry.* San Francisco: Harper & Row, 1986.

Sweetser, Thomas, and Carol Holden. *Leadership in the Successful Parish.* San Francisco: Harper & Row, 1986.

Tavris, Carol, and Carole Wade. *The Longest War: Sex Differences in Perspective.* Rev. ed. San Diego, CA: Harcourt Brace Jovanovich, 1989.

Thompson, Mary R. *The Role of Disbelief in Mark.* New York: Paulist Press, 1989.

Tichy, Noel M., and Mary Anne DeVanna. *The Transformational Leader.* New York: Wiley, 1986.

Tracy, David. *Plurality and Ambiguity.* San Francisco: Harper & Row, 1988.

Tracy, Diane. *The Power Pyramid: How to Get Power by Giving It Away.* New York: Morrow, 1990.

United States Catholic Bishops. "Partnership in the Mystery of Redemption." *Origins* (Oct. 6, 1988): 757–88.

———. "One in Christ: A Pastoral Response to the Concerns of Women for church and Society." *Origins* (April 5, 1990): 717–40.

———. "Report of Hunthausen Commission." *Origins* (June 4, 1987): 40–44.

Urrabazo, Rosendo. "Hispanic Ministry." *Origins* (Aug. 17, 1989): 202–6.

Ury, William, Jeanne M. Brett, and Stephen B. Goldberg. *Getting Disputes Resolved: Designing Systems to Cut the Costs of Conflict.* San Francisco: Jossey-Bass, 1989.

Varney, Glenn H. *Building Productive Teams: An Action Guide and Resource Book.* San Francisco: Jossey-Bass, 1989.

von Rad, Gerhard. *Genesis: A Commentary.* Philadelphia: Westminster Press, 1961.

Walton, Richard E. *Management as a Performing Art: New Ideas for a World of Chaotic Change.* San Francisco: Jossey-Bass, 1989.

———. *Managing Conflict: Interpersonal Dialogue and Third-Party Roles.* 2nd ed. Reading, MA: Addison-Wesley, 1987.

Weisbord, Marvin R. *Productive Workplaces: Organizing and Managing for Dignity, Meaning, and Community.* San Francisco: Jossey-Bass, 1987.

Whitehead, Evelyn Eaton, and James D. Whitehead. *Christian Life Patterns.* New York: Image Books/Doubleday, 1982.

———. *Seasons of Strength: New Visions of Adult Christian Maturing.* New York: Image Books/Doubleday, 1986.

———. *A Sense of Sexuality: Christian Love and Intimacy.* New York: Image Books/Doubleday, 1990.

Whitehead, James D. "Stewardship: The Disciple Becomes a Leader." In Michael Cowan, ed., *Leadership Ministry in Community*, pp. 69–80. Collegeville, MN: Liturgical Press, 1987.

Whitehead, James D., and Evelyn Eaton Whitehead. *The Emerging Laity: Returning Leadership to the Community of Faith.* New York: Image Books/Doubleday, 1988.

———. "The Gift of Prophecy." *Spirituality Today* (Winter 1989): 292–304.

———. *Power and Conflict in the Church.* Kansas City, MO: Credence Cassettes, 1990.

Wink, Walter. *Naming the Powers: The Language of Power in the New Testament.* Philadelphia: Fortress Press, 1984.

Wright, Wendy M. *Sacred Dwelling: A Spirituality of Family Life.* New York: Crossroad/Continuum, 1989.

Index

About the Authors

Evelyn Eaton Whitehead is a developmental psychologist with a doctorate from the University of Chicago. She writes and lectures on questions of adult development and aging, leadership development, and collaboration in ministry.

James D. Whitehead is a pastoral theologian and historian of religion. He holds a doctorate from Harvard University, with a concentration in Chinese religions. His professional interests include issues of contemporary spirituality, pastoral leadership, and theological method in ministry.

The Whiteheads are authors of *Christian Life Patterns, Marrying Well, Seasons of Strength, Method in Ministry, Community of Faith,* and *The Emerging Laity.* Their recent book *A Sense of Sexuality* received the Book-of-the-Year award from the journal *Human Development* in 1989. Through Whitehead Associates, they have since 1978 served as consultants in education and ministry in the United States and elsewhere. They have been members of the associate faculty of the Institute of Pastoral Studies at Loyola University in Chicago since 1970. The Whiteheads make their home in South Bend, Indiana.